Hitler's
Panzers
East

Anvil: *The Red Army forces.* With approximately 20,000 tanks, 15,000 combat aircraft, and huge reserves of tough peasant riflemen politically indoctrinated by a meticulously organized political party, the Red Army stood in 1941 as the most formidable anvil that had ever been struck by an attacker. Shown above, a smoking KV-I heavy Soviet tank, a victim of combat early in the German offensive against the Soviet Union. (Bundesarchiv Bestand)

Hammer: *The German armed forces.* With mission-oriented leadership (*Auftragstaktik*) and decisive historical style characterized by the strategic concept of the great battle of decision (*Entscheidungsschlacht*), the German armed forces achieved near-fatal results against the Soviets in the first twenty-four days of Barbarossa. Shown below is an example of German tactical flexibility: a Luftwaffe-served 88mm antiaircraft gun used in the ground-firing role, especially against Soviet tanks and fortifications. (Bundesarchiv Bestand)

Hitler's Panzers East

WORLD WAR II REINTERPRETED

By R.H.S. Stolfi

University of Oklahoma Press : Norman and London

By R. H. S. Stolfi
(F. W. Von Mellenthin and R. H. S. Stolfi with E. Sobik) *NATO Under Attack: Why the Western Alliance Can Fight Outnumbered and Win in Central Europe Without Nuclear Weapons* (Durham, 1984)
Hitler's Panzers East: World War II Reinterpreted (Norman, 1991)

Library of Congress Cataloging-in-Publication Data

Stolfi, Russel H. S. (Russel H. S.), 1932–
    Hitler's panzers east : World War II reinterpreted / by R.H.S. Stolfi.
        p.   cm.
    Includes bibliographical references and index.
    ISBN 0-8061-2400-8 (alk. paper)
    1. World War, 1939–1945—Campaigns—Eastern   2. World War,
1939–1945—Tank warfare.   3. Strategy.   4. World War, 1939–
1945—Germany.   I. Title.
D764.S866   1991
940.54′21—dc20   91-50308
                                                                      CIP

Text and jacket design by Bill Cason.

Maps by GiGi Bayliss.

Contents

Illustrations

Tables

Chart

Preface

The conventional wisdom on World War II in Europe sees little prospect of the Germans' winning in 1939–1940 and virtually none after the attack on the Soviet Union in June 1941. This wisdom uses the term *blitzkrieg* to describe the intellect, discrimination, and style of Adolf Hitler from 1939 to 1941 and marks the turning points of the war as the battles associated with Alamein, Stalingrad, and Kursk. I reject this view and present instead a fundamental reevaluation of the period, inviting a new perception of World War II.

Most historians have considered victory beyond the capabilities of the Germans. My purpose is to show that the German armed forces had beaten the Soviet field armies defending Moscow in June to July 1941, and could have advanced through Moscow into the Moscow-Gorki space in August to October 1941. The corollary of this thesis is that the main concentration of the Red Army would have been destroyed and Soviet mobilization terminated by the German advance, leading to the revisionistic view that the Germans would have defeated Soviet Russia by the end of October 1941. By the magnitude of the victory and its timing, the Germans would also have won the war in Europe.

The political and social consequences of this outcome would have been epochal—the suffocation of liberal democracy on the European continent and the probable extinction of marxian socialism. Notwithstanding the eventual defeat of the Germans, if it could be shown that they had the capability to win the battle of Russia in June to August 1941, we would have to reevaluate the significance of these events. One lesson to be drawn from my interpretation is that the superiority of the Germans in war-fighting tactics and operations was greater than previously thought. Consequently, German tactics and operations as exemplified by the vast battles at the beginning of the advance into the Soviet Union deserve to be studied more thoroughly for application in future conventional war.

In recasting World War II to include the thesis that the Germans had the physical capabilities at the right time and place in Europe to win, I was forced to reinterpret the turning point in the war and the mentality and style of Adolf Hitler. I credit the substantial German capability to win in August 1941 to strength in men and weapons, skill in tactics and operations, and effecting surprise and concentration of effort by seizing the strategic military initiative. The Germans exerted these factors against the Soviets in the summer of 1941 and had the opportunity at that moment to win the war in Europe. At a time when France was defeated and Britain crippled, isolated, and with little chance of bringing the United States into the war (June 1941), the Germans had the single opportunity in time and place to win against the heavy odds they faced during the period.

The Germans had no comparable opportunity to win the war between 1939 and 1945. It follows that *the* turning point of World War II occurred in the opening stages of the Barbarossa initiative, in the brief period from the opening day of the advance to approximately 29 July 1941, a day on which Hitler had only to order the continuation of the attack toward Moscow to inflict fatal damage to the Soviet state. It will become apparent that the battles of Alamein, Stalingrad, and Kursk were only incidental junctures in a war lost by Germany in August 1941 and irretrievable thereafter.

Barbarossa, whether successful or unsuccessful, had the tactical, operational, and strategic qualities that make it the hinge of fate in World War II. For several decades, I have believed that the Germans had the fundamental physical strength to defeat the Red Army and seize the Moscow-Gorki mobilization space, and yet, they neither took Moscow nor won the campaign. At that time, the Soviets had no control over their own destiny, fighting hard but ineffectually against German field armies that advanced relentlessly through their defense. Under such circumstances, the Germans must have failed for some reason, some outlandish misjudgment or aberration demanding a fundamental reevaluation of World War II.

Adolf Hitler alone made the decision. In that judgment, he halted German Army Group Center and misdirected it away from Moscow. His procrastination added to the time lost by the Germans in making the eccentric move south into the Ukraine. Virtually every officer in the German army having an opportunity to influence the decision opposed it. Hitler came close to reversing it. Had he gone on vacation in June and July 1941 or been incapacitated, it is difficult to resist the conclusion that the Germans would have won in Europe in 1941.

Hitler's decision was less whimsical and aberrant than might appear at first glance. He operated in a pattern largely unsuspected to the present day, but which is obvious when the Ukrainian decision is connected to other important ones in 1939 to 1940. Universally considered to have been directing a blitz war from 1939 to 1941, Hitler must be reevaluated as having had no such war in mind. In the great campaigns in which he intervened militarily in the German phase of the war—Norway, France, and Soviet Russia—it is not possible to explain several of the more important decisions from the viewpoint of a blitzkrieg strategy. Hitler conceptualized a quick victory over Norway not as part of a blitz war against Britain and France but to secure Swedish iron ore. Initially, he ordered an attack in the west for 12 November 1939 but conceptualized it as a push into Belgium to secure that state as a buffer for the industrial Ruhr. He directed a surprise attack against Soviet Russia, demanding a quick victory, but defining success in terms of seizing Leningrad, center of an important industrial area and key to control over Baltic communications but scarcely a blitz victory in the east.

The Germans nevertheless executed largely blitz-style military operations in the Norwegian, western campaigns and the opening stages of Barbarossa. The campaigns are usually viewed as elements of a series directed toward a lightning defeat of the British and French in the west and the Soviets in the east. The French campaign illustrates especially well the potential for misinterpretation. During four decades, observers have analyzed the quick German victory in the west and linked it to a German intention to knock France out of the war. The original German plan in October 1939 for an attack in the west was not intended to defeat France, let alone quickly. The Manstein plan, approved in February 1940, the follow-up of the original plan, was designed to defeat France quickly, but few German officers had confidence that it would achieve so extreme an end. Most importantly, Hitler did not intend the plan to result in the conquest of France, seeing the operations as a better means to achieve his original objective of seizing Belgium. Hitler's intentions remained ultraconservative: to improve the siege position of Germany by systematically expanding the siege lines around it. Such a mentality—Hitler as siege Führer—explains the earlier decision to take Norway and the later one to pace an attack against the Soviet Union to the conquest of Leningrad and the Ukraine.

In this work, I found myself in the unenviable position of proving a case rather than dispassionately presenting events within a chosen historical period. *Hitler's Panzers East* presents a new interpretation of the European war that claims the Germans were capable of winning in the opening stages of Barbarossa and that Hitler was governed during the war by a siege rather than a blitz mentality. These interpretations demand convincing arguments. I advance the arguments to support an interpretation of the war that explains the observable historical phenomena of 1939 to 1941 more effectively than the existing conventional treatments.

During the years of research for this book, I examined materials at the library and archives of the Hoover Institution on War, Revolution, and Peace, the adjacent libraries of Stanford University, and the special collection of German records of World War II on microfilm at nearby San Jose State University. These materials, together with interviews with participants, and supplemented by documents examined in Freiburg, Germany (National Military Archive and Military Historical Research Office), are the basis for my arguments.

The greatest potential for bias in the results probably lies in my conscious decision to concentrate on German documentation to support conclusions about the summer of 1941. The dearth of materials from the Soviets on this period caused me to make a virtue out of necessity and use original German sources—diaries, memoirs, war diaries, supplementary message traffic, and prisoner of war interrogations, among others. I consider it fundamental to the thesis that the Germans controlled events during the summer of 1941 to the degree that most significant points needed for verification can be derived from German sources. The Germans were so strong relative to the Soviets and so successful in overrunning battlefields, taking prisoners, seizing documents, conducting aerial reconnaissance, and intercepting Soviet radio—and even telephone message traffic—that German records provide a picture of the possibilities for Soviet survival.

R. H. S. STOLFI

Pebble Beach, California

Part I

Hitler, the Soldiers,
and German Decisions, 1939 – 1941

Chapter One

Hitler's Decision to Attack the Soviet Union: Reaction to British Survival or Drive for Final Supremacy in the East?

Point: "For success the operation depended heavily on daring and surprise. Those elements won campaigns but were not enough to win wars."

Earl F. Ziemke, *The German Northern Theater of Operations*

Counterpoint: "On July 7th . . . I ordered an immediate attack across the Dnieper. Kluge appeared at my headquarters . . . absolutely opposed to my decision . . . and ordered that the operation be broken off . . . I told him my preparations had already gone too far to be cancelled . . . furthermore, I was convinced that the attack would succeed and decide the Russian campaign in this very year."

Heinz Guderian, *Panzer Leader*

Could the Second World War have been won by operational decisiveness, daring, and surprise, or was it preordained that the logistical enterprises of the Western Allies and the systematic battering of the Soviets would triumph? Through bold operational concepts, daring, and surprise, the Germans won victories from 1939 to 1941 that led toward victory over a Soviet Union on the verge of military collapse in the summer of 1941. Had the Germans defeated the Soviet Union in 1941, the historical interpreter would have been presented with a montage of brief ground battles leading in a short time to complete German control over Europe and victory in the Second World War. Presented with such a picture, he would generalize that the Germans won battles more effectively than any other combatants,[1] but that the hypothetical German victory depended on elements of chance and personality unique to the times—a rare combination of Prussian military tradition and the messianic political leader, Adolf Hitler—to explain the hypothesized German victory. The Germans did not win, but it is my thesis that they came so close that the premier lesson of the Second World War is how near to victory the German field armies were in the battle for Russia in July 1941. It is tempting to generalize, for example, that the Soviets took almost four years to recover from the first four weeks of Barbarossa, a traumatic time exemplified by the German entry into Smolensk, on the land bridge to Moscow, on 16 July 1941.

Hitler's Decision-Making

Probably the most important decision that Hitler made from 1919 to 1945 was to invade the Soviet Union. Clearly the most important military decision that Hitler made in the Second World War was to abandon the great operational concept of destroying the Soviet armed forces in the forefield of the Moscow-Gorki space during the battle for Russia and to substitute limited operations with limited goals for the destruction of the Russian armed forces and collapse of the Soviet state. These two generalizations are indispensable for understanding Hitler, a man still incompletely understood, and reinterpreting the Second World War in Europe. Such a reinterpretation can show the decisive possibilities in Barbarossa and reshape the war into a more realistic story from which accurate historical lessons can be extracted. At the most general level of interpretation, for example, the lessons of the Second World War are not so much that the Allies won and how they did so, but that the Germans came so close to winning.

With Hitler, it can be shown that he made decisions from 1919 to 1945 in which his own life was at stake, others in which the survival of the National Socialist movement in Germany was questionable, and finally some in which the survival of Germany was affected. Hitler's judgment to seize political power by armed force in Munich on the evening of 8 November 1923 placed his life in jeopardy and threatened the existence of national socialism in Germany not only though the possible death of its leader but also because of damage to the party.[2] The decision was so important that it could have destroyed Hitler and national socialism. One could argue that the decision to make the *Putsch* (armed uprising),

and the correlated determination by Hitler after release from fortress detention to steer the National Socialists into power legally,
constituted judgments that, through luck and skill, set him on his
meteoric rise to national and international prominence. The clear-
est argument supporting Hitler's most important decision, however, would probably be that in which the greatest immediate consequences of Hitler's action could be shown.

The *Putsch* of November 1923 and Hitler's related decision of
1925 to enforce a National Socialist strategy of attaining legal control over the German government had immediate consequences,
largely in Bavaria, and were not as important on their own merits
as later decisions. Hitler garnered great publicity in the German
press from writers covering the trial and became a nationally
known figure, but the *Putsch* affected Germany largely because of
the newsworthiness of a Bavarian uprising rather than its decisive
impact on German politics. In February 1933, shortly after becoming chancellor of the German Republic, Hitler decided to hold new
elections to the Reichstag and use the anticipated gains to push
through a change to the constitution, proroguing the legislature
and enabling him to enact and promulgate legislation. This decision had immediate and direct consequences for Germany, giving
him and the National Socialists effective control over the state by
Christmas 1933. Several important centers of power eluded this
process of synchronization with the party, principally the army
and the church. As important as Hitler's decision was to gain control of the German state, it had no direct, immediate consequences
for Europe similar in magnitude to those in Germany. As Hitler
consolidated his control, he developed a forceful foreign policy,
including a coherent drive to control Europe that would lead toward several of the great political and military decisions of the
twentieth century.

As Hitler's successes mounted, he made decisions with ever-
greater impact on the world. His decisions in the great military
campaigns of 1939–1941 escalated from those affecting Bavaria to
those influencing Germany, Europe, and the world. His bold decision to move German troops back into the German Rhineland in
March 1936, with its attendant risk of war with France and Britain, closely parallels in its essential qualities of risk, breadth, and
consequences the even greater decision to invade Poland in 1939.
Hitler did not intend in either case to draw Germany into a war

with France and Britain. He won the first gamble, but lost the latter and found himself in a war with two major European powers on 3 September 1939. In control of Germany and its armed forces, and on the offensive from 1939 to 1941, Hitler made his most important decisions concerning Germany and Europe. Within the strategic calculus of a Europe-wide war after 3 September, he made grand political decisions, and, as self-appointed commander of the German armed forces since February 1938, he made self-imposed military decisions that would determine the outcome of the war. Because of Hitler's accumulated power by 1939, these decisions would determine the survival of Germany and the future of every state in Europe.

Faced with the 1939 British guarantees to Poland and the French alliance with that state, Hitler nevertheless ordered the invasion of Poland to begin on the morning of 1 September 1939. He made this political decision—when and where to go to war—based on his political masterstroke of several days earlier, the Russo-German nonaggression pact. That pact isolated Poland and made it difficult for any rational statesman in the west to fight a war to safeguard the territorial integrity of Poland. Faced with the British and French ultimatums of 2 September 1939 to halt military operations against Poland, Hitler decided to continue the battle of Poland. The British and French governments declared war on Germany on the afternoon of 3 September 1939. The decision by Hitler to invade Poland and expand the invasion into an Europe-wide war, with time and place largely choices of the Western Allies, might have been Hitler's final great action had it not been for the astounding military successes of the Germans in 1939 and 1940 and the continuation of the German offensive into 1941.

Instead of leading to the defeat of Germany, Hitler's decision to continue the invasion of Poland led to the defeat of the armed forces of Poland, Denmark, Norway, Luxembourg, Holland, Belgium, and France and the physical occupation of those states by early July 1940. The German army's war-fighting style and weapons technology won battles against those armed forces. The German armed forces' planning and execution of great surprise offensives drove everything before them and presented Hitler with the opportunity in July 1940, after the battle of France and the retreat (evacuation) of the Allied amphibious force from northern Norway, to make what would be his most important political decision. In

July 1940, Hitler held the initiative in the war in Europe to make a single decision that could result in German political control over the continent. Hitler chose the correct one in July 1940, to attack the Soviet Union—a decision that, if executed successfully by his armed forces, would give Germany control over the space and resources of Europe from the French coast to the Urals.

The Strategic Potential of Britain in Europe in 1940: A Study in Weakness

Hitler made the correct judgment in July 1940 to attack the Soviet Union, but not, as it might have been projected at the time, because Britain would be forced into some face-saving accommodation with Germany. He made the right judgment because defeating the Soviet Union would have been a decisive event notwithstanding virtually any action taken by Britain to stay in the war. After Germany defeated the Soviet Union, any British posture, even with the continued support of the British Empire, would be meaningless in the face of German control of the fuel, iron ore, and agricultural resources of the entire continent. It could be generalized that Britain would have suffered fatal deficits in strategic space and resources in Britain and fundamental disadvantages in any continued ground campaign in North Africa. In the latter case, powerful, continent-scaled German air and ground forces freed from the continent could be projected into North Africa from closer German-controlled and Italian space.

German destruction of the Soviet armed forces and seizure of the bulk of industrial and natural resources of the Soviet Union would have been the most decisive event of the Second World War in Europe because of the enormous space and productive capabilities coming under German control. The advantages for Germany would have been so great that Britain's traditional trump—sea power and naval blockade—would have been rendered obsolete. In the circumstances, Germany would have been self-sufficient with the contiguous resources of Europe, a situation of economic autarky, which was Hitler's basic reason for expansion into European Russia. The term used by Hitler and others in describing this expansion—*Lebensraum*, or living space—is misleading because it implied that Germany was overcrowded. Hitler's concept was far more decisive, for it saw that Germany lacked resources within its 1914 boundaries and would require greater resources to survive as a great state.

Britain, then, was outmatched after the German victory in Soviet Russia but held two other possible trumps that might have been played. In its European war Britain had been joined by the empire, whose vast but distant resources must be counted in Britain's powers of resistance. Perhaps the single most important comment on the empire is that it was spread worldwide, and under the postulated circumstances Germany, without a land front, could have concentrated air and naval resources against the limited British Isles and blockaded it effectively enough to prevent the empire from sustaining a war. The other possible British trump, one played with decisive effect in April 1917, would have been drawing the United States into the war. After the planned German victory over the Soviet Union of September 1941 and the threatening strategic situation for the United States in the Pacific, the trump would not have been promising for a U.S. declaration of war against Germany. Even with the (unlikely) intervention of the United States at the end of 1941, it is questionable that Britain could have supported "spatially" the effort required to conduct a successful amphibious operation against the three million square miles of territory under the control of the Germans, with a German army free to concentrate against that landing.

Hitler's Use of Britain After the French Campaign (1940)to Justify an Attack Against the Soviet Union

When Hitler made the decision in July 1940 to invade Russia, he must have sensed that victory there, in and of itself, would have ended the war in Europe. Yet from July 1940 to June 1941, he reiterated with impressive consistency the argument that the Soviet Union was Britain's last hope for continuing the struggle and that its defeat would force Britain out of the war. Based on ample sources, historians and analysts trumpet a consensus that Hitler attacked the Soviet Union to deny Britain its last potential strong ally on the continent.[3] That interpretation has not been challenged, yet it does not stand up to the logic of the imbalance in resources between Britain and a German-dominated continent and to views formulated by Hitler in writing as early as 1924. With awe-inspiring consistency, Hitler made it clear that German destiny would be realized one way or another in European Russia—the east. Hitler was impressed with the economic power that Germans could extract from the east; he perceived economic self-sufficiency resulting from German control over European Russia. He lavished twelve months of preparation on the campaign, which included widespread deception and an unprecedented concentration of forces for a military offensive.

During the long period of planning and concentration for the attack, Hitler monotonously repeated the theme that the invasion of the Soviet Union was forced on him by continuing British resistance. This does not mean that in his own mind it was the real or the most important reason for the attack. Hitler has been quoted as saying no person would ever know what he was really thinking.[4] The most important decision he made prior to the order to begin planning for the invasion of the Soviet Union was his decision to attack Poland, with the resultant outbreak of the Second World War. From the autumn of 1938 through the last few days of August 1939, he hewed to the line that Germany required the return of Danzig to the Reich and certain other changes in the territory held by Poland in Pommerania, referred to as the "Polish corridor." Shortly before the invasion, Hitler succinctly commented, with virtually no later elaboration, that the invasion of Poland had nothing to do with Danzig[5] but was intended to smash the Polish state and realize the German destiny in the east.

Many people in the political and military spheres close to Hitler in his capacity as the supreme decision-maker in Germany remarked that they never knew what Hitler was really thinking, for example, the cool and brilliant Generalfeldmarschall Erich von Manstein, in the second volume of his memoirs. In a similar vein, the intelligent, tough, political soldier of fortune, Hermann Göring, commented that when it came to making important decisions in the Third Reich, he and all others had as little to say about those decisions as the stones on which they stood.[6] Göring's comment implies that not only were those around Hitler unable to influence the great decisions, but also that they were unaware of the thought processes, rationale, motivations, driving forces, and ultimate goals behind them.

A thesis of this work is, however, that the Barbarossa decision was the most important made by Hitler. First, it was made extraordinarily soon after the fall of France, which occurred in the last days of June 1940, but slightly in advance of serious, coherent preparations for a projected amphibious operation against England. As usual, the beginning of any process is important, and a sapient question is: In July 1940 did Hitler envision the leisurely start of alternate possible future operations, or did he see himself willing Barbarossa to commence at the earliest time and with the best weather for effective campaigning in the east in 1941? Strong arguments support views that Hitler never intended to launch an amphibious attack against England[7] and had no realistic opportunity for such an invasion because of the approach of autumn and adverse weather. But the idea that Hitler did not have his heart in an amphibious invasion of Britain does not help to prove either that he conceptualized Barbarossa as independent of Sea Lion (code name for the projected amphibious attack) or as a means to the end of defeating Britain. Even before he could be certain that Britain would continue a war at sea and in the air, but no land war on the continent, he had alerted the army for an invasion of the Soviet Union. This and the unwavering emphasis he placed on Barbarossa from July 1940 onward support a thesis that he considered the campaign in the east the primary direction for German war strategy independent of Britain and the sea-air campaign in the west.

The fact remains that Hitler gave the successful conclusion of the war with Britain as the rationale for the battle of Russia. As a successful German politician and leader of a patriotic movement, and later as dictator, Hitler was acutely sensitive about his popular image and the effects of his actions. He portrayed Danzig and the corridor as causes of the confrontation between Germany and Poland in late 1938 and 1939, and ordered an elaborate "incident" to serve as an immediate stimulant for launching a counterattack in defense of the Reich. Why, considering Hitler's political acumen and decisiveness, did he not announce to the German public that the time had arrived to smash the Polish Slavs and expand into Polish space? Hitler seems to have been driven by a finely tuned sense of what would satisfy most Germans, not just national socialists, as the reasons for war and the various campaigns during the German initiatives from 1939 to 1941. Hitler was dismayed by the lack of enthusiasm in Berlin for the war in Poland on the morning of 1 September 1939.[8] He must have been frustrated that his demands against Poland had been moderate, at least until the last days of August 1939, and that these demands were not enough to result in a popular decision against an opportunistic, chauvinistic neighbor, which had expanded at German expense after the First World War.

On 22 June 1940, armistice day between (victorious) Germany and France, one sees Hitler in an immensely strong position and on the verge of making the great decision of the war—to attack the Soviet Union. He faced a defeated France and a crippled Britain and was already ordering the final, decisive move. He informed a few around him on 21 July 1940 of his intention, from which he never varied down to the predawn of 22 June 1941, when the earliest attack began in Army Group North. Since Hitler personally directed the commander in chief of the army, Generalfeldmarschall Walter von Brauchitsch, on 21 July 1940 to prepare a campaign in the east, he must have formed his decision earlier than that date, probably sometime after the armistice with France. Based on documented comments and known wartime outcomes, many have propagated the interpretation that Hitler stood mesmerized by Britain and its continued resistance in the war and, as evidenced by the Sea Lion directive of 16 July 1940 for the invasion of England, bent all efforts to defeat it.

Based also on documented comments and known wartime circumstances, an alternate interpretation suggests that Hitler turned immediately toward the final great showdown with the Soviets (ideologically) and the Russians (spatially), having defeated France and neutralized Britain. It would be more in accord with Hitler's consistently avowed goal of expansion in the east, and the defeat of France and neutralization of Britain, to see him moving east immediately to accomplish the self-appointed task of seizing the resource base for a thousand-year Reich. Hitler was a middle-aged man in a hurry, driven by personal fear of an early death through incurable disease, his primary concerns probably being cancer in the early 1930s and heart problems thereafter.[9]

Hitler Faces the Historical Necessity to Attack in the East in 1941

In any event, Hitler made the decision in July 1940 to attack the Soviet Union. The decision came after two decades of rhetorical philosophizing about the eastern solution to the German problem of living space and followed Hitler's self-willed judgment to smash Poland. Hitler then faced a declaration of war by the British and French governments, a western decision that mirrored Britain's determination to fight a war against Germany at the time and place of its choosing rather than at some other, less opportune time. Hitler found himself in the nightmarish situation, described in his writings and discussions in the 1920s and 1930s, of being forced to fight Britain and France. In Hitler's writings, these two powers, through hate, envy, and fear, would not allow Germany to gain living space in the east necessary for Germany's long-term security and development. Hitler voluntarily took the first step toward eastern expansion on 1 September 1939 and two days later found himself in an unwanted but forecast war with Britain and France. Nine months later, he had maneuvered himself into strategic freedom of movement to complete the drive to the east.

Hitler found it circumspect to portray the crisis over Poland in 1939 as one thing (friction over Danzig and the corridor) while actually heading relentlessly toward a different goal of either smashing Poland in a quick battle or enticing it into joining an eastern crusade against Bolshevik Russia. Despite his penchant for being decisive politically and grandiose ideologically, Hitler was deeply concerned over what reasons Germans would accept for his great independent decisions—those which he had full freedom to conceptualize and control. In Czecho-Slovakia in March 1939, he gave the reason for the invasion (and resulting *Blumenkrieg*, or flower war) as the inability of the Czech government to maintain order, which few can accept today as real. In Poland, under virtually identical political conditions of sudden invasion, he likewise misrepresented the real reasons—which were difficult for the German people to accept—for a military invasion. One must suspect that Hitler did not believe he could present the actual reasons for the invasions of Czecho-Slovakia (March 1939); Poland (September 1939); and the ultimate move, Barbarossa planning and the invasion of Soviet Russia (July 1940-June 1941). Conventional wisdom on the buildup, outbreak, and early progress of the war rather contemptuously ignores Hitler's reasons for the occupation of Czecho-Slovakia, utterly rejects Danzig and the corridor as the motivation for Hitler's invasion of Poland, but then accepts without reservations Hitler's statements that he invaded the Soviet Union to force Britain out of the war.

When the British government, through pique, pride, annoyance, and concern, determined that there would be a Europe-wide war on 3 September 1939, Hitler found himself hurtling toward the

final showdown in the east several years ahead of his probable
1943–1945 schedule. He also found himself in a war with France
and Britain that did not promise much hope of success, let alone
quick success. Retrospectively, it is easy to forget that the German
plan (*Fall Gelb*, or Case Yellow), for offensive operations in the
west from October 1939 to February 1940 was a woefully inadequate document. The German plan of attack was a half-measure
that almost certainly would have mired in a stalemate in northwestern France with the additional hazard of a British naval blockade. It is difficult to state conclusively what the outcome of *Fall
Gelb* would have been in its original inadequate form, but one can
generalize that Hitler would have had precious little opportunity
to extricate himself from a war of attrition in the west, leaving
him no chance of attacking in the east.

In the event, through a rare combination of luck and strategic
insight, Hitler adopted Manstein's ideas for the offensive in the
west. Using Manstein's concepts, in a revised operations plan, the
German armed forces knocked France out of the war and handled
Britain so roughly that they presented Hitler with the initiative to
make the next move. Few can doubt that Hitler saw his ultimate
political mission as the invasion and conquest of European Russia.
The task was historic and legendary, based on the towering pre-
sumption and idealism of national socialism, an idealism so great
that Hitler consciously adopted the anomalous position that no
one would ever know what he was really thinking. One could say
that if Hitler had been presented with the opportunity to attack in
the east after the frenetic pattern of 1938 and 1939, he would have
seized the opportunity with his typical political decisiveness and
moved east. This can be said with special confidence because Hitler
made the decision in July 1940 to attack the Soviet Union.

Yet, in counterpoint, Hitler also made it clear in writing and
conversation that Germany's most important enemies were Britain
and France. In this apparent inconsistency among Germany's most
important enemies, Hitler saw not only Bolshevik Russia but also
Britain and France as dangers because the two countries would
probably never give Germany a free hand in the east. It is difficult
to understand how Hitler hoped to solve this dilemma, particularly
with the half-measure qualities of the original *Fall Gelb*—which
lacked even the goal of defeating the Allied armed forces on the
continent—and his devastating indecision during the Manstein

Plan evolutions. Having come full circle through various exoteric analyses of Hitler's decision in July 1940 to attack the Soviet Union, one can suggest the revision that if Hitler's great final goal were the conquest of European Russia, and French defeat and British neutralization in June 1940 presented Hitler with that opportunity, the consensus that Hitler attacked the Soviet Union to finish off a partly crippled Britain is not credible.

A basic difficulty with the current interpretation is that it places the horse and the cart of the known strategic situation in reverse; it makes a wounded Britain (the cart) more important than the Soviet Union (the horse). It is difficult to accept that Hitler did not see the defeat of the Soviet Union as the decisive event of the war after June 1940. Hitler conceived the invasion of the Soviet Union as a complete surprise, out of peace into war in overwhelming strength, obsessed by the ambitious national socialist goal to colonize large areas of European Russia. The reasons for the invasion were so radical that Hitler could not pass them to either his distinguished senior military commanders and staff or the German people to explain the attack. At the risk of being trite, one can suggest that had Britain not been in the war in July 1940, Hitler would have had to invent it as a convenient, plausible, and acceptable explanation to attack the Soviet Union.

Chapter Two

German Calculation of the Rigors of an Attack Against the Soviet Union: Accurate Appraisal or Underestimation?

Point: "It is of decisive importance for the breakthrough to push forward as far as possible without regard to the danger from the flanks, with maximum use of the mobility afforded by our tank engines, without rest or rest days, with movement at night, and mobility limited only by the distance which fuel supplies will allow."[1]

Army Group Center, Panzer Group 2, XXXXVIIth Panzer Corps, Order Number 1 for the attack against the Soviet Union, dated 13 June 41

HISTORIANS and analysts today interpret the Second World War as one that the Germans could never have won. In September 1939, Germany faced a gloomy crisis, in which Hitler blundered into a war with Britain and France while simultaneously fighting in Poland. But in July 1940, when Hitler decided to attack the Soviet Union, circumstances in Europe had changed so radically to the advantage of the Germans that Hitler had the historic opportunity to make a decision that could have led to German victory. Observing the Second World War through conventional sources but a unique perspective, one can see that Germany's trumps in war were few but formidable. The most important were Adolf Hitler's political decisiveness and the battle-winning capabilities of the German army. In July 1940, Hitler had to make the right political decision, and the German army had to plan and concentrate effectively to give Germany a reasonable chance of winning a Russian campaign.

The Unique Synthesis of Hitler and the German Army: 1939–1941

Hitler showed impressive decisiveness in ordering the attack against the Soviet Union, an indomitable will for which he has not received adequate recognition for the potential consequences. In historical parallels, when the Japanese launched their surprise attack against Russia in February 1904, the operation comprised an attack by naval and amphibious forces against Imperial Russian forces in northeast China to seize and hold territory far from the heartland of Russia and only recently occupied. In contrast, Hitler ordered an all-out attack across a land boundary into the heartland of the state, with the intention to destroy it. Hitler employed the army as the instrument of decision against the Soviet Union, providing it with the advantages of surprise and concentration of effort, factors that ensured the quick success of the German army even over a large, well-armed country like the Soviet Union. By making the decisive political decision, Hitler gave the German army the parallel opportunity to make decisive gains, exploiting surprise and concentration into victory.

Historians have inadequately correlated Hitler's political daring in Poland, the west, and the Balkans with the stunning military victories, tending to suture off the periods during which the campaigns developed into one compartment of political considerations and another filled with the gunsmoke of battles. Blockaded by British sea power, Hitler made a dramatic political decision, with few parallels in boldness, to seize Norway from Larvik to Narvik and presented the German armed forces the opportunity to execute a daring surprise attack. My point is that the sensational attack in Norway was possible only because of Hitler's political will. In short, without a politically decisive Hitler, there would be no brilliantly decisive military success. A subtle extension of my point is that the attack's success depended almost solely on the offensive will and daring of the German army and the fundamental operational style transferred to the German navy and air force. Without battle-winning German commanders and combat soldiers there could be no successful battles, no brilliantly decisive political victory.[2] Against Soviet Russian land power in July 1940, the delicately balanced synthesis of Hitler and the German army faced the great test of defeating the Soviet armed forces in the brief summer campaigning season of high-latitude Europe.

The Germans Gauge the Strength of Russland: July 1940–June 1941

Serious German planning for the attack on the Soviet Union began as early as 22 July 1940, when Generaloberst Franz Halder, chief, Army General Staff, began to study the problems of an offensive in the east. In one brief week, from 22 to 29 July 1940, Halder devised perhaps the most effective scheme of maneuver possible for a rapid conquest of the Soviet Union—simple, direct, and remarkably concentrated for a front expanding in breadth as one pushed eastward into Russia. Having studied the problem briefly, Halder assigned the talented chief of staff of the 18th Army on the Dutch front in the west, *Generalmajor* Erich Marcks, to study the problem further. Marcks completed a plan by 5 August 1940 that was the basis for the final army plan submitted to Hitler on 5 December 1940. "Halder concluded that an attack launched from assembly areas in East Prussia and northern Poland toward Moscow would offer the best chances of success."[3] After destroying the Soviet armies defending Moscow and seizing the city, the attacking German field armies would compel Soviet forces pinned in the Ukraine to fight battles with reversed fronts. The initial German attacks would be concentrated on surprisingly narrow fronts, and the main attack, in the center, would remain that way on the advance toward Moscow. Wisely, Halder knew that for success the German plan would depend heavily on the Soviet reaction to it. He felt that if the Soviet military high command had a strategy of immediate, systematic withdrawal into the hinterland, the German field armies could not intercept its forces enroute to Moscow. Then, the war would drag out somewhere in European Russia to the detriment of the Germans. In the event, with astonishing good luck for Halder, Hitler, and the Germans, the Soviets chose to defend strongly everywhere, as far forward as possible, retreating only when forced by tactical disintegration or when breaking out of several large encirclements set by the Germans.

It is difficult today to judge what the German military planners thought of their chances of success in a war against the Soviet Union. Historians and analysts tend to judge, beclouded by Germany's defeat in the Second World War. Influenced by the ultimate German defeat and the initial German timetable of approximately ten weeks for victory over the Soviet Union, commentators usually generalize that the German army underestimated both the

Russian armed forces and campaign conditions, falling prey to naive overconfidence. German veterans of Barbarossa, many of whom experienced the misdirected culmination of the offensive at Moscow in December 1941 and took part in almost four years of half-victories and full defeats on the eastern front, complicate the scene by generalizing that the Soviet Union could never have been defeated.[4] Analysis of the planning for Barbarossa and the course of the offensive itself do not support a contention that the German army underestimated the Russian armed forces or that it could not have defeated them.[5] Personal diaries and other documents of the time show the Germans soberly gauging the challenges of a campaign in Russia.[6] Many middle- and senior-ranking German officers had fought on the eastern front during the First World War, and virtually all were impressed by the physical hardness, primitive stoicism, and resistance of the Russian forces and their willingness to take casualties.

Contrary to the prevalent interpretation that the Germans underestimated the Soviet armed forces and the rigors of a campaign in Russia, the German High Command (OKH) approached the campaign with respect and trepidation, evidenced by such details as its purchase of 15,000 Polish light wagons and horses suited to the unpaved tracks posing as roads in Russia and hiring 15,000 Poles to energize the primitive but effective, eastern-style transportation system.[7] Similarly, Hitler discovered in the early stages of planning that the Luftwaffe surprisingly intended to maintain a significant number of its antiaircraft guns (Flak, or Fliegerabwehrkanone) in a reserve pool in the German home defense area. With his inimitable decisiveness in many situations, he ordered every gun in the pool to be turned over to the army and used in the east against both ground and air targets, commenting that every available gun would be used against the Soviets.[8] These details of German planning for Barbarossa do not support the interpretation that the Germans underestimated the Soviets.

Franz Halder, chief, Army General Staff, kept a personal diary covering the preparations for Barbarossa from 22 July 1940 to 22 June 1941, and it does not contain a single remark on the pending eastern campaign that can be read as underestimating its rigors.[9] Approximately two weeks into the campaign, on 3 July 1941, Halder noted that "after two weeks of war the Soviets have in fact been beaten," and this comment has been lifted by numerous historians to illustrate the German underestimation of the Soviet Union in war. Halder's comment is equated naturally, but not necessarily correctly, with an assumed parallel underestimation of the Soviets by Halder and Germans in general. A more effective interpretation of Halder's remark is that it was accurate, alerting us to some almost incredible resurgence by Soviets and Russians or some catastrophic blunder at the highest level in the German command, a Titanesque mistake in both timing and direction, in the opening weeks of the Russian campaign.

German military planners displayed a healthy respect for the Russians and accurately sensed the challenges of a war against them. Heinz Guderian, who led the largest armored group in the east directly toward Moscow in the *Schwerpunkt* (point of main effort) of the Halder plan, published a book on tank warfare in 1937 in which he estimated the size of the Russian tank force at approximately 10,000.[10] Guderian had visited a Soviet tank factory in 1933 that produced 22 tanks daily of the Christie-derived, fast-cavalry type, and he had few delusions about the size of the Soviet tank force and the qualities of most of the vehicles. Guderian must have been prepared to face the actual number of Soviet tanks available for combat in June 1941, based on his realistic appreciation of the numbers in the late 1930s.[11] Other German planners displayed similar realism. The junior Major Rudolf Loytved-Hardegg, a Luftwaffe intelligence officer, who for reasons of deception, secrecy, and achieving surprise was responsible for estimating the size and quality of the Soviet air force and creating the target folders for every Luftwaffe target planned for attack on 22 June 1941 north of the Pripyat Marshes, passed on his responsible, "front line" estimate of the size of the entire Soviet air force as 14,000 military aircraft, a remarkably accurate figure, not an underestimate.[12]

Hitler Calculates Russian Strength

These accurate estimates reflect solid realism among the German military planners of Operation Barbarossa in appraising the important dimensions of the Soviet armed forces. The OKH led the planning for Barbarossa, which would be an immense ground forces operation, and OKM (Navy High Command) and OKL (Air Force High Command) fell in smoothly with the overall scheme of maneuver of the ground forces, notwithstanding in the latter the special influence and sensitivity of Hermann Göring, designated successor to Hitler in the event of Hitler's demise or incapacity. The sober and realistic appraisals of a wide range of military planners, represented by Halder, Guderian, and Hardegg, contrast with some statements and actions by at least one key figure. Hitler can be quoted to prove that he underestimated the Soviets, but equally decisive comments can be produced to show his perceptive concerns for the dangers of a campaign in the east. At a conference on 9 January 1941, Hitler was quoted in a war diary as saying, "The Russian Armed Forces are like a headless colossus with feet of clay but we cannot with certainty foresee what they might become in the future. The Russians must not be underestimated. All available resources must therefore be used in the German attack."[13] The first part of the first sentence has been quoted misleadingly by writers anxious to buttress the idea that the Germans underestimated the challenges of a campaign in the east. Quoted in its entirety, the estimate comprises a remarkably succinct and effective analysis of the dangers and necessities of an attack against the Soviets.

Hitler's conversations, speeches, and decisions during the planning and concentration of forces for Operation Barbarossa reflect a realistic appraisal of the chances of success. It is also easy to forget that Hitler made the right decision, the only decision that gave him a realistic opportunity to win, dependent almost completely on playing Germany's trumps rather than awaiting certain defeat by losing the initiative and eventually encountering the strength of an overwhelming enemy coalition. Hitler played the trumps—his political decisiveness and audacity in ordering a timely 1941 attack on the Soviet Union and the superior operational style of the German army to beat the Soviets—and it must be assumed that he had alternate fits of pessimism and optimism about the whole business reflected in both moderate and immoderate statements on the outcome of the invasion. The obvious criticism that Hitler should have finished Britain first is not convincing, for when Sea Lion was cancelled indefinitely on 17 September 1940, he faced a six-month wait before launching an amphibious operation against a high-technology, Athenian-style state, which would have regained its psychological balance after the disasters in France and Norway. Hitler displayed correct instinct *and* reason in the choice of a surprise attack, but in doing so he decided to engage a colossus and must be suspected of having a clear appreciation of the risk.

German Timetables of Advance

Writers dedicated to the proposition that the Germans had little chance of success in Barbarossa point to the timetables of 6 to 10 to 17 weeks to conquer the Soviet Union as perhaps the strongest evidence of a gross underestimate of Soviet Russia. Personalities as different as the mercurial Hitler and the sober-minded Halder estimated during the planning for Barbarossa that the campaign would be over in from 6 to 10 weeks. Taking the estimate of 6 weeks as a base for consideration, one must be struck by the actual 195 additional weeks the war continued beyond German estimates.

The cutting edge of analysis cuts several ways in this case: If the Soviets were so much stronger than the Germans estimated, why did it take them 195 additional weeks after Barbarossa, with the notable assistance of Britain and the United States, to defeat the underestimators? Almost any answer to such a question must imply that even if the Germans failed in Barbarossa, they caused enough widespread and extensive damage to the Soviets in the course of the eastern campaign to restrain the eventual Soviet victory and reduce it to frustratingly indecisive proportions. After all, Hitler and Halder, representing Germany politically and militarily, respectively, envisioned the goal of Barbarossa as the conquest of European Russia. One cannot be certain of the goals of Josef Stalin and the Soviet Communist party in the war, into which they blundered and which took so long to finish, but the Soviet leadership achieved nothing as decisive as the Germans almost achieved in a few weeks. Instead, after four years of war, the Soviet leaders found themselves in control of only half the continent and, most importantly, not occupying Germany and France.

Citing German estimates of 6 to 10 weeks to defeat Soviet Russia, conventional views proffer no convincing argument that the German advance fell behind schedule and conclude that the capabilities of the Soviets were underestimated. The interpretation sees in the continuation of fighting beyond 6 to 10 weeks, and the defeat of the Germans 195 weeks later, a natural, essentially gradual decline of the Germans toward inexorable defeat. The first weeks of Barbarossa, however, instead of showing German underestimation of the Soviets, demonstrates that the *Schwerpunkt* army group of the German invasion met the most sanguine expectations of the hardheaded and restrained Halder. Army Group Center had advanced toward the Moscow-Gorki space and inflicted striking casualties and damage to the defending Soviet field armies, great enough to equate with impending defeat of the Soviet Union.

Hitler's Fundamental Underestimation of the Offensive Capabilities of the German Army

A revisionist comment about Hitler and Barbarossa is that in the planning and in the execution of the invasion, the more important decisions he made reflect a fundamental underestimation of the offensive capabilities of the German army and a concomitant overestimation of Soviet armed forces. This generalization is juxtaposed against the main weight of the opinion that the Germans underestimated the Soviets, and, largely for that reason, a campaign they planned to last six to ten weeks dragged on for almost four years and ended in (German) defeat. Besides this general view, the more detailed conventional interpretations offer supporting evidence that Hitler underestimated the Soviets, marshalling his words in conferences, conversations, and written directives.

The evidence is a mixed bag to be handled with care in considering the possibilities of Barbarossa to end the war in Europe in the summer of 1941. Discussions and directives show Hitler organizing part of European Russia for occupation and ordering reductions in armaments in anticipation of a successful conclusion to the campaign. Historians offer such evidence to support the view that the Germans were out of touch with reality in planning and executing the invasion. Many writers comment that the Germans failed to provide winter clothing for their field armies and offer this as evidence of underestimation of Soviet resistance. The logic is strained, however, because the Germans are accused of underestimation when they planned in advance for occupation of the Soviet Union and underestimation when they did not plan in advance.

The most effective analysis of this situation probably shows Hitler inefficiently and overoptimistically dissipating the German effort in Barbarossa instead of concentrating on achieving a quick victory. Regarding winter clothing, neither Hitler nor the Army General Staff can be criticized fairly for not having ready stocks of winter clothing. In planning for Barbarossa it would have been reasoning from false and irrelevant premises to stock special clothing for a winter campaign. Beyond the initial six to ten weeks of battle, and by the autumn offensive in early October 1941, the Germans can be criticized for failing to gather clothing for winter field operations but not for underestimating the rigors of a campaign in Russia. By October 1941, Barbarossa had miscarried because of Hitler's fear and uncertainty earlier in the campaign. By then, the Germans can be criticized only for not adjusting to the actual circumstances. Even in October, however, and concerned with a factor categorized under "weather," the Germans might have been better served by concentrating on a special effort to get through the autumn rains en route to Moscow rather than tying up transportation and personnel to get winter clothing. Operation Typhoon of October 1941 was a late, finely tuned effort to push into the Moscow-Gorki space and destroy the Soviet forces defending it. Gathering a mass of agricultural and engineer-style tractors might well have pulled the Germans through the mud of October.[14]

Earlier, during the time of the final planning for Typhoon and still within the expanded context of Barbarossa, Hitler set some objectives for the German field armies and made comments that betray unrealistic optimism. When he should have been concerned with the defeat of the Soviet armies defending Moscow and the seizure of the capital and communications center of the Soviet Union, he was assigning unrealistic territorial targets divorced from the strategic reality of October 1941 (although, interestingly, not from the earlier reality of July). Hitler set targets for the field armies in several cases that were so outlandish that one must suspect that he based them on some combination of wishful thinking and sublimation of his own doubts on the capabilities of the army to reach the "assigned" territorial objectives. The stated objectives nevertheless stand as a kind of monument to Hitler's underestimation of the rigors of the campaign by October, that is, when under the Halder Plan it probably would have been completed successfully.

The OKH plan of 5 December 1941[15] was presented to Adolf Hitler as the basis for the directive for the invasion of the Soviet Union signed by him on 18 December 1941. It can be referred to as the Halder plan. For an undertaking as vast as the land invasion of the Soviet Union, the Halder plan was monumentally simple and direct. As such, it contained no inherent flaws such as over-complexity or misdirection and was within the capabilities and style of the German army to accomplish in the necessarily short time required to prevent the recovery of the Soviets from the ini-tial trauma and head off the development of a lengthy two-front war. Under the Halder plan, German Army Group Center was to advance quickly and directly into the Moscow-Gorki space—just as simple as that.

The arrival of Army Group Center at and beyond Moscow on roughly 28 August 1941 in the communications center of European Russia would have disintegrated the resulting isolated Leningrad and Ukrainian fronts. The Germans would have interrupted rail communications there and forced the Soviet armies to fight with reversed fronts while simultaneously pressed on their original fronts by Army Groups North and South. With a stroke of the pen, on 17 December 1941, Hitler modified the Halder plan by halting Army Group Center after it had broken the Soviet armies in White Russia and turning its mobile forces north to annihilate the Soviet forces in the Baltic area.[16] The Germans were committing them-selves to a battle, however, in which surprise, speed, and daring would be the indispensable necessities for victory, and such ti-midity and scattering of force were out of place. Halder never var-ied from his position before (or after) this time that "major opera-tions should have been directed exclusively toward Moscow,"[17] but he failed to enforce his view on Hitler.

In Operation Barbarossa, the Germans had the capability to win the Second World War in Europe in 1941. Hitler's planning deci-sion to halt the *Schwerpunkt* army group to assure the progress of Army Group North—a side showforce from the viewpoint of the defeat of the Soviet Union—was *the* planning decision of the war. This assertion is made in the face of the great Allied planning decisions made later in the war that led eventually to coalition victory. Those decisions, in effect, were made possible by the ear-lier unforced error of Hitler in the planning of Barbarossa and, after some reversals and tortuous gyrations, in the execution of the campaign. How is it possible that a man of Hitler's daring and aggressiveness politically could apparently have been so indecisive and confused within the framework of the planning and execution of the accompanying military campaigns? One purpose of this book is to suggest an answer to this intriguing question in later chapters, but first, it is necessary to point out on the basis of such a question that Hitler, from the moment he engaged in military campaigning, showed exaggerated, indecisive, and irrelevant concerns in executing blitz campaigns.

Chapter Three

Hitler and the Opening Battles of Three Great Blitz Campaigns: Comparing the Strategic Picture in Barbarossa with that in France and the Balkans

The German army's virtuosity in winning the battles of 1939–1941 has masked the eccentric pattern of Hitler's concern with local crisis and immediate detail at the expense of the grand concepts of the early campaigns. Except for a few high points, such as the Dunkirk decision, Hitler's apprehensive intrusion in the war's direction from 1942 onward in the losing stages is better known than his earlier interference with success. The earlier meddling was characterized by a fatuous pattern of dissipating the main effort in campaigns in extraneous excursions and mistaken alarms. The earlier meddling also had far more important consequences than the later. It resulted in the turning point—the loss of the war for the Germans in August 1941—and his anticlimactic but better-known half-measures from 1942 onward.

Hitler's Indecisive Objectives in the West, 1939–1940: Setting the Pattern for Russia

At the highest level, perhaps the best pre-Barbarossa example of Hitler's fear of grand military concepts in continental war was his initial move into serious military strategy—his unrealistic directive of 9 October 1939 to launch an attack in the west by 12 November 1939. Not only did Hitler order an attack with bad timing that gave little chance of success, but he also approved a plan of military operations whose truncated aim was to achieve, roughly, the occupation of Belgium. The OKH operation order issued on 19 October 1939 in conformance with Hitler's earlier directive contains the following indecisive German aim for an offensive in the west: "To defeat the largest possible elements of the French and Allied Armies and simultaneously to gain as much territory as possible in Holland, Belgium, and Northern France as a basis for successful air and sea operations against Britain and as a broad protective zone for the Ruhr."[1]

At first glance, this timorous half-measure, disguised as the German armed forces' aim in launching an offensive against the combined strength of two major world powers, indicts Hitler, Brauchitsch, and Halder as less than competent to fight a war in 1939. Few writers have addressed the ramifications of a German offensive in the west conducted according to the aim highlighted above— to seize roughly forty miles of Belgian seacoast so that the most powerful land power in Europe could conduct more efficient sea and air operations against Britain. Although that aim was extended by an amendment of 29 October 1939, the amended OKH operations order contained no hint of fighting a French campaign to victory. The amended operations order was the basis for a German offensive in the west from the end of October 1939 to the last half of February 1940, a period of four months. It is difficult to escape the conclusion that had the German army executed the operations order of 29 October 1939 and achieved its stated aim, the result would have been stalemate in the west.[2] That would have been a strategic dead end for Germany in the autumn of 1939 or spring of 1940, when the offensive could have been launched under the defective order.

At second glance, then, Hitler and OKH, but especially Halder as army chief of staff, are still indicted as less than competent in planning the quick victory in the west required to prevent German defeat through blockade and attrition. But how could Hitler, with his penchant for the dramatically decisive political move, and Halder, with his expressed emphasis on grand operational concepts, have been parties to the October operations order? Regarding Hitler, who seems more complex and remains hidden farther from view, the answer is clear. He fearfully perceived early in October 1940[3] that the French would occupy Belgium during the onset of winter fog and, apparently on that dread perception, decided to launch an offensive to forestall it.[4] Although concerned with a realistic potential action by the enemy. Hitler was obsessed by that detail to the exclusion of a decisive plan to defeat the Allied forces in France and occupy it. From the beginning of the war it is clear that he ignored a principal aim of military strategy, the destruction of the enemy armed forces, and instead chased less important objectives.[5] Well before the planning and execution of Barbarossa, he can be seen in a pattern of going for every tempting objective at once on the offensive, then overreacting to crises in the ensuing battle.

If any important question remains unanswered in the war from 1939 to 1941, it is probably: How could the Germans win *anything* from September 1939 to October 1941 with Hitler's nervous instability, British possession of Ultra, and the incapability of the Italians to conduct their part of the war? The answer lies partly in the need to reevaluate upward the quality of Germany's trumps. Hitler's decisiveness in the great political moves of the period must be seen as even more important in explaining the German victories than suspected. The battle-winning capabilities of the German army also must be seen as extraordinary because the army had to overcome first-class opposing armies and the unique combination of factors noted above.

Hitler proved a frail reed in his capacity as military commander by his inability to back the vital line of operations in the "lightning" campaigns of 1940–1941. Halder, in contrast, must be represented as capable of seeing the vital line of operations in any military campaign. Yet, reacting to Hitler's directive of 9 October 1939 to attack in the west immediately, he was largely responsible for producing the ineffectual OKH operations order of 19 October 1939. Halder, whose competence can scarcely be doubted, produced an operations order that was a classic half-measure. The combination of Halder and half-measure is an unlikely one, demanding an explanation, which, in turn, could produce a better interpretation of the war and similar situations in other wars.

In October 1939, Brauchitsch and Halder (commander and chief of staff, German army, respectively) found themselves directed by the supreme political authority of the state to carry out an almost immediate attack in the west. Neither man showed great confidence in the attack prepared in October 1939, but neither left any comprehensive comments on what he felt was wrong with it.[6] Halder kept an extensive diary and wrote several pieces for the

U.S. Army after the Second World War. He gave an incomplete picture in which he makes clear that the army required more time to recover from the Polish campaign than a November 1939 attack date would allow. The army also needed better weather for offensive operations. With all his operational skills, he does not comment on the circumscribed, utterly indecisive aim set for the offensive in the west. It is not clear, therefore, whether Halder lacked confidence in the attack directed by Hitler because of the unrealistic timing and season or because the Hitler-directed attack was an impossible half-measure and could not defeat the French even if its aim were accomplished.

In an argument that casts a favorable light on Hitler, Halder may have been the prisoner of his historical condition in the German army of 1939, one that involved enormous respect for the French army[7] and reflected no room for strategic maneuver against a France shielded by the Maginot line and alerted to a German attack through Belgium. As prisoner of that condition, and faced with the strained and premature concerns of Hitler to prevent a French coup in Belgium, Halder must have lacked confidence in the success of the half-measure forced on the German army. In fighting for better timing and season for the offensive, and probably for an indefinite postponement of any attack in the hope of a negotiated political settlement, Halder can be seen as pessimistic about the war and unwilling to examine the possibilities of another decisive Schlieffen plan.[8]

Hitler's Indecisive Objectives in the West, 1939–1940: The Analogy Between France (1940) and Russia (1941)

The German offensive against France can be employed to understand the grander possibilities of the offensive against the Soviet Union. Hitler can be shown, for example, more willing than the commander and chief of staff of the army to combat the French. It appears that Hitler, as usual, displayed unerring instincts in his aggressive will to attack France but erred in almost every detail of the battle against the French army. Brauchitsch and Halder showed neither confidence in a battle in Belgium and northern France nor willingness to fight it. They get high marks for humanitarian instincts in seeking a peacefully negotiated political settlement and lower marks for their warfighting energy. Fundamentally disagreeing with an attack in the west, Brauchitsch and

Halder did not have the courage to confront Hitler and tell him that his winter attack was militarily unsound, despite his political panic over the possibilities of a French advance into Belgium. The soldiers did not clarify that the attack ordered was unsatisfactory for three overriding military reasons. First, it had unacceptable chances of succeeding because of faulty timing; second (with more important ramifications), it stood no chance of defeating the French because of its own indecisive objectives; and third, it entailed a commitment of forces and the possibilities of losses out of balance with desired gains. Under contemporary circumstances, Brauchitsch and Halder can be excused philosophically for their devious ploys to delay and discourage an attack in the west. Under historical scrutiny they stand characterless and at the borderline of incompetence in failing to insist on the necessity for a decisive attack in the west in the event that Hitler persisted in the political decision to continue the war. They also stand indicted for not modifying the order to achieve the complete defeat of Allied forces on the continent of Europe.

Too close to Hitler in the chain of command, and subject to immediate pressures, Brauchitsch and Halder were incapable of translating Hitler's call for an offensive into a winning military plan. The vagaries of chance and the battle-winning talents of the German army helped Hitler and OKH transform the impotent amended order of 29 October 1933 into the ultradecisive order associated with the ideas of Generalmajor Erich von Manstein and the battlefield energy of General der Panzertruppe Heinz Guderian. Bad weather forced numerous postponements of the October order, and the capture of the order by the Belgians on 10 January 1940 gave the Germans both opportunity and reason for change.[9] The final act in the transition to an effective plan seems to have been the meeting of 17 February 1940 between Manstein and Hitler, in which the former advanced his ideas on a decisive attack in the west.[10] For reasons that are less clear, Hitler seems to have edged toward establishing the Schwerpunkt of the attack in the west with Army Group A, between Sedan and Dinant, rather than Army Group B, farther to the north. On 18 February 1940, the plan for the attack in the west was changed by Hitler, who issued a new directive for the attack, Number 10, of 20 February 1940, in its final successful form.

The planning for the French campaign repeats a pattern in the preparations for Barbarossa. In the planning and execution of the French campaign, Hitler displayed epic determination to launch a surprise offensive against a major world power within an ongoing war. He set indecisive aims, however, for the military offensive. The OKH showed a reprehensible inability to present a grand operational concept to Hitler but followed up with brilliant direction of the final order. The German field armies came to the rescue of everyone German, Manstein constructing an alternate operations plan and Guderian executing a decisive tank attack. In the planning and execution of the Russian campaign, Hitler similarly showed epic determination to launch a surprise offensive against a major power. He demanded, however, an indecisive halt of the main concentration of the German armies to assist ancillary forces in seizing subsidiary objectives. The OKH produced an elegantly simple and direct operational concept for the campaign but followed with a reprehensible failure to sweep aside Hitler's objections to their decisive formulation. The German field armies again came to the rescue with effective enough handling of the main concentration of the tank force to achieve the decisive objectives of the army plan. Unlike the case in France, though, Hitler managed to misdirect the German tank force far enough and long enough to lose the Russian campaign.

This comparative summary of political decision and military planning for two campaigns supports a view that none of the important factors in the later campaign predetermined a German defeat in Russia. It shows Hitler as the key figure, with the authority, will, and characteristic indecisiveness to ruin the battle of Russia. In the French campaign, however, the German army surmounted both the French and the Führer to win almost immediately. From the aspect of Hitler, OKH, and the army, the factor decisively different from that in the French campaign was the absence of a Manstein to focus on the potential for disaster in the planned halt of Army Group Center. No Manstein emerged to modify the Hitler directive, but the army operations order gave Bock, Hoth, and Guderian the green light into the Moscow-Gorki space. Even if the Hitler directive and the army operation order had been modified to direct an unfettered drive of Army Group Center to Moscow, Hitler probably could not have overcome his "fascination" with subcritical detail and local crisis, and a battle with Hitler would still have been fought by the German army as part of the battle of

Russia. As a special irony, based on its performance in the opening engagements of Barbarossa, the German army proved capable of defeating the Soviet armed forces and winning the battle against the Russians but incapable of triumphing in the double battle suggested above.

Hitler Caught by Surprise in the Balkans, 1941: Contrasting the Balkans with the Opening of the Russian Campaign

The Balkan campaign, another important way station along the road to Barbarossa, showed a similar pattern of German factors but also a difference or two that help us to understand the possibilities of a German victory over the Soviet Union. In the special circumstances of the Balkan campaign, Hitler played a less obtrusive role than he did in the planning and conduct of the French and Russian campaigns.[11] Although the Germans had planned an armed intervention in Greece since December 1940, designated Operation Marita, they had not originally considered the undertaking overly challenging, and Hitler was not engrossed in details. Yet, in accord with his aggressive political talents, he ordered a buildup of combat forces (as opposed to military advisory forces) in Romania and Bulgaria to provide an option of seizing part or all of Greece. He needed that option as a prudent measure to forestall an opportunistic British landing to support Greece, using the excuse of the war between Italy and Greece since October 1940. Hitler had not shown overwhelming interest in Marita, probably because of his growing preoccupation with Barbarossa and the success of his policy in Yugoslavia until 26 March 1941, the latter success a factor that reduced the chances of British intervention in Greece. Hitler also was considering other operations in the Mediterranean, including action at Gibraltar, Malta, and in Libya, and he had already dispatched a small motorized force under Generalleutnant Erwin Rommel to assist the Italians in Libya.

This unstable but relatively quiet situation in the Balkans changed suddenly with a political coup in Belgrade on 26 March 1941 in which the revolutionaries overthrew the pro-German government of the regent, Prince Paul, and proclaimed Peter II as king. The deposed government had just signed the Rome-Berlin-Tokyo Pact, but the revolutionaries announced that the new government would follow a policy of neutrality. Hitler was personally offended by the government and its action, and the British government had new incentives to reinforce the Greeks. The Germans faced an uncomfortable contretemps that undermined the security of their pending operations against the Soviet Union. The situation called for action and showed the Germans at their "best" in the Second World War.[12] Hitler, in his unequivocal style, ordered the immediate smashing of the Yugoslav and Greek states, with emphasis on immediate destruction and little concern about how the task should be done.

One could argue that the Balkan campaign was important for the similarity between it and Barbarossa in the patterns of advance, exploitation, and style of the actors; hence it enforces the understanding of the Germans' winning in Russia. It might also be argued that the Balkan campaign was important because of its concrete results—the destruction of opposing armed forces and seizure of territories—and how those results conduced to German success in the battle of Russia (Barbarossa proper). In pattern and style, the Balkan campaign illustrates the near-ideal situation for the Germans, when Hitler made an immediate, decisive political decision, and the army was freed from either a whimsical change in the thrust of the army plan or his stubborn concern with operationally irrelevant detail. The German army executed the quickest draw and fired the most efficient shots of the Second World War in Europe. In eleven days (26 March–6 April 1941), the Germans reinforced their troops in Bulgaria and massed new forces in Romania, Hungary, and southern Germany (Austria) in time to commence an eighteen-day battle (6–23 April 1941). In the fight, the armed forces of two states were bagged, a quality British expeditionary force was withdrawn from the continent, the Italian army was freed from a major theater of operations, and German casualties totalled only about 5,655 in killed, wounded, and missing.[13]

The point is that it was a brilliant campaign, showing in April 1940 how the Germans could perform in Barbarossa. Reappraising the Balkan campaign, however, one could denigrate the German performance by positing that the quality of opposition and the challenge of geographical space made the German accomplishment less impressive. One could elaborate that Serbians and Greeks were not Russians, implying less toughness and technology among the Balkan peoples, and point out that Yugoslavia and Greece were smaller states. These reasonable points are overshadowed by the toughness of the Greeks in fighting against the Italians, the difficult mountainous terrain over much of Yugoslavia and Greece, and the dimensions of the theater of operations, comprising an 800-mile "front" from northern Yugoslavia to southern Greece. Other factors add luster to the German performance, notably the short time for German planning and concentration, the thinly developed, almost primitive communications network, and the intervention of a significant first-rate British expeditionary force. On reevaluation, the Balkan campaign retains its luster, and set in the context of Barbarossa, it displays the formidable nature of the Hitler-army synthesis in war-fighting when Hitler did not intrude into military operations.

Hitler Opens the Russian Campaign: German Trumps and Strategic Timing

The Balkan campaign, thus, is important not so much for its results in Yugoslavia and Greece but for Hitler's political decision and the German planning and concentration for battle on the southeastern front, which won it without campaign-losing interference by Hitler. Because it took place on the eve of Barbarossa, the Balkan campaign suggests a "Hitler-on-vacation" reevaluation of the Second World War. In that reevaluation, it could be generalized that the German army would have defeated the Soviet armed forces and occupied enough territory to cause the collapse of the Soviet Union had Hitler been absent from the scene from 22 June to approximately 31 August 1941 for whatever reason. In the Balkan campaign, the key to German success was the effectiveness of the Hitler-army synthesis, not so much the weakness of the opposition. Being reoriented into the sequence of events leading to Barbarossa, the Balkan campaign serves historical purpose by illuminating the possibility that the Germans would have won the war in Russia very quickly had they used their trumps more effectively. A major objection to that generalization is that the Germans would have faced tougher resistance from a larger army in a more expansive theater in the battle of Russia. Part of the thesis of this book, however, is that the Hitler-army synthesis was so strong that no combination of Soviet forces in the short offensive could check the Germans, and it follows that only a mistake by the Germans could have led to a German defeat.

The thesis must be jarring for the reader brought up on a fare of the great natural strength of the Russian fatherland, the organizing abilities of the Communist party, and the stubborn courage

of numerous Russians, especially when the logic behind it demands that the Russians could save themselves no more than the
Poles, French, British (of the expeditionary forces in France and
Greece), Greeks, and Yugoslavs. It is difficult to find situations in
which the Greeks might have survived the German attack, but two
suggest themselves immediately. If Hitler were so important in the
German victories of 1939–1941, it is possible he might have faltered in his political decision to intervene in the Balkans, thus
giving the Greeks, Yugoslavs, and British time to organize effective
defenses in the mountainous terrain. Using a parallel military argument, one could say that the German army may have faltered in
battle due to special circumstances in the advance or, more likely,
might have been held up by Hitler with his penchant for being
distracted by tangential objectives.

Strategic timing is an important consideration in evaluating
Hitler's realism in his decision to move east. Hitler announced his
decision in July 1940 to attack the Soviet Union and confirmed in
writing in December 1940 that the attack would take place by
approximately 15 May 1941. The well-chronicled Balkan campaign
contributed to the delay of Barbarossa more than five weeks, to 22
June 1941. It is less well known that the winter of 1940–1941 was
severe and the spring of 1941 exceptionally wet. Weather conditions combining late thawing of the eastern European rivers, late
melting of snow, and spring rains conspired to keep rivers at flood
levels until well into May and the surrounding land almost impassable for large-scale military movements.[14] The Bug River and
its tributaries stood in the path of Panzer Group 2, the largest organized for the invasion, and farther north the Nieman River stood
in the path of Panzer Group 3. These two panzer groups comprised
the armored wedges (*Kielen*) of Army Group Center and carried
the hopes of the army for a quick victory in the Soviet Union. The
river flood levels and wet ground conditions would probably have
delayed Barbarossa at least three weeks to allow the natural barri-
ers in front of Army Group Center to clear up even if the Balkan
campaign had not taken place.[14] One authority recently noted that
German weaknesses in the production of important weapons and
other equipment (notably motor vehicles) would probably also
have delayed the start of the campaign beyond the directed ready-
date of 15 May 1941.

Historians and analysts have emphasized this delay in the German attack, the consensus being that the Balkan campaign was a critical factor in the collapse of the German winter attack against Moscow in the first week of December 1941. Virtually every book, article, and report taking the Russian campaign as its major theme notes the Balkan war, relates it to a delay in opening Barbarossa, and often links it with the collapse of a German offensive close to Moscow later in December. The subtle but important point made in only a few of the more perceptive and knowledgeable German works—and with startling candor in several Soviet works—is that the great offensive of 22 June–16 July 1941 had achieved the necessary preconditions for a German victory over the Soviet Union. The important element, then, is not the delay in opening the campaign in June but the results achieved by July.

At a higher level of consideration than the month of attack in 1941 is the year itself. Hitler showed a combination of prudence and exaggerated concern for economic matters and war production from 1939 to 1941. He lifted Germany out of its great depression in 1933 by armaments and other large-scale, state-supported economic programs, such as *Autobahnen* construction. Hitler claimed in a Reichstag speech in 1939 that he had invested 90 billion reichsmarks (one reichmark equaled approximately 20 cents at that time) in armaments production from 1933 to 1939, an impressive figure for the uninflated currencies of the day. The actual figure was closer to approximately 56 billion reichmarks, a sensational amount also, but one seen retrospectively to have been near the minimum necessary for Germany to survive the first part (1939–1940) of the war.

Hitler had been more modest in his rearmament of Germany than was generally supposed from 1933 to 1939 and had not intended to get embroiled in a war with Britain and France as early as September 1939. He placed great importance on his popularity with the German people, and an explanation for his modest armaments effort was his concern with straining that popularity by a burdensome, belt-tightening economic policy. He had acute instincts about the importance of economic matters in political movements and war. The invasion of Norway (to secure Swedish iron ore), drawing a line with Stalin over Romania (to secure Romanian oil), and at an even higher level of consideration, his stress on securing living space for Germany to maintain its political greatness illustrate his concerns. One can sense a nervous ambivalence in Hitler's views about war production to secure a thousand-year Reich and also maintain his contemporary popularity. With the fall of France in June 1940, Hitler was probably most concerned with the military balance between Germany and Soviet Russia. In setting levels of war production adequate to win the battles in 1939 and 1940 while maintaining his popularity on the home front, he seemed acutely aware that such levels and the associated size of the German armed forces would not be satisfactory should the Soviets expand their defense production and armed forces in anticipation of a war against Germany.

Hitler's instincts, reasoning, and timing of Barbarossa for 1941 were striking because further Soviet preparations for war, including 1941 and most of 1942, would have been disastrous. The Soviets would have had at least twelve months to develop border fortifications, expand their peacetime army, improve tanks and aircraft, deploy frontier forces more effectively, and take steps to prevent a surprise attack by the Germans. A useful historical analogy illustrates the probable adverse situation for Germany. When the elder Helmut von Moltke, chief, army general staff (1859–1888), faced the increasing possibility of a two-front war with France and Russia in the 1880s, he conceptualized an initial main attack against Russia to knock it out of the war quickly and then turn on France. His successor (once removed), the decisive Count Alfred von Schlieffen (1891–1906), faced an Imperial Russian program to improve fortifications and communications on the Russo-German border, which changed the strategic calculus in Schlieffen's mind. He felt compelled to launch the opening main attack in a two-front war against France, then move against Russia. The analogy shows the decisive effect of a moderate increase in preparations for war by the Russians in the early 1890s on Germany's eastern front and suggests adverse effects for the Germans had the offensive been delayed until 1942.

In timing Barbarossa for 1941, Hitler judged that the battle of Russia would be fought under the best strategic circumstances regarding the military balance between the two states. He also calculated that success would automatically secure the National Socialist *Weltanschauung* living space, probably force Britain out of the war, reduce German war production even if Britain remained in the war, and have a significant effect on keeping the United States out of a war in Europe even should Britain remain in the war. By timing the attack for 1941, Hitler also escaped the criticism by German military officers planning the invasion and later commentators that he embarked on a two-front war that could not be won. Hitler conceptualized a campaign to last six to ten weeks, with consolidation stretching to approximately seventeen weeks. But Germany would not have been in a two-front war at all in 1941 because of Britain's inability to bring significant pressure to bear on Germany by land, air, or sea during the planned battle period.

Hitler pointed out early in the planning for Barbarossa that the campaign would make sense only if it were finished quickly. Halder and the army planners put together a battle intended to accomplish the political goal of quick defeat of the Soviet Union. But how can planners contrive to put the armed strength of a great power in a bag like a cat? That would be a formidable feat. The German general staff assumed the planning, however, and added realism to the chances of defeating even a great power like the Soviet Union. The general staff, thanks to weather-induced delays in the battle of France and providential changes in the plan of attack by the former operations officer of the general staff (Manstein), put the French army in a bag in June 1940. Certainly European Russia was different from France, and Russians from Frenchmen, but it could be deduced from general principles that the Russian armed forces were no more than a bigger cat in a bigger bag, and subject to the same principles of war exploited by the Germans in France in 1940.

Part II

The Opening Stages of the Russian Campaign

Chapter Four

Barbarossa North, the Great Opportunity in the Baltic: June 1941

Point (winning): "Exactly four days and five hours after zero hour [the 56th Panzer Corps] had actually completed as the crow flies a non-stop dash through 200 miles of enemy territory ... if at the same time Panzer Group H.Q. pushed the [41st] Panzer Corps straight through Dvinsk behind us, it seemed likely that the enemy would have to keep opposing us with whatever forces he had on hand at the moment and be incapable ... of fighting a set battle."

Erich von Manstein, *Lost Victories*

Counterpoint (losing): "27.6.41. The immediate mission for the *Kampfgruppe* [of 6th Panzer Division, 41st Panzer Corps] ... move to Iluksti 15 km northwest of Dvinsk.... 28.6.41. New orders for division to advance from Roskispic to reach the Dvina by Livani [not anywhere near Dvinsk] and build a bridgehead there [there had been a bridgehead at Dvinsk since noon on 26.6.41]."

U.S. National Archives, Records German Field Commands.

Counter-counterpoint: "This was the 'safe,' staff college solution."

Erich von Manstein, *Lost Victories*

During the blitz in Russia, momentum characterized German offensive operations, combining swiftly paced advances with the destruction of opposing forces. To break the momentum of Army Group Center in its drive to Moscow by halting and redirecting it away from the capital in an ancillary mission could be described as operational suicide. The Soviet armed forces were too strong for the Germans to present them with a gratuitous opportunity to survive the panzer attack through Russia, designed to destroy the field armies defending Moscow and seize the indispensable strategic space around it.

Nevertheless, on 17 December 1940, Hitler changed the army plan submitted to him by halting Army Group Center after its move through White Russia. The Barbarossa directive, signed by Hitler and issued by the High Command of the Armed Forces (OKW) on 18 December 1940, contains the outlandish and fatuous order for Army Group Center to advance with powerful armored and motorized formations from the area around Warsaw and rout Soviet forces in White Russia blocking the road to Moscow. This would make it possible for operations to continue (by Army Group Center and Army Group North) toward Leningrad to destroy the enemy forces operating in the Baltic area.[1] The most extraordinary aspect of the Hitler Barbarossa directive is that Brauchitsch and Halder at OKH, and Bock at Army Group Center, who received the directive or were aware of it, did not object that carrying out the mission would make it impossible to achieve the highest-level intent of the war against the Soviet Union: "*to crush Soviet Russia in a rapid campaign* [italics in original]."[2]

Hitler Paces Barbarossa to the Seizure of Leningrad

Hitler served notice early in the planning for Barbarossa that he believed Leningrad to be a tempting target. On closer investigation it is clear that he developed a compulsion to secure German communications in the Baltic Sea by seizing Leningrad and destroying the Soviet fleet there. Hitler's capacity to dilute the main effort of a blitz campaign is exemplified by his insistence on taking that city, an action remote from defeating the field armies of the Soviet Union. With questionable concern for the war in general, and a blitz campaign in particular, Hitler explained to the chief of the Armed Forces Operations Staff, Generalleutnant Alfred Jodl, that it was vitally important for "large numbers of the mobile troops of the Army Group in the center to pivot north after they penetrated the enemy front in White Russia. Not until this most vital mission had been accomplished should operations against Moscow be continued."[3] Fortunately for the Germans and their chances of success in Barbarossa, Army Group North drove back the Soviets in the Baltic, essentially freeing the movement of Army Group Center toward Moscow.

If followed as Hitler directed, the Barbarossa directive would have ensured the survival of Soviet Russia by immobilizing Army Group Center probably for about five weeks, a period similar to that originally determined as necessary (six to ten weeks) to end the whole campaign. Neither Brauchitsch nor Halder had the temperament or spirit to ensure setting a decisive task for the army in the Barbarossa directive. To their credit as professionals, however, they assumed that the defective plan would be overtaken by events, in which the aggressive Army Group Center leaders would press on for Moscow and the panzer groups then drive beyond into the Moscow-Gorki space. The army plan placed the *Schwerpunkt* with Army Group Center, and even Hitler agreed to include the statement under tasks in the Barbarossa directive, specifying that "only a surprisingly rapid collapse of Russian resistance could justify the simultaneous pursuit of both [Moscow and Leningrad]."[4] Hitler acknowledged in this revealing sentence that Leningrad would be the priority target for Army Groups North and Center but that it was conceivable that a collapse of Russian resistance would allow Army Group Center to drive uninterruptedly for Moscow.

Army Groups North and Center advanced so rapidly in the opening days of Barbarossa that little question arose of diverting forces from Army Group Center to assist the northern army group in its advance through the Baltic. Through operational skill and luck, Army Group North was presented in the first four days with unforeseen opportunities. The fluid situation gave it an excellent chance of seizing Leningrad within two or three weeks of the beginning of the campaign. This result was possible even though the army group was numerically inferior to the Russians in the occupied Baltic republics and faced an unpaved road system and forested, swampy terrain unsuited for panzer operations. German Army Group North, under Generalfeldmarschall Wilhelm Ritter von Leeb, was the weakest army group organized for the advance into the Soviet Union, having one panzer group comprising only two panzer corps, in turn holding only three panzer and three motorized infantry divisions. The Soviets faced problems of their own, defending themselves in foreign territory among unfriendly populations anticipating liberation from recent occupation (1939).

German Operational Possibilities on the Baltic Front

Army Group North employed the mobile forces in Panzer Group 4 under Generaloberst Erich Hoepner as the spearhead of the advance toward Leningrad. The most important obstacle it would have to master was the Dvina River, flowing westward from Vitebsk through Dvinsk and Jakobstadt to the Baltic at Riga, in Latvia. This huge obstacle was too far from the German border to be crossed in a one-day coup de main, as the Germans in Panzer Group 3 under Hoth had done at the Nieman River, farther south in Army Group Center. The Germans needed a drive that would seize Leningrad at a blitz pace, destroy the Soviet fleet, and secure German communications once and for all in the Baltic. More important, though, the Germans required quick success to prevent the diversion of forces from Army Group Center. A quick German victory at Leningrad would speed the drive of Army Group Center on Moscow and, more importantly, the impetuous seizure of Leningrad and Moscow would collapse Soviet resistance in northwest European Russia.

Such possibilities are speculative and, while interesting, are of small merit in any reinterpretation of German success probabilities in Barbarossa unless it is clear that the Germans had the battle-winning capability to defeat the Soviets in the northwest. One can analyze the German capabilities to win on the Army Group North front by examining the actual advances and the concomitant destruction of Soviet forces. To win outright in the north by quickly seizing Leningrad, or to win in the minimally acceptable sense of pinning down the Soviet field armies so that they could not interfere with Army Group Center, the Germans had to pass two tests in the Baltic. They first had to prevent the Soviet buildup of a coherent, blitz-halting defensive system along the Dvina River. Then, having ruptured that system in an acceptably brief period, they had to drive toward Leningrad while simultaneously pinning down Soviet armies on the Baltic front to prevent interference with the German forces moving toward Moscow. The important element for reinterpreting the Russian campaign is, therefore: Did the Germans pass the two necessary tests in the Baltic?

Hoepner's Panzers Seize the Dvina River Bridges at Dvinsk

Army Group North assigned Panzer Group Hoepner the mission of seizing bridgeheads across the Dvina. Hoepner, in turn, assigned his stronger 41st Panzer Corps the mission to cross at Jakobstadt and the weaker 56th Panzer Corps farther east at Dvinsk. The latter corps was approximately 290 km from the center of its assembly area on the Soviet-Lithuanian border to Dvinsk. It also faced serious terrain obstacles such as the gorge on the intervening Dubissa River, inferior roads, and strong Russian forces with many tanks.[5] In perhaps the most impressive coup in Barbarossa (or any other operation by either side in the Russian campaign), the 8th Panzer Division, 56th Panzer Corps, seized the road and rail bridges over the Dvina River at approximately 0530 on 26 June 1941. Moving about 350 km by road and using innovative tactical subtlety, a small combat team of the Brandenburg Reigment (special forces) reinforced by engineers seized the bridges and prevented their destruction long enough for stronger forces to pass over the bridges and seize the city quickly, preventing it from being turned into a rubble fortress by the Soviets.[6] Halder noted the achievement laconically in his diary: "Confirmed report passed on to Führer: 8th Panzer Division penetrated into Dvinsk at 0800, occupied town at 1250 after hard street fighting."[7] Halder did not comment on the war-winning strategic opportunity presented the Germans in Barbarossa by this stunning operational and tactical performance of the German troops in Army Group North.

The Analogy Between the Meuse and Sedan in the French Campaign and the Dvina in the Russian Campaign

In several ways, the coup at Dvinsk was analogous to the German drive to the Meuse in France and a similar coup near Sedan on 13 May 1940. In retrospect, it is easy to forget how the Germans agonized over their chances of crossing the Meuse and how differently the campaign would have turned out had not the early pace been maintained. On 7 and 14 February 1940, the Germans conducted war games, attended by the chief of the army general staff and the commander of Army Group A, in which they argued over the timing and operational techniques for crossing the Meuse. Following these war games, in March 1940, Hitler called the leaders of Army Group A, the *Schwerpunkt* force for the advance in the west, and directed them to outline the tasks for the attack and how they would be carried out. German attention was again riveted on the challenge of crossing the Meuse, to the exclusion of the overall strategy to follow after the crossing, to defeat France.

The commander of the 19th Panzer Corps, the spearhead of Panzer Group Kleist, describes the German uncertainty and nervousness over early success at the Meuse and noted in an amazing scene before Hitler that the commander of the 16th Army, the formation that lay to the south of the armored wedge, cried out: "Well I don't think you'll cross the river in the first place."[8] The almost exclusive attention devoted to crossing the Meuse stands out in the authoritative claim made by the redoubtable panzer corps commander, Heinz Guderian: "I never received any further orders as to what I was to do once the bridgehead over the Meuse was secured. All my decisions, until I reached the Atlantic seaboard at Abbeville were taken by me and me alone. The Supreme Command's influence on my actions was merely restrictive throughout."[9]

In the analogous case of Panzer Group Hoepner driving for Leningrad, the Germans had to negotiate quickly a major river, the Dvina, for blitzkrieg-pace success. They concentrated on a swift crossing of the Dvina while scarcely considering the continuation of the attack in the event of immediate success at the river. The commander of the 56th Panzer Corps, which must be considered because of its successful advance to be the spearhead of Panzer Group Hoepner, comments in his memoirs exclusively on the task of reaching the Dvina River. Inexplicably, for a man of his talents, the panzer commander, General der Infanterie Erich von Manstein, fails to connect the operational goal to seize the Dvina crossing with the strategic end of winning Leningrad. Manstein notes that before the offensive started he had been asked how long it would take to reach Dvinsk, assuming it were possible to do so. He answered, "If it could not be done inside four days, we could hardly count on capturing the crossing intact."[10] He does not mention why it was important to capture the bridges intact, nor does he comment on why it was necessary strategically to secure the crossings intact and immediately in a successful advance to Leningrad. What appears in the most important opportunity offered the German attackers in Barbarossa is that, like the earlier case of the Meuse in France, they were engrossed in the details of crossing the Dvina.[11] Unlike in France, where Guderian kept the strategic goal of an advance to the sea clearly in mind and pressed on unhesitatingly through powerful but confused and dislocated French and British forces, Manstein made the astounding offhand comment that he was less exercised by his initially isolated position, "which would not continue indefinitely, than by the problem of what the next move should be."[12] The next day, 27 June 1941, Hoepner arrived in Dvinsk and could not set a deep strategic objective for Manstein, or for the 41st Panzer Corps—far behind, but effectively disengaging from a tough tank battle around the town of Rossenie.

Faced with the historical analogy suggested between the Meuse and the Dvina, it is tempting to state that, had Guderian crossed the Dvina four days and five hours into the campaign with unscathed forces, he would have projected himself directly toward Leningrad, dragging a reluctant high command to a collapse of the Soviet Baltic front, or at least the severe dislocation of Soviet forces and encirclement of major forces by the German 18th Army along the Baltic Sea. The aggressive continuation of the march by Manstein's 56th Panzer Corps would have forced the switch of Reinhardt's delayed 41st Panzer Corps from a side-by-side advance to the Dvina at Jakobstadt to a commitment in depth behind Manstein. With that echeloning of forces, the Germans would have automatically cleared the supply and communications lines to Manstein and added enough strength, with three additional mobile divisions and one attached hard-marching infantry division, to drive immediately through Dvinsk to Pskov and Leningrad.

The Greatest Unforeseen Opportunity Presented to the Germans in Barbarossa

It is difficult to avoid the conclusion that Soviet forces cut off to the west and south of Pskov from resupply and movement through that town would have been overtaken and broken up by the German 18th Army advancing on the Baltic side of Panzer Group Hoepner. It is equally difficult to escape the conclusion that German tanks, arriving in Pskov about 4 July 1941, would have broken down Soviet command and control. The Soviet Baltic command, for example, could no longer have been reinforced from reserves mobilizing in the interior of Russia. The Finnish armed forces, aided by several German divisions, advanced against the Soviet Union on 10 July 1941, adding support to the view that a more decisive handling of Panzer Group Hoepner after 26 June 1941 would have led to the seizure of Leningrad in July 1941.

This possibility was the greatest unforeseen opportunity presented the Germans in the Russian campaign. It was made possible by Manstein's success at Dvinsk, but it was not seized by the Germans, and it is worthwhile to examine the reasons why. In an analysis of the hypothetical situation—the most important "what if" situation with German Army Group North—one could ask: Were these conjectural moves realistically possible? Could the Germans, who proved capable of partially encircling Leningrad in September 1941 and besieging it for 900 days, have seized the city or effected a total land encirclement in July 1941? The operational situation to be clarified is whether the 41st Panzer Corps could have been extricated from the tank fight at Rossenie and pushed through behind Manstein's 56th Panzer Corps to the northeast at Dvinsk. This little-discussed possibility ranks as one of the most important in the Second World War in Europe. If the Germans were capable of shifting the 41st Panzer Corps through Dvina, it may be concluded that the concentrated 4th Panzer Group would have taken Leningrad in July 1941. Army Group Center would have been assisted in its drive on Moscow by that success, and, after the fall of Moscow and the parallel collapse at Leningrad, the Soviet strategic position in northwestern Soviet Russia would have been untenable.

Much has been written in the west on the campaigns and engagements of 1942–1945 in the Mediterranean and northwestern Europe, with similar outpourings in the Soviet Union over Stalingrad, Kursk, and other momentous battles in the east during the same period. Study of the campaigns, battles, and engagements remain important, indeed irreplaceable in understanding modern conventional war and the deployment of conventional forces on a tactical nuclear battlefield. But none of the engagements in the European theater from 1942 to 1945, some of which, such as Alamein, Stalingrad, Kursk, and Normandy, can be important because it influenced in any significant sense the issues of victory or defeat. The most that can be claimed for the battles of 1942–1945 is that a special few brought Germany closer to defeat assured by the summer of 1941 or in some significant degree delayed the virtually assured outcome of the war. The shift of the 41st Panzer Corps behind Manstein in late June 1941, however, transcends entire later campaigns in importance on the issue of victory or defeat in the war and not merely the advance or delay of Allied victory. Yet because of an interpretation of the Second World War that does not distinguish between issues of greater and lesser importance, the shift of the 41st Panzer Corps to capitalize on the Manstein opportunity remains little known and thinly analyzed.

The Issue of a War-winning Drive by Panzer Group Hoepner Through Dvinsk to Leningrad

On 22 June 1941, assigned to seize a bridgehead over the Dvina River at Jakobstadt, the 41st Panzer Corps advanced into the Soviet Union until, on the third day of its drive, on 24 June 1941 at 1500, it bumped into powerful counterattacking Soviet tank forces, compelling it to fight a major tank battle around Rossenie.[13] The corps had its hands full against approximately 300 Soviet tanks and comparable strength in infantry and artillery. At this stage of the war in the east, a German panzer corps, with its two panzer and one motorized infantry divisions at full strength, should have finished off the Soviet force in a tough but crisis-free battle ending on 25 June 1941. The Soviet force, however, included approximately twenty-nine heavy tanks with thick armor, big guns, and wide tracks, which translated into impressive survivability, fire power, and tactical movement on the battlefield.[14] The two German panzer divisions, with their large complement of Czech-manufactured, medium-light tanks and additional modestly gunned German medium tanks, found it difficult to master the Soviet heavy tanks. Nevertheless, with characteristic German tactical virtuosity, the panzer corps managed to encircle the Soviet 3d Mechanized Corps by 0830 on 26 June 1941 and annihilate it the same day.[15] The stage was set for the decision of the war in the north—in which direction to commit the 41st Panzer Corps on 27 June 1941, and what would be the resultant mission for Panzer Group Hoepner.

Earlier, on 23 June, after air reconnaissance revealed the powerful Soviet tank force in the path of Panzer Group 4, Hoepner decided not to turn around the leading 8th Panzer Division of the 56th Panzer Corps to assist in the impending tank battle but to direct it toward Dvinsk as planned. The decision paid off handsomely because on 26 June, as the tank battle at Rossenie ended, the 8th Panzer Division had crossed the Dvina, seized the city of Dvinsk, and enlarged the resulting bridgehead to the north. By 27 June 1941, Hoepner had already ordered his Panzer Group reserve, motorized infantry division, *Totenkopf*, to push through to Dvinsk and support the successful drive of the 8th Panzer Division. On 27 June, Hoepner, visiting Manstein in the Dvinsk bridgehead, had the chance to make the fateful decision, which would probably have led to the July seizure of Leningrad.

The war-winning decision would have been to order the 8th Panzer Division and accompanying 3d Motorized Infantry Division to take Pskov immediately, then keep the Soviets off balance the remaining distance to Leningrad. One might fairly ask: Did the two German mobile divisions have the necessary mobility and strength to drive through to Pskov? The second part of Hoepner's super-decision, to order the 41st Panzer Corps immediately forward along the same axis of advance, answers the question. The dangerously exposed and distant 8th Panzer and 3d Motorized Infantry divisions of Hoepner's concentrated Panzer Group would have been followed by Totenkopf and the three mobile divisions of the 41st Panzer Corps. That force—six German mobile divisions—would have the capability against surprised, confused, and disrupted Soviet defenders of 27 June 1941 and the following days to drive through to Pskov.

Hoepner carries a heavy burden for not ordering the 56th Panzer Corps forward out of Dvinsk on 27 June and redirecting 41st Panzer Corps behind it. By not exploiting the great achievement of the 8th Panzer Division, Hoepner paralyzed Panzer Group 4 and invited strategic disaster for the Germans in the Baltic. On 1 July 1941 Hoepner informed his panzer corps generals that "the army group commander is strongly influenced by the idea that the panzer group in the existing situation cannot alone break the enemy resistance between Duna [Dvina] and Leningrad and is taking measures to lead the infantry armies even closer to the panzer corps." In not forcing the hand of Leeb on 27 June 1941, Hoepner allowed him to curb the "operational freedom of movement" of the armor by 1 July.[16] Instead of driving through Pskov by approximately 4 July, Hoepner had just begun to move beyond the Dvina and toward that city, a week behind the schedule made possible by the coup at Dvinsk. German armor at Pskov on about 4 July 1941 would have severely reduced the Soviet chances of knitting an effective defense between Leningrad and the fast-moving mobile divisions.

There are objections to the picture I have drawn, including the nonconjectural point that the Germans did not encircle Leningrad until September 1941. It can be argued that the Germans did eventually encircle Leningrad even though they did not exploit their initial grand opportunity at Dvinsk. That the Germans reached the great Russian city on the Baltic in September supports my argument that they would have been similarly successful in July 1941 had they exploited their earlier, equally nonconjectural opportunity at Dvinsk. Manstein, the gifted commander of the 56th Panzer Corps, argues convincingly that "a tank drive such as [the] panzer corps made to Dvinsk inevitably generates confusion and panic in the enemy's communication zone; it ruptures the enemy's chain of command and makes it virtually impossible to coordinate his countermeasures."[17] Others, including the former operations officer of the 6th Panzer Division, 41st Panzer Corps, have argued to the contrary that the Rossenie battle disrupted that corps just enough[18] that it could not reach Dvinsk fast enough to contribute decisively to an effective drive of the entire panzer group concentrated for an advance to Pskov.[19] The argument is not convincing because parts of the 41st Panzer Corps pushed on so rapidly after the Rossenie battle that they reached Jakobstadt only two days after Manstein crossed the Dvina.[20] At Jakobstadt they did not seize any bridge intact and took until 2 July 1941 to cross and recapture momentum. Had the 41st Panzer Corps pushed through to Dvinsk on 28 June as it had moved to Jakobstadt, it would have been able immediately to cross the bridges already seized by the 56th Panzer Corps and found itself part of a concentrated thrust to Pskov led by the latter corps, now almost two days ahead.

The Historic Moment: Hoepner and Manstein Fail to Act in the Baltic

Presented with the grand opportunity to develop the operations noted above, Hoepner opted instead for a safe, staff-college solution in the north, ordering the 41st Panzer Corps to advance on Jakobstadt, while the 56th Panzer Corps eventually spent seven days waiting for its companion corps to force a crossing of a river bridged a week previously. When every hour counted at the start of the blitz to keep the Soviet forces in the Baltic off balance, Hoepner and his commander at Army Group North, Ritter von Leeb, allowed a panzer corps to sit in a bridgehead. Soviet forces were attracted to it, regained their composure, and launched strong attacks against the voluntarily immobilized German tank forces. The circumstances present several ironies, foremost among them that

Hitler, through OKW on 27 June 1941, ordered Army Group North to redirect 41st Panzer Corps through Dvinsk to exploit the great opportunity created by Manstein's troops. Hitler, who, with this noteworthy exception, served as a brake on forward momentum in Barbarossa, escapes blame for the indecisive handling of Panzer Corps Hoepner. The soldiers—Hoepner, his commander, Leeb, and to some degree, OKH—must shoulder the blame for the war-losing conservatism at Dvinsk. Perhaps equal in irony, Manstein, who argued in retrospect for continuation of the drive, commenting that Hoepner "could tell us nothing" about future objectives after crossing the Dvina, under reevaluation is no longer the hero of the piece.

Manstein knew that the destruction of the Soviet forces blocking the way to Leningrad, and the city itself, were the objectives of the panzer drive. He did not need Hoepner to enter into the bridgehead to reiterate that or, worse yet, to claim the panzer group was bound to be cautious about future moves because of uncertainties about keeping the attack marshalled. One does not need a weatherman to tell which way the wind is blowing, and Manstein required no elaboration from his immediate senior on a drive aimed unambiguously at Leningrad. This lack of initiative by Manstein stands up poorly compared with Guderian's uninterrupted exploitation of the earlier Meuse crossing, particularly since Guderian never received instructions on what to do after he crossed the Meuse. German operations were so finely tuned that had Guderian waited for instructions from another conservative commander (Kleist) in the bridgehead over the Meuse on 13 May 1940, it is doubtful that the French campaign would have been a German success. The analogy shows that Manstein realistically could have been expected to forge ahead out of the bridgehead, dragging a reluctant high command in Army Group North along the road to Pskov and Leningrad as Guderian dragged Kleist and the Führer himself to the English Channel in 1940.

Instead, Manstein sat tamely in his bridgehead, losing seven irretrievable days that should have been used to deepen the shock in the opposing field armies and to tear up the command and control capabilities of the Soviet Baltic military district. When action could have resulted in the immediate seizure of Leningrad, the associated uninterrupted advance of Army Group Center through Moscow, and quick victory over the Soviet Union, he did not move on his own initiative. In 1942 and 1943, Manstein would achieve astounding operational success on the eastern front with his meticulously planned and utterly determined attacks at Sevastopol and on the Kerch Peninsula. His supreme achievements as a commander were the combined extraction of German armies from the Caucasus, near-relief of the 6th Army at Stalingrad, and the great counterstroke south of Kharkov in March 1943. As a staff officer, Manstein drafted the German operation plan for the successful advance into France. This achievement, along with his successes as a commander of the 38th Army Corps in France, gave him the reputation of the premier operational mind of the war in Europe.

Manstein's paralysis at Dvinsk in 1941 and his desperately unimaginative attack against known Soviet defenses in the Kursk battle of 1943 lower his reputation. These lapses contrast badly with Guderian's instincts at the Meuse in May 1940 and throughout Barbarossa, but especially in crossing the Dnieper in early July 1941, supporting the grand strategical concepts to conquer France and the Soviet Union. The German supreme successes in the Second World War were the battle of France and the opening two months of Barbarossa. In the former, the Germans eliminated a great continental power from further contention in the war, and in the latter they seized the initiative and presented themselves an opportunity to win the war in Europe. Guderian was the man of the moment when the Germans had the opportunity to win; Manstein peaks as operational commander in 1943, when any battle fought, no matter how brilliantly, could not have won the war.

Writing after the war on the campaign in the Baltic, Hoepner does not mention the opportunity presented the Germans at Dvinsk, commenting only that "the first intermediate operational target" of the panzer group had been reached for the time being at an important point and that a great river barrier had been overcome. The chief of staff, Oberst Charles de Beaulieu, implied that it was important to get a bridgehead across the Dvina River as quickly as possible as an end in itself. Astoundingly, his comments on the first two weeks in the Baltic support a conclusion that if the quick crossing of the Dvina were an end in itself, it would have been to mop up Russian forces south of the river. After that, while leisurely waiting for the infantry to complete its task, the Germans would consider moving on toward Leningrad. These comments are savage satire on Beaulieu's sense of urgency in the Baltic. Beaulieu notes that the quick thrust of the panzer group to the Dvina "had succeeded and won at the same time an adequately wide basis . . . for further mobile operations in the direction of Leningrad." The word in the quotation above translated as "wide" also means "diffuse" in German, and the reader must suspect that the panzer chief of staff and his commander were more concerned with the breadth and safety of their operations than depth and concentration.[21]

Aftermath of the Paralysis at Dvinsk

Presented with the heaven-sent opportunity at Dvinsk, the panzer leaders should have driven the panzer group toward Leningrad until compelled by Soviet resistance, terrain, or logistics to halt. Unlike Hoth and Guderian, who could operate quickly and in depth, Hoepner, his chief of staff, and the commander of Army Group North stood planted in a more leisurely past, unable to exploit their new mobility. On 28 June 1941 the lst Panzer Division, 41st Panzer Corps, freed from the Rossenie tank battle, had the technical capability and tactical energy to advance 150 km toward Jakobstadt in a twenty-four-hour period for no decisive operational purpose. The 41st Panzer Corps did not move northward out of its bridgehead until 2 July 1941, allowing the 56th Panzer Corps to move forward and renew the war. It was a disgrace for the panzer group that infantry divisions of the neighboring 18th Army thrust combat detachments across the Dvina into Riga, capital of Latvia, only three hours into the morning of 29 June and two days before the armor moved out of the bridgeheads around Jakobstadt and Dvinsk.

In spite of his conservative command of the Panzer Group, Hoepner placed his forces on the Luga River near Porietschje, only 110 km from Leningrad, on 14 July 1941. This was an advance of 750 km from the border of 22 June. Although operations slowed at this point, Army Group North had pushed back all the Soviet forces mustered on this important front. In September 1941, in other operations, the army group came close to seizing Leningrad outright. They were deterred at the last minute largely by Hitler's aberrant judgment to besiege the city rather than risk heavy casualties in a possibly unsuccessful coup de main. To understand the Second World War in Europe at its turning point in mid-1941, it can be generalized that the Germans missed a unique opportunity to win immediately in the Baltic and that terrain and road conditions favored the defenders. Army Group North battered the opposing Soviet forces effectively and quickly gained so much ground that the Soviets never achieved operational freedom of maneuver. Nor were they ever able to interfere significantly with the advance of Army Group Center. On the contrary, the German forces set siege lines around Leningrad in September 1941 and had a strong chance of seizing it outright shortly before the siege.

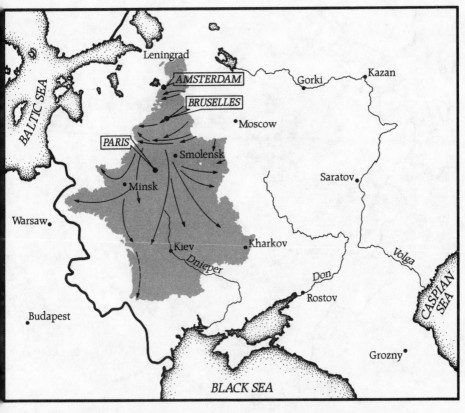

Map 1. Spatial dimensions of the German campaign in the lowlands and France superimposed on a map of European Russia

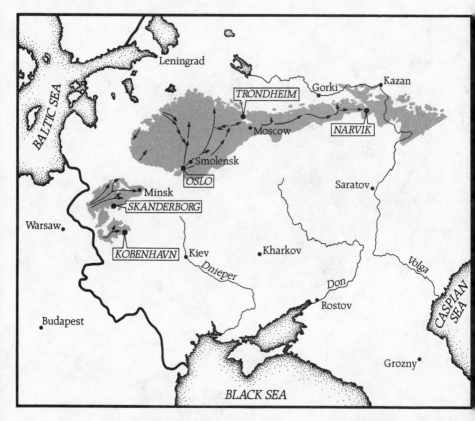

Map 2. Spatial dimensions of the German campaign in Scandinavia (1940) superimposed on a map of European Russia

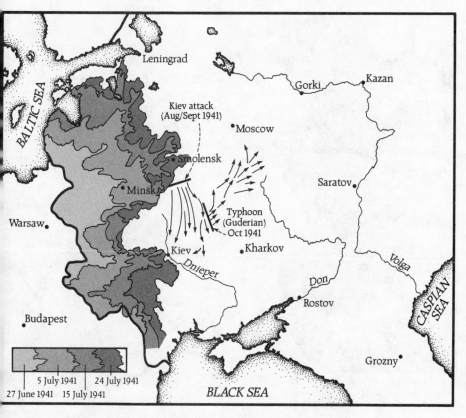

Map 3. Movement of German Panzer Group 2 (Guderian) through European Russia from 25 August to 29 November 1941 against strong Soviet resistance

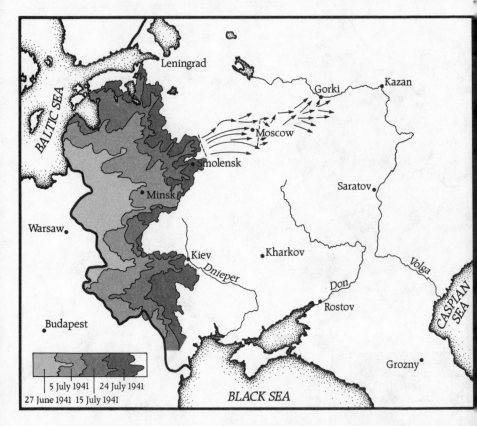

Map 4. Movement of German Panzer Group 2 (Guderian) through European Russia from 25 August to 29 November 1941 hypothesized as directed eastward through Moscow from positions actually seized by Panzer Groups 2 and 3 by 21 July 1941

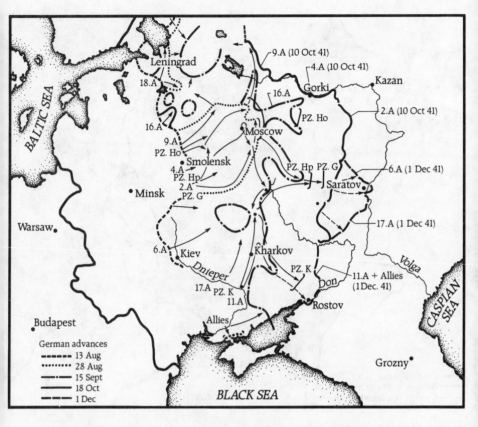

Map 5. Hypothesized German offensive of German Army Group Center Against Moscow on 13 August 1941 and resultant collapse of the Soviet armed forces

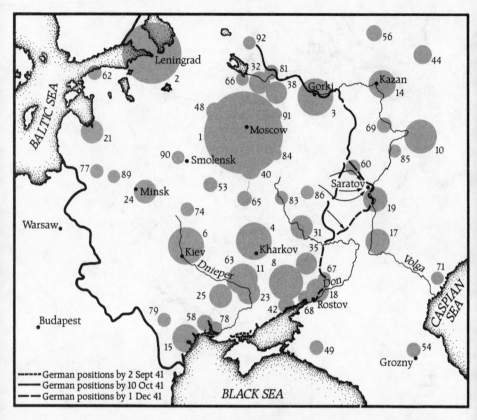

Map 6. Hypothesized German positions based on offensive of Army Group Center beginning on 3 August 1941 into Moscow-Gorki space. The German positions are superimposed on a map showing the location of Soviet industrial centers in about 1955. The circles are directly proportional to the industrial output; for example, the Moscow circle is 8.2 percent of total Soviet output.

The map is based on Lydolph, *Geography of the U.S.S.R.*, p. 330, from Lindsdale and Thompson, "A Map of the U.S.S.R.'s Manufacturing," *Economic Geogra-*

phy, January 1960, facing p. 36. The manufacturing outputs of the areas centered in the circles are within German territory hypothesized as having been seized by 1 December 1941, and are the following percentages of Soviet manufacturing:

Rank	City	%	Rank	City	%
1.	Moscow	8.20	58.	Nikolayev	0.35
2.	Leningrad	4.90	60.	Penzya	0.35
3.	Gorki	1.65	62.	Tallin	0.35
4.	Kharkov	1.65	63.	Dneproderzgh	0.30
6.	Kiev	1.60	65.	Kursk	0.30
8.	Donetsk	1.30	66.	Rybinsk	0.30
11.	Dnepropetrovsk	1.10	67.	Shakhty	0.30
15.	Odessa	0.95	68.	Taganrog	0.30
18.	Rostov	0.85	74.	Gomel	0.25
21.	Riga	0.75	77.	Kaunas	0.25
23.	Zaporozhye	0.75	78.	Kherson	0.25
24.	Minsk	0.70	79.	Kishinev	0.25
25.	Krivoy Rog	0.65	81.	Kostroma	0.25
31.	Voronezh	0.65	83.	Lipetsk	0.25
32.	Yaroslaval	+0.65	84.	Ryazan	0.25
35.	Lugansk	0.60	86.	Tambov	0.25
38.	Ivanovo	0.55	89.	Vilnyus	0.25
40.	Tula	0.55	90.	Vitebsk	0.25
42.	Zhdanov	0.50	91.	Vladimir	0.25
53.	Bryansk	0.35	92.	Volvzdn	0.25
	Total	29.90		Total	5.55

Grand Total———34.45%

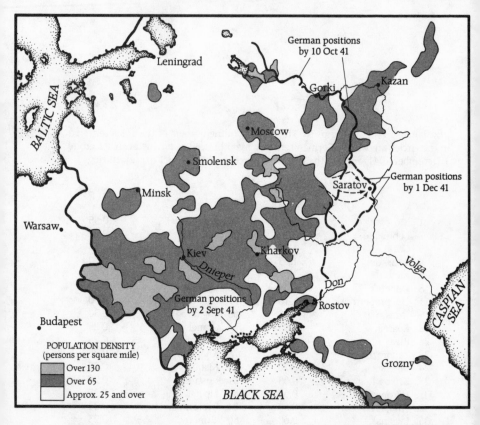

Map 7. Hypothesized German positions based on offensive of Army Group Center beginning on 13 August 1941 into the Moscow-Gorki space. The German positions are superimposed on a map showing the distribution of Soviet population in about 1941.

Chapter Five

Barbarossa South, the Fight in the Ukraine: June 1941

THE Germans would win or lose the Russian campaign based on the progress of Army Group Center in the summer of 1941. Yet, what about the progress of the wings and the possibilities of operational disasters that might adversely affect the advance toward Moscow? In June and July 1941, German Army Group South was advancing against an enemy that outnumbered it in every significant way. Soviet forces south of the Pripyat Marshes outnumbered the Germans in men; numbers of major infantry, tank, motorized, and cavalry formations; and tanks, aircraft, and artillery pieces of like sizes. On 17 March 1940, Hitler intruded to the severe detriment of German operations south of the Pripyat Marshes by a dilettante whim unchallenged by OKH and Army Group South. Concerned that the strong German 12th Army, scheduled to advance out of Romania into the southern Ukraine, would be held up by the Dniester River, Hitler ordered the German offensive concentrated largely in the restricted gap between the Pripyat Marshes and the Carpathian Mountains.[1] German military professionals in OKH and Army Group South had not seen any exceptional challenge in the Dniester and planned a great double envelopment of the Soviet forces in the Ukraine west of the Dnieper using the 12th Army as the southern arm. Because of Hitler's ill-advised, nervous dabbling into an effective plan of operations, Army Group South was forced to attempt a single envelopment out of the gap between the marshes and the mountains against numerically superior forces.

Extraordinary Strength of the Red Army in the Ukraine, 1941:
Unanswered Questions

The immense numbers and fighting qualities of the Soviet forces massed in the Ukraine remain at least an interesting curiosity and at most a possible decisive clue to Soviet plans and intentions in 1941. In a state noted for ideological conformity and bureaucratic discipline, Soviet historians have hewn the unwavering line that the Soviet Union, as early as August 1939, began to play for time and position against an impending attack from an ultraimperialist, National Socialist Germany. Conveniently for the peace-seeking, socialist image affected by the Soviet government, the Germans attacked the Soviet Union in 1941. Thus, the Soviet position on the period from 1939 to 1941 to 1945 was set since 1941 in the interpretive concrete that the Soviets seized vast territories in eastern Europe in 1939 and 1940 in anticipation of just such a German attack. The argument continues that seizure of all or part of five countries was necessary to successfully defend the Soviet Union and was justified by events that unfolded in 1941.

With striking inconsistency, Soviet and Western writers who subscribe to that interpretation of Soviet actions in 1939–1941 fail to connect the Soviet takeover of huge territories totalling approximately 180,000 square miles for defense against German imperialist invasion with the mutually incompatible German surprise attack massing 157 German divisions in peacetime close to the Soviet border by June 1941. Hitler, indeed, has remained such a historical villain that virtually no serious consideration has been given to the possibility, even knowing Hitler's acknowledged aggressive intentions in the east, that the Soviet Union—which took more than half of Poland (1939); invaded, occupied, and built up military bases in the three former Baltic republics (1939); attacked and absorbed significant parts of Finland (1939–1940); and invaded and occupied Bessarabia (1940)—might have had corresponding, aggressive intentions in the west.

Soviet writers slavishly hew to the line that the Soviet Union consciously prepared for an attack by National Socialist Germany. Western writers, rather timidly by comparison with themes of Soviet aggression in postwar eastern Europe, the Cold War, etc., generally accept the benevolent interpretation that Stalin was buying time to increase the Soviet defenses. Neither interpretation is overly convincing, particularly since each depends for its automatic acceptance on the indisputable truth that Germany attacked the Soviet Union in 1941. Still, historical truth can be misleading, for although the Germans invaded the Soviet Union, one can make a strong case that the strategic calculus in Europe favored the Soviet Union, which was in a far better position to attack Germany. In 1939 and part of 1940, the Soviets faced a Germany at war with two other major European powers and, seen through the eyes of historical contemporaries, with little chance of winning it. Circumstances were favorable for aggressive action by the Soviet Union and presented exceptional opportunities for expansion westward. That the Soviets seized an area in eastern Europe larger than California during 1939 and 1940, when they had the opportunity and the armed force to do so, does not necessarily prove aggressive intent. Considering, however, that Germany was at war with two major European powers in a struggle that promised to be challenging, exhausting, and lengthy, the historical interpretation that the Soviet Union seized large territories to the west between September 1939 and May 1940 to prepare for certain attack by Germany is not credible.

Soviet Offensive Strategic Actions and Options: 1939–1941

It is credible is that by September 1939 the Soviet government, with an opportunistic and flexible foreign policy and an immense armaments effort, dwarfing the weapons and manpower of National Socialist Germany, could do more than just defend itself. When France fell in June 1940 to the exploitive offensive capabilities of the German army, one might argue that the Soviet government again faced possible great danger from Germany. Further, the Soviet interpretation of the events of July 1940 to June 1941, in which a dedicated Communist party and a courageous Russian people struggled to prepare for an imperialist German onslaught, is more credible than in the preceding years. Even here though, the Soviet government was favored by the providential British perseverance in the war. The consensus showing the Soviets playing for time to defend themselves does not track with the historically contemporaneous picture of a Germany involved in an aerial campaign over Britain and preparations for a challenging cross-channel invasion. From September 1939 to June 1941, the Soviet government had more options than cowering pusillanimously before the prospects of a German attack. The revisionist must note that the Soviets moved very aggressively during this period and certainly had offensive intentions limited only by immediate opportunities and long-term, deep-seated respect for the German army. The revisionist would also probably record that the seizure by the Soviets of 180,000 square miles of territory, while cowering, was only moderately pusillanimous.

Missing Information on Soviet Offensive Intentions: 1939–1941

The Soviets moved aggressively in 1939–1941 along their western boundaries into east Europe, their militant intentions limited only by selective fear of German counteraction. Why has historical interpretation stalled at the unlikely premise that the Soviets were preparing to resist a German attack? Why were enormous Soviet field armies deployed in the Ukraine in 1941, and Soviet forces in the Western Military District opposite German Army Group Center, in a defensively unconvincing arrangement? The answer is perhaps that the Soviet government was on the winning side in the Second World War and able to ensure that the Soviet-East European historical interpretation of behavior and motivation from 1939 to 1941 basked in the light of socialist defense against unprovoked, imperialist, fascist aggression. Western writers early succumbed to the temptation to consider the war in Europe as Hitler's, while the tough, aggressive foreign policies of France, Britain, and (Soviet) Russia tend to be ignored. That generalization does not mean that the governments of those three powers were not impressed with German military capabilities under a nationalist leader like Hitler in the 1930s. The generalization warns that the traditionally tough, self-confident foreign policies of those states were not inverted because modern historians determined that the Second World War was Hitler's: He wanted it, planned it, and started it. These factors are accepted today but were largely unknown to the decision-makers of the 1930s and early 1940s.

At the insistence of the Western Allies, the grand coalition partners of the Second World War convened an International Military Tribunal at Nuremberg after the war to try German political and military leaders for conspiracy to commit aggressive warfare. The tribunal included one Soviet judge and was incompetent to deal with the well-documented and similar Soviet aggression in 1939 and 1940. It is difficult to gauge the effect of the tribunal and its widely known activities on the interpretation of Soviet intentions and actions in 1939 and 1940. Still, it can be generalized that the western governments and writers were influenced by the nature of the immediate postwar period and the burgeoning revelations of Hitler's radicality to accept a "defensive" version of Soviet action in Europe from the Polish summer to the summer of 1941. All agree that the Soviet government deployed an immense army in the path of the Germans in June 1941 and entrenched it in so peculiar a way that it could be interpreted as being ready for either defense or offense. Because the Soviets have not, and may never, provide any other view than a defensive arrangement for their armies, one must rely on the brief opinions found mostly in German accounts of the early days of Barbarossa, when it was fashionable to comment briefly on the initial Soviet dispositions. The German accounts note that Soviet dispositions were highly unusual and could have been used for either attack or defense.

Awkward Deployment of the Red Army in the Ukraine and White Russia, 1941

It is difficult to explain why the Soviets in June 1941 deployed more powerful forces in the Ukraine than in the Western Military District, on the Polish border, and on the direct road to Moscow. One can conjecture that they were familiar enough with Hitler's views on the grain, raw materials, and industrial plant of the Ukraine to gamble defensively on a major German invasion or a heavy probe pointed into the Ukraine from southern Poland. Yet, it is possible that, given the tensions and provocations in Romania, the Soviets were planning an offensive of their own to ensure inheriting territories within their traditional sphere of influence. With the Soviet propensity for defensive interpretation of events and denigrating the German invasion, it would be difficult to get documentary verification of Soviet offensive intentions and the attendant unusually strong military deployment in the Ukraine. One of the few sources would be Soviet armed forces personnel captured during Barbarossa, when it seemed so probable the Germans would win that damaging information might slip out in systematic and lengthy interrogation of Soviet prisoners.[2] On 20 September 1941, German troops of the 11th Army Corps, upon the German encirclement of five Soviet armies around Kiev, captured a Soviet first lieutenant, a technical expert on the rail system. He was familiar with higher-level troop deployments and stated that the Soviets were planning an attack against Romania in the autumn of 1941.[3] Soviet planning for that attack or exercising similar offensive options against territory in southeastern Europe could explain the powerful Soviet forces in the Ukraine more reasonably than defense.

The awkward unbalanced deployment of Soviet field armies in the west, where forces blocking the corridor to Moscow were weaker than those in the Ukraine, may explain more readily Soviet offensive intentions in southeastern Europe. The Soviets, for example, demonstrated sensitivity about the defense of Moscow from the beginning of the German invasion. It is difficult, knowing the desperate Soviet defense of Moscow from the beginning of the campaign, to explain the relatively weaker forces in the Special Western Military District opposite German Army Group Center. Any interpretation in which the Soviets were committed in advance exclusively or even just largely to defend against a feared German attack is difficult to sustain. The great strength of the Soviet forces opposite German Army Group South and the ability to employ them offensively toward Romania lend support to an aggressive and opportunistic political strategy by the Soviets involving offensive options as well as defense for the field armies in the west. The forward concentration of the Soviet formations opposite German Army Group Center, which unnecessarily exposed those forces to double envelopment in the Bialystok salient, and the dearth of fortifications before them, lend credence to a view that the Soviets anticipated an advance into eastern Europe while being prepared by the size and disposition of their field armies to repel a possible German attack. This spectacle of Soviet forces on the eve of Barbarossa implies an illustrative misreading of Hitler's aggressive political intent in the east combined with an almost incredibly ingenuous underestimation of the offensive capabilities of the German army.

Among possible interpretations—Soviets solely on defense, Soviets with offensive and defensive strategic options, and Soviets prepositioning for their own offensive—German Army Group South faced powerful Soviet forces in the Ukraine. The army group was already hobbled by Hitler's intrusive meddling stemming from his concern over delays crossing the Dniester River between Bessarabia and the Ukraine. It was a baseless fear, like that which contributed to the ill-famed decision to stop German mobile forces short of Dunkirk on 24 May 1940 for fear of difficult terrain. Playing for bigger stakes now, especially after his successes in Poland, Norway, and France, Hitler continued loading operational crosses on the ample but not infinitely broad back of the German army. In this case, he ordered all German forces, except for a weak infantry army, away from the Dniester front. This forced Rundstedt to advance frontally with the bulk of his forces in Army Group South and every one of its mobile divisions against numerically superior Soviet forces. Rundstedt's unenviable and challenging mission was somehow to encircle the Soviet forces west of the Dnieper River and destroy them.

The Mission of Army Group South in Barbarossa

Perhaps the crucial factor in Barbarossa for Rundstedt and the other commanders in Army Group South was to clarify the relationship between the powerful, predominantly German forces in the south and the even stronger forces of the Army Group Center *Schwerpunkt*. Rundstedt indicated that he could contribute most to the progress of Army Group Center and winning the war by trapping and destroying Soviet forces west of the Dnieper. As an absolute minimum for success in the Russian campaign, he had to pin down and deny operational freedom of maneuver to the forces opposite him. To gauge Barbarossa's potential for success through defeat of the Soviet armed forces, one has to estimate the capabilities of the German forces on the northern and southern flanks of Army Group Center to defeat the Soviet field armies opposed to them and help keep Army Group Center on schedule.

Already constrained by Hitler's decision to redeploy the bulk of the German forces in Romania, including every mobile division, to the gap between the Pripyat Marshes and the Carpathian Mountains, Army Group South faced aggressive, numerically superior Soviet forces, attempting to hold as far west as possible. From the start, Army Group South encountered fierce resistance and innumerable, aggressive local attacks by Soviet tank forces that vastly outnumbered the Germans'. The forces of Panzer Group 1 and the 6th and 17th Armies, advancing on a narrow front with impassable terrain on both flanks, attacked frontally into the mass of the Soviet forces. They advanced slowly, with little chance of a breakthrough in the north and less opportunity for a single envelopment from that direction to destroy west of the Dnieper the huge

Soviet forces in the Ukraine. The Soviet defense west of Kiev has led interpreters to generalize that the fierce Soviet resistance forced the Germans to break off the *Schwerpunkt* advance of Army Group Center to clear up the southern flank of the Barbarossa operation before pushing on toward Moscow. The generalization, important in interpretation of the Russian campaign, is not supported by the operations of Army Group South.

Disintegration of the Soviet Field Armies West of the Dnieper, 1941

Although slowed by powerful Soviet forces, at first skillfully directed at higher level, German Army Group South advanced relentlessly into the great mass of the Soviet field armies. Fighting with impressive determination, the Russian troops soon took prohibitive losses in less skillfully led counterattacks, and defense at the operational and tactical levels. The strong Soviet 8th Armored Corps, on 29 June 1941, struck boldly behind the German 11th Panzer Division into the right flank of Panzer Group 1 near Dubno, forcing the group to destroy it. The chief, German general staff, monitoring the southern front two days earlier, had identified the Soviet armored corps and noted its apparent intention to attack at Dubno. He remarked that in doing so it was marching straight to its own destruction. The action is instructive, representative of the fighting in Barbarossa and an indicator of the potential outcome of the campaign. The action at Dubno shows the Soviet command in the Ukraine willing to sacrifice a major formation in the overoptimistic expectation of halting temporarily the German advance toward Kiev, directly to the east but some distance away. It shows the Russian troops fighting toughly, often to the last round of ammunition and drop of fuel, and absorbing catastrophic casualties. Conversely, it shows the Germans appalled by the operational sacrifice of the Russian unit but impressed by the determination of the troops to press home an attack doomed to failure. Last, it shows the Germans willing and able to destroy the formation and still maintain an advance that threatened to destroy Soviet resistance through irreversible casualties, damage, and loss of territory.

Although it took a while, the Soviet forces disintegrated under the impacts of their losses and the pace of the German advance. After putting up effective resistance for fifteen days, from 22 June to 6 July 1941, the Soviet command in the Ukraine began to lose control over events. German reports on 7 July show the 11th Panzer Division of the 48th Panzer Corps in Panzer Group 1 breaking "clearly through the enemy positions east of Polonnoje and ... pushing right through fleeing Russian columns to Berdichev."[4] Meanwhile, the Germans had pushed back and inflicted immense casualties on the Soviet armies in the Ukraine but had neither seized Kiev nor encircled a great body of troops as in the Bialystok and Minsk battles by Army Group Center. It is tempting for observers to generalize that Army Group South was in difficulty, but the forward movement it achieved by 6 July, the casualties it had inflicted, and the breakthrough to Berdichev on 7 July do not support that view. Rather, it suggests that Army Group South had severely mauled Soviet forces in the Ukraine and pinned them down, foreclosing operational freedom of movement by the defender and, of course, any opportunity to interfere with the progress of Army Group Center farther north.

On 7 July 1941, the Soviet position in the Ukraine deteriorated rapidly, from being pinned down and forced back into avoiding the disaster of a great encirclement west of the Dnieper. By now, German Army Group South had "equal strength due to the heavy losses inflicted on the enemy and soon [would] add numerical superiority to tactical and operational superiority."[5] At this crucial juncture, the Germans were poised to achieve operational freedom of movement, facing the great decision in the south of where to pivot and in which direction to proceed to trap the Soviet armies west of the Dnieper. Two days later, on 9 July, at Army Group South, Rundstedt stated his intention to strike with the bulk of Panzer Group 1 for Belaya Tserkov, approximately 110 km farther east of Berdichev, and then to push south or southeasterly as dictated by the situation. Earlier in the day, however, Hitler directed the commander of the German army (ObdH), Generalfeldmarschall Walter von Brauchitsch, to execute a timorous halfmeasure advance south from Berdichev with about one-third the armor of Panzer Group 1, splitting the remainder of the armor into two formations in widely divergent directions of advance. By the evening of 9 July, Brauchitsch and his chief of staff, Halder, who had immediately protested Hitler's concept of further operations, and Rundstedt, who protested against splitting his armor and the timid nature of the attack south from Berdichev, faced their toughest enemy in the Ukraine—Adolf Hitler.

Hitler seemed destined to prevent the disorderly retreat and large-scale encirclement of a significant part of the Soviet forces in the Ukraine. The Soviet command and the Russian soldier had shown substantial skill and casualty-absorbing toughness, respectively, but finally met disaster west of the Dnieper the second week of July 1941. Hitler's decision probably would not have adversely affected Army Group Center's advance toward Moscow. However, it would have allowed the Soviet forces to avoid the severe casualties and substantial weapons losses associated with a big German *Kessel* (pocket) and the psychological disequilibrium and sense of inferiority caused by precipitous retreat across the Dnieper. Hitler would have let the Soviet command and Russian soldier regain their composure. That, so reassuring to bureaucratically oriented commanders and peasant-based soldiers, was dangerous to the deep feints and daring advances of the German blitzkrieg attacker.

As commander in chief of the German armed forces after February 1938, Hitler passed his orders mostly to Brauchitsch and Halder. Except for the support the latter two men could marshal from senior field commanders affected by the orders, they stood as almost the only bulwark against the whimsical instability, nervousness, and unfocused energy of the supreme commander. Since November 1939, Brauchitsch was largely incapable of standing up to Hitler in confrontations over the conduct of the war, leaving his chief of staff largely responsible for maintaining effective direction in military operations. Halder was shielded from most immediate confrontations with Hitler, who dealt initially with Brauchitsch. Halder nevertheless proved a tough, determined, and generally effective antidote to Hitler's esoteric scattering of military effort and fear of risks. On 10 July 1941, Hitler reiterated in writing that he thought it "advisable and necessary to swing the leading elements of Panzer Group 1 promptly to the south." Although Brauchitsch disagreed with this blitzkrieg-diluting directive, he would make no decision that did not have the Führer's approval.

Unlike the many later Hitler decisions examined ad infinitum and ad nauseum concerning Stalingrad and Kursk, which had virtually no effect on winning or losing the war, Hitler's interference in Army Group South is relatively undiscovered[6]—though it took place when the Germans were winning the campaign in Russia and the struggle in Europe. The decision, in effect, conjoined by a few similar ones, could have affected decisively winning or losing the war. In the immediate confrontation of 10 July 1941, Halder noted laconically in his diary that "it is now up to me to get the Führer to agree."[7] Unable to contact a sleeping Führer at 1100 (!), Halder reached Generalfeldmarschall Wilhelm Keitel, chief, OKW, and, interspersing logic and persistence, pointed out that the Führer had directed OKH to destroy the largest possible enemy elements west of the Dnieper and therefore demanded an envelopment farther to the east. Surprisingly, within an hour after Halder's call to OKW, Hitler agreed to Halder's concept, and Army Group South continued operations in a bolder pattern. These operations led into the great encirclement at Uman (west central Ukraine) at the end of July and the disorderly retreat of the Soviet field armies across the Dnieper. Most significantly, for a more effective interpretation of the Second World War in Europe, it is clear that despite Hitler, Army Group South continued successful operations in the Ukraine and pinned down—indeed, severely mauled—Soviet forces. Army Group Center retained complete operational freedom of movement to advance on Moscow, limited only by its own immediate problems of reorganization, rest, and resupply.

Chapter Six

Army Group Center Destroys the Soviet Field Armies on the Road to Moscow in June and July 1941, Dragging a Reluctant Hitler Toward Victory

Point: "The situation supports the assumption that the enemy does not have sufficient forces left for a sustained defense of [White Russia]. This theory is borne out also by a Russian order, intercepted yesterday, to the effect that the Dvina River will be held only by groups concentrated at the crossings."

Chief of staff, German army, on 4 July 1941. Franz Halder, *The Halder Diaries.*

Point: "Only in one place on the eastern front—in front of Army Group Center—is the enemy really smashed. . . . Now is the time to attack with all of the mobile troops toward Moscow."

Commander of Army Group Center on 13 July 1941. Fedor von Bock, *Tagebuchnotizen Osten I.*

On the flanks in Russia, Army Groups North and South routed the opposing Soviet forces and allowed Generalfeldmarschall von Bock to push forward with Army Group Center uninhibited by lesser events. Unlike in the Baltic and Ukraine, where Germans were outnumbered by opposing Soviet field armies, Army Group Center was stronger than the powerful Soviet forces confronting it and by 2 July 1941 had smashed them. The two biggest pieces emerged as the Bialystok pocket, eliminated by 29 June 1941, and the pocket west of Minsk, which was near surrender by 2 July.

These pockets caught the attention of Adolf Hitler and reduced him to quavering concern over their sealing and elimination.[1] Hitler ordered strong lines of encirclement around the Soviet pockets and cautioned against sending the German armor east.[2] Almost perversely, with extraneous alarms, excursions, and halts, Hitler did more than any man to prevent the Germans from smashing the main concentration of the Soviet armed forces in front of Moscow. He attempted to ensure more certain half-successes in the early weeks of the war and did irreparable damage by preventing the Germans from fighting a timely, decisive engagement before the Soviet capital.

Army Group Center Defeats Both Hitler and the Russians at Bialystok and Advances Toward Moscow, June, July 1941

In Barbarossa's opening encounters in the Bialystok-Minsk battles, Bock, Guderian, and Hoth formed the most effective offensive command team of the war. It was so effective from 22 June to 3 July that it not only routed the Soviet forces blocking the way to Moscow, but also won the first battle of Hitler in the Russian campaign—the battle to overcome Hitler's self-destructive fear of decisive victory. With political aggressiveness and daring that were unmatched in his generation, Hitler looked with contempt on the generals' cautions in the risky advances and narrowly averted wars in the Rhineland, Austria, and Czechoslovakia. Once he found himself in war, he discovered that the politically timid generals included war-fighting lions whose military aggressiveness and daring were unexcelled.

After Bock and Hoth had considered the complexities and requirements of the Russian campaign, and until German seizure of the high ground northeast of Minsk on 26 June 1941, the two generals visualized Army Group Center executing the first great encirclement of the Russians all the way to Smolensk.[3] For boldness, daring, and fearlessness, the projected battle of decision has few peers in war. One can test the success of his move by asking if the panzer commanders were capable of the projected task. If the Germans had the technical capabilities to succeed, the greater human factor assuring success would be the self-confidence of the commanders, staffs, and troops. With Guderian and Hoth commanding the panzer groups, Bock may well have succeeded in an opening super-battle, and the answer to the question is a tentative yes. Major Klaus Graf von Stauffenberg provided a highly informative report on his visit to Guderian's group on 17 July 1941, when he noted: "Troops subject to great strain. Striking power is gradually diminishing, self assurance is continually growing."[4]

In projecting the first great battle all the way to Smolensk, Bock proved he could keep the battle at the necessary blitz pace beyond Minsk. Bock defeated the Soviets in the Bialystok and Minsk battles not so much by capturing 324,000 Russians and 2,500 tanks as by doing so decisively. Did it make a difference that Bock won decisively? Those Russians and tanks were the same whether taken vigorously or lackadaisically. Bock conceived a victorious drive through Smolensk into the Moscow-Gorki space and decisively extracted the bulk of his mobile troops from the encirclement and retained operational freedom for the panzer groups to drive on to Moscow. Bock won at Bialystok and Minsk while simultaneously moving toward Moscow on 3 July 1941.[5] He presented Germany on that fateful Thursday with the immediate collapse of the Soviet Union. While Hitler fixed on the fanatical resistance of the Russians in the pockets and probably slept fitfully,[6] perhaps imagining Russians jumping over fences and escaping, Bock ordered his mobile forces to converge on the high ground east of Smolensk.

With the elimination of the Bialystok-to-Wolkowysk pocket, the near capture of the Novgorod-to-Minsk pocket, and the resumption of the attack to the east by the panzer groups on 3 July 1941, the Germans completed the first phase of the planned lightning war against the Soviet Union. Under Hitler Directive Number 21 for the attack on the Soviet Union or the very different directive issued by Army Group Center, the Germans had achieved decisive success, maintaining a blitz schedule and breaking up the Soviet field armies in White Russia.[7] In the Hitler directive, Army Group Center had the task of "routing the enemy forces in White Russia," making it possible for strong mobile formations to advance northwards and, in conjunction with Army Group North, destroy enemy forces in the Baltic area. The Bock directive for Army Group Center directed the immediate destruction of the Soviet forces in White Russia, seizure of the Smolensk land bridge in the Russian Soviet Federated Socialist Republic, and continuation of the drive for

Moscow. The success of both Army Group Center and Army Group North by 3 July brought both the Hitler directive and the Bock directive (representing essentially the German army position) on the campaign in the east into enough congruence to keep the German offensive moving at a blitz pace. They focused on a single decisive objective—the Moscow-Gorki space and the forces massing to defend it. Bock had been so successful by 3 July, and Army Group North had also done so well, that even Hitler with his nervous urge to dissipate the drive of the Army Group Center could not divert Bock from moving toward Moscow.

Bock fought a furious battle with Hitler and Halder to continue the drive to the east. Halder noted as late as 2 July that success measured in large numbers of prisoners had to be shown the Führer to allow continued movement east. Halder explained that Hitler did not feel that success would develop and asked, "Where are the prisoners?" Frustrated, Bock replied he had already locked up more than 100,000—which was not a trifle—and the number growing daily. He exclaimed, "Haven't the colossal amounts of material been reported to the Führer?" He noted that on 2 July they had already waited too long to move out from Minsk and pleaded with Halder not to let Hitler stop the panzer divisions.[8]

The Soviets In Extremis: Stalin and the Communist Party Call for a Great Patriotic War

As the Germans pressed on toward Moscow on 3 July 1941, Josef Stalin called on the Russian people to participate in a great patriotic war against the invading Germans. It is tempting to generalize that Army Group Center's drive toward Moscow was so successful and menacing that Stalin was forced at the highest level of political strategy to extract the national (bourgeois) energies of the Russian people to defend the world's leading socialist state. Stalin was impressed by the German drive to Minsk when he made the decision to fight a national, patriotic war and was probably also impressed by his own decision as the Germans moved out again with their mobile forces toward Moscow on 3 July. Less than two weeks later, the Soviets would implant war commissars in every regiment, division, staff, and training and materiel command of the Soviet armed forces. War commissars were civilian communists, responsible for the political loyalty of the Soviet armed forces.

They countersigned every order issued and signed by military commanders, down to regimental or equivalent level.[9] These Soviet actions paralleled extravagant lies about Germans shooting all military prisoners and deserters and were correlated with Soviet shooting and maiming of German prisoners, so commonplace as to suggest policy. The Soviets launched tactically senseless attacks and accepted catastrophic losses to slow the Germans and convince their people that they could halt the invader. The actions support a view that the Communist party considered its political and military situation in July 1941 as in extremis.

At this crucial juncture, Hitler had the initiative in the war and the ability to render the military decision to end it successfully. One man launched the Germans into the Second World War in Europe; one man positioned the Germans to win the war in Europe through his timely political decision to invade Soviet Russia, and now he could win or lose by his military decision in July 1941. Hitler had played his politico-strategic cards brilliantly in 1939–1941 by his unexcelled political press into one campaign after another, each contributing to a better position for Germany in a final showdown with the Soviet Union. Even the controversial Balkans campaign removed any realistic chance that the British could rekindle a land war on the continent during Barbarossa. Politically, Hitler committed Germany to a war against the Soviet Union under extremely favorable circumstances—a one-front war during the planned duration of approximately six to seventeen weeks and a timely struggle that prevented further Soviet military buildup.

With the War Won in the East, Hitler Lapses into a Fortress Mentality

Having decided to commit Germany to a short war against the Soviet Union, Hitler faced a problem akin to putting the fabled bell around the cat's neck. Although the metaphor is strained—Hitler and Germany are unlikely mice and the Soviet Union a somewhat weak cat—it illustrates the abused relationship among politics, war, and the armed forces in any state. Hitler, the political leader of Germany, had plunged the state into a war with the Soviet Union, in accordance with Clausewitz's dictum that war is the continuation of politics by other means. In effect, having decided to establish German hegemony over Europe by defeating the Soviet

Union, Hitler now needed the army and the military operations to succeed. Hitler's war, a political decision against the Soviet Union, could succeed politically only through military victory. It was a decisive political idea to bell the Soviet cat, but it could be placed only by the German army.

Unlike political questions of why, where, and when to fight wars, winning wars revolves almost entirely around military means and military strategy. Wars are politically determined but once begun are the province of armed violence and the uncertainty and chance associated with violence. Once a civilian government has determined to use the logic of war to achieve its political policy, it must employ military grammar effective enough to win. By 3 July 1941, Hitler had planned and executed a war against the Soviet Union, but did the grammar on which he now depended for success promise victory? The German army had the numbers, qualities, position, direction of advance, and time to win against the Soviet Union,[10] but the strategy controlling events from that point on was coming up for final determination.

Since 4 February 1938, Hitler had worn two hats, one political and one military, as head of state and commander of the armed forces. From July 1940 to June 1941, he intruded into the military planning for Barbarossa and diluted the army plan presented to him on 5 December 1940 into the indecisive half-measure of 18 December. In accordance with the more decisive army plan for defeating the Soviet Union, Bock moved out Army Group Center on 3 July 1941 to seize the high ground northeast of Smolensk and continue the drive against the remnants of the Red Army defending Moscow. At the same time, Hitler continued his own strategy of time-consuming half-measures on the flanks, a military strategy out of keeping with his political goal of a short war against the Soviet Union.

Well before the Russian campaign, Hitler had developed a style of strategic military thinking that could be described as a fortress mentality—stubborn concern with the securing of areas contiguous with fortress Germany. The term is useful to characterize his military thinking about the Russian campaign, but it also describes his pattern of military leadership beginning with decisions from the end of the Polish campaign to the end of the war. An important example of Hitler's fortress orientation in strategy before Barbarossa was his insistence in October 1939 on an immediate attack in the west. Hitler was seized by fear that the Allies were planning a preemptive military occupation of Belgium,[11] and he reacted by ordering a great general attack.[12] The general staff, still unaware of the enormous potential of the mobile divisions and the tactical air force,[13] and facing difficult problems of redeployment and late autumn campaigning weather after Poland, saw little chance of a successful advance in 1939.[14] Hitler stubbornly insisted on an attack in the west that he intended primarily to secure Belgium. This style of great, general attack with limited goals would repeat itself in the Russian campaign.

In 1940, well before the campaign in the Soviet Union had begun, Hitler was transfixed by the importance of Leningrad and started to devise a military strategy for seizing that city.[15] In the months before Barbarossa, he also began to harp on the importance of the Don River basin and the Crimea, noting the raw materials and industrial plants of the former and the strategic location of the latter. The Germans would have to take Leningrad early in any successful campaign against the Soviet Union, but taking that city would not cause the collapse of the Soviet Union. Its fall would give Germany control over the sea communications in the Baltic. Seizure of the second largest industrial city in the Soviet Union would be an impressive achievement but not equal to the defeat of the Soviet Union or the focus of a vast but short campaign in the east. Yet, in late March 1941, in discussions with his higher military commanders in Berlin, Hitler stated, "The Panzer Armies' push on Leningrad is to be regarded as the ideal solution of the strategic problem."[16] Halder referred to such statements as "the same old refrain,"[17] and they show that Hitler never intended to win the war in Europe immediately and decisively. In the planning for Russia, this fortress mentality comprises the Leningrad syndrome—a rejection of the grand risk of the immediate seizure of Moscow and flight to the more assured but still uncertain half-success of Leningrad.

Army Group Center Advances Toward Moscow and Victory over the Soviet Union

To compound a developing set of contradictions, in his Barbarossa directive Hitler had approved the concentration of German strength in Army Group Center to rout the Soviet forces in White Russia while advancing on Moscow. German army planners had accurately pinpointed Moscow as the confluent focus of the Soviet nation, which it could not afford to lose and would be forced to defend with its main armed forces. The same planners had been disabused by Hitler's Barbarossa directive but assumed until 3 July 1941 that Army Group Center would be given the green light to move on Moscow. Privy to the Barbarossa directive of Hitler and OKW and the army order of OKH with its halt of Army Group Center to allow mobile forces to seize Leningrad, Bock makes no mention of a possible diversion in his Army Group Center order for Barbarossa.[18] At the high level of leadership of Panzer Group 3, Hoth makes the astounding comment that he assumed—based on his orders from Army Group Center—that the only objective of Panzer Group 3 and Army Group Center was the destruction of the Soviet forces defending Moscow and its capture.[19]

As Panzer Groups 2 and 3 (now organized under a new head-quarters designated 4th Panzer Army) moved out from Minsk on 3 July 1941, followed by the 2d and 9th Armies, the German rank and file believed they were headed singlemindedly for Moscow. At the same time, Brauchitsch (the only senior to Bock in the army chain of command), Bock, and Halder hoped that Army Group Center would continue its spirited drive into the courageous but disintegrating Soviet armies and reach Moscow by the end of August 1941. Simultaneously, with his staff having no influence on him, Hitler operated under the premise that he would halt Army Group Center after it seized the Smolensk land bridge and, in yet a further twist, redirect the largest elements south to ensure control of the eastern Ukraine and Crimea. Explaining these circumstances recasts the existing interpretation of the Second World War in Europe into more realistic propositions and clarifies the Soviet achievement. It also highlights the full potential of modern lightning war from 1939 to 1941 and more clearly exhumes facets of the giant historical figure, Adolf Hitler.

Strong cases can be made for German victory over the Soviet Union in summer 1941. Directed politically by Hitler to defeat the Soviet Union in a quick military campaign, the German army, dominant service of the German armed forces, planned to do exactly that.[20] It is difficult to believe that, with the collective experience it brought to bear on an attack against the Soviet Union, the German army could have deluded itself into making an attack that had little chance of success. The army was a determined proponent of war games, especially since the First World War,[21] and played them at theater, army group, field army, and panzer group levels during planning and concentration for Barbarossa. These games confirmed that the German army could quickly defeat the Soviet armed forces. Every game played by OKH and subordinate army units was based on the assumption of an uninterrupted drive by Army Group Center on Moscow, and the Soviet armed forces' then being forced to fight with reversed fronts in the Baltic and Ukraine. German forces would also use the Moscow communications net against them. The German war games showed the Germans successfully carrying out the advances necessary to capture Moscow. During the campaign, Army Group Center advanced in accordance with the army plan for the first five weeks of the war, evidence that the advances played out in the games by competent, battle-tested professionals would match advances actually achieved in combat against a determined enemy.

In the first phase of Barbarossa, from 22 June to 3 July 1941, Hitler and the Russians had done everything possible to slow the forward progress of Army Group Center, but it had been difficult to restrain. The Germans had achieved tactical and operational surprise along the entire frontier. Every bridge on the Bug River—and on the entire river frontier between Germany and the Soviet Union—was taken intact.[22] On the first day of the war (approximately 0305–2200, 22 June 1941) 1,811 Soviet aircraft were shot down or destroyed on the ground according to Luftwaffe daily reports.[23] Reichsmarschall Hermann Göring rejected these claims as exaggerated and ordered an investigation by damage teams and observers into the areas hit on the first day to prevent subsequent embarrassment to the Luftwaffe. The investigation revealed that the number of Soviet aircraft destroyed was actually higher than the compiled reports, approximately 2,000 aircraft.[24] During the same period, the Germans lost approximately 17 aircraft to enemy action,[25] representing an astonishing exchange ratio of 123 Soviet aircraft to 1 German. The Germans achieved air supremacy along the front of Army Group Center, adding an another potentially decisive element to support its advance toward Moscow.

The Most Important Operational Question for the Germans in the Attack on the Soviet Union

The most important operational question of the projected war against the Soviet Union is one infrequently discussed in existing literature. It was whether the Red Army would disengage from the Germans along the border and reengage at a time and place of its own choosing, deep in the hinterland. The question was crucial because had the Soviets disengaged opposite Army Group Center, dropping off powerful rear guards to slow the Germans, they would have retired intact to the great natural obstacles of the Dvina and Dnieper rivers.

The escape of Soviet forces opposite Army Group Center was the great fear of both Hitler and the army. The escape would have been a disaster for Hitler, considering his deep-seated fear of missing those half-measures, exemplified by the quick seizure of Leningrad. He was determined to achieve those half-successes by multiple diversions of Army Group Center in three directions after it destroyed the Soviet field armies west of the upper Dnieper. Had it been forced to engage Soviet field armies that had retired unscathed to the Dnieper and Dvina, Army Group Center would not have been available for diversion to Leningrad or the Ukraine. For Army Group Center, Soviet escape would have been a disaster because it would confront intact Soviet field armies behind natural defenses 500 km inside the Soviet Union. The Germans would have had scant chance of breaking through these defenses to reach Moscow quickly with the mobile divisions of Army Group Center. They would have been forced to wait for the horse-drawn, foot-marching infantry armies en route to the upper Dvina and Dnieper rivers. These armies would require two weeks just to march there without resistance from Soviet rear guards. They also would need time to prepare for an attack against an enemy with no flanks, with at least three weeks to prepare the area for defense, with reserves and levies fed from the interior to reinforce the frontier armies.

In the great war game run by Bock on 9 and 10 April 1941 in Posen, where Army Group Center headquarters lay disguised as an eastern area defensive command, he, his staff, and senior commanders agreed that a quick victory over the Soviets would be chancy if the Soviets traded space for time and made their first stand on the upper Dnieper.[26] Not knowing what Soviet strategy would be, the German leadership determined that the panzer groups would have to move rapidly in anticipation of the worst case, to prevent the escape of major Soviet forces trying to disengage under predetermined strategy. In his dairy, Bock notes as the high point of his entry for 22 June 1941, "The question of whether the Russians planned to get away was not yet to be answered."[27] The OKH was equally concerned, and Halder agonized for two days, noting darkly on 23 June 1941 that all the reports to that time "indicate that an enemy attempt at disengagement must be expected." He added, "Army Group North even believes that the enemy may have made this decision as far back as four days ago."[28] Then, on 24 June 1941, Halder wrote: "Generally speaking it is now clear that the Russians are not thinking of withdrawal but are throwing in everything they have to stem the German invasion."[29] The assistant operations officer of Army Group Center, instrumental in setting up the April 1941 war game, noted even more emphatically: "We were astonished in the war that the Russians fought on the border."[30]

Uncertain whether the Soviets would run for it, trade space for time, or fight and trade casualties for space and time, OKH and Army Group Center sketched out the battle for White Russia. Somewhat optimistically, but accurately as events proved, the army assumed that it could outrun the Soviets and pondered where to complete the encirclement, creating the first great *Kessel* in the east. Bock's problem of the campaign was whether the Soviets would run or fight, but within that heavy uncertainty he saw the great initial decision was where to encircle the Russians in White Russia. At OKH, Brauchitsch and Halder with similar concern had decided by late March 1941 that the destruction of the Soviet forces in White Russia would follow an encirclement at Minsk.[31] Bock and his remarkable panzer group leaders, Guderian and Hoth, personified the energy and will to defeat the Soviets, and they were uncomfortable with the decision. Bock believed the encirclement at Minsk would allow the Russians who escaped to set up the defenses that the Germans were so anxious to avoid on the Dvina and Dnieper.

Bock and Hoth favored the possibility of only incidentally

smashing the enemy west of the rivers and driving immediately into the area east of the upper Dvina and Dnieper.[32] That drive promised to put all the Russians fighting in White Russia in the bag while simultaneously blocking a Russian stand on the rivers. Bock glimpsed in that advance a pace of operations that would disintegrate the Soviet field armies, cut off their escape into the hinterland, and prevent the buildup of any significant defensive front before Moscow. The strategic possibilities of the drive were enormous, and had the Germans been successful in an initial drive, they would have reached the area around Smolensk only nine days into the campaign. The disruption of Soviet command and control would have incalculably great consequences, implying rapid Soviet military collapse before Moscow. Still, the Germans would have difficulty providing the ammunition and probably also the fuel for the panzer groups.[33] The Germans also would have monumental problems capturing the Soviets in the super-*Kessel* notwithstanding the disruption of the Soviet rear area and probable fragmentation of the withdrawing enemy field armies.

At OKH, Brauchitsch and Halder held firmly to the Minsk encirclement, and the war-winning possibilities of the wider drive remain, of course, conjectural. However, it is not conjecture that Bock and Hoth, setting their sights on operational targets far beyond Minsk, were successful in achieving them despite determined but disorganized Soviet resistance and the overweening restraining influence of Adolf Hitler.

The Soviets Commit the Red Army to the Defense of Moscow: 22 June–27 July 1941

Toward the end of March 1941, thus, as OKH decided to link up the two panzer groups of Army Group Center at Minsk, Bock railed at the limited scope of the encirclement and voiced concern about maintaining the advance to the east after the two panzer groups set the outer lines of encirclement.[34] Bock, not lacking self-confidence, was genuinely dismayed when the army leadership would not opt for a greater victory on the frontier. From 22 June to 16 July, the divisions of Army Group Center would take Minsk and Smolensk. They stood on the latter date with the morale, logistics, weapons, and advanced position to destroy the shattered Soviet forces before them. The Soviets lay operationally helpless in White

Russia, essentially incapable of launching attacks or conducting defensive operations under adequate control. This devastating situation has remained obscure because Soviets under general, desperate orders to stop the Germans launched numberless local attacks, which eventually merged into the self-imposed German halt beyond Smolensk. The hiatus stretched to an extravagant seventy-eight days and led some historians to misconstrue that "Russian resistance stiffened" and the "exhausted" Germans took the time to recover and only then press on toward Moscow.

Army Group Center inflicted casualties and havoc on the opposing Soviet forces from 22 June to the end of July 1941 that are difficult to exaggerate. The Soviets moved most of their armed forces opposite Bocks's army group with instructions to halt the Germans, prevent the loss of Moscow, and disregard casualties. By 19 July, the Soviets had situated their defensive forces in a way that reflects the striking power of German Army Group Center and its successes on the Central front. Between 22 June–19 July 1941, the Soviets had committed the following forces to defend the state:[35]

Table 1. Red Army Forces Committed
to the Defense of the Soviet Union
(22 June–19 July 1941)

German Front	Infantry Divisions	Tank Divisions	Mecha- nized Brigades[36]	Cavalry Divisions	Totals
North	46	7	2	1	56
Central	123	24	10	3	160
South	74	23	1	5	103

Table 1 shows that the Soviet leadership had committed most of the Red Army division- and brigade-level formations against German Army Group Center. From the beginning, the Russians had fought almost instinctively for every foot. The Communist army commissars reinforced the instinct by compelling resistance regardless of the tactical situation or losses to maintain control and prevent the distintegration of forces held together initially by iron discipline. Psychologically shocked and physically displaced by the German advance, and without effective control over their divisions, the Soviet corps and army headquarters enforced a formula of movement to the sound of guns and unquestioned, immediate attack against the advancing Germans. The capacity of the Russians to absorb losses, the strengths of the commissar system in enforcing discipline, the impracticality of coordinating significant disengagement, and the lack of space to survive against the mobile enemy led the Soviet high command to make a virtue of the inflexible dictum to hold on to every inch of Russian soil.

Of the German army groups, Army Group Center made the most dramatic advance and attracted the most Soviet forces. It also advanced directly on Moscow. The Soviet government policy of holding every inch of territory forced it to defend the capital, and once committed, the government could give it up only at risk of losing credibility with its people. If a tough dictatorship could not defend the Soviet capital, approximately 1,000 km from the German border, it could scarcely hope to force the Russian people to resist farther to the east against an obvious winner.[37]

Moscow was the communications and transportation plexus of European Russia and the core of a surrounding area accounting for more than 18 percent of the industrial production of the Soviet Union.[38] Independently of the political and psychological shock associated with losing Moscow, these factors would have forced the Soviets to defend it. This defense would have presented the German army with the opportunity to destroy the Red Army west of that great city. By 19 July 1941, the Soviets had poured in 160 division-level formations to halt Army Group Center, which had started the war with a strength of fifty-one divisions, only modestly exceeding that number in later months, and then including three rear "security divisions."[39]

What was the result of the Soviet bid for political and military survival after the Soviet high command committed to combat the bulk of its armed forces? Army Group Center had advanced 650 km into the Soviet Union (along the route of advance of Panzer Group 2) and destroyed or severely punished (*schwer anzuschlagen*) and removed from the front approximately 114 Soviet division-level formations, which had inserted themselves between the army group and Moscow. Based on wireless interceptions, captured maps, orders, and prisoner interrogation, the 4th Panzer Army, deployed along almost the entire front of Army Group Center, reported that it was in combat against "about 35 infantry divisions and 9 panzer divisions" on 19 July 1941.[40] Army Group

Center had become an insatiable consumer of Soviet divisions and Russian space. Virtually any analysis by 19 July 1941 would have had to forecast annihilation of most Soviet armed forces and the impending seizure of Moscow. Bock's army group was not held up by excessive losses. On 16 July 1941, the day it captured Smolensk, it had suffered a modest 43,000 casualties.

How had this come to pass, and what details can flesh out the picture sketched above? The German army achieved complete tactical and operational surprise against immensely powerful Soviet ground and air forces strategically massed to take advantage of any opportunity offered by the war between Britain and Germany. Attacking out of the edge of darkness into the first twilight of 22 June 1941, the Germans caught the Soviets at the tactical level asleep in and around barracks, out of bunkers, and without ammunition for combat.[41] In peacetime, ammunition, even for infantry weapons, is kept out of the hands of troops due to the danger of accidental firing. As the first day wore on, the Russians, comprising the overwhelming majority of the Soviet peoples, fought with characteristic tenacity in prepared defenses and determined attacks that would characterize their combat style for the war. Similarly, the Germans would attack with matchless élan based on individual initiative and a flexible sense of the general mission to be accomplished in any combat situation. In Army Group Center, German infantry would march and fight 40 km into Lithuania and White Russia,[42] and the armored spearheads would drive 80 km by midnight of the first day. These deep advances splintered the Soviet telephone communications network, displaced command centers, broke up Soviet army formations, and caused a breakdown of command and control in the Soviet army on the central front. Opposite Army Groups North and South, relatively stronger Soviet forces held together more effectively except for the extraordinary advance of the 8th Panzer Division, 56th Panzer Corps, in the north, which presented the Germans with an unforseen opportunity—immediate penetration to Leningrad.

Stubborn Courage of the Russian Soldier Despite the Germans' Taking Three Million Prisoners

On the darker side, in the first hours of the campaign, without similar provocation, Red Army soldiers committed atrocities against

German ground and air force personnel. The accounts of murder, mutilation, and maiming come entirely from German sources but are so general, from so many different observers and commentators, and in so consistent a pattern as to be exempt from serious question.[43] In the second volume of his memoirs, Manstein comments, "On this very first day of the war . . . our troops come across a German patrol which had been cut off by the enemy. . . . All of its members were dead and gruesomely mutilated."[44] He added that he and his aide, who spent much time on the road in uncleared territory, agreed they would never allow the Russians to capture them alive—an astounding comment by a *General der Infanterie* (equivalent to a three-star American general). Manstein also commented that in a counterattack made by his troops on 28 June 1941 near Dvinsk, his men recovered the bodies of three wounded officers and thirty men who had been overrun the previous day in a field dressing station. All the wounded Germans had been mutilated and killed by their captors.[45] German units from every army group reported this pattern of behavior.[46] The Russian actions have been muted by the Allied victory in the war, the activities of the German General SS Sicherheitsdienst (security service) units in systematically searching out and killing Jews in the Soviet Union, and the enormous casualties incurred by the civilian population and armed forces in the east.

Killing captured and often wounded Germans was so pervasive that it raises the question of whether it was an inherent, spontaneous characteristic of the Russians, who dominated the field armies, or part of a systematic policy by the Soviet Communists to encourage resistance and maintain control over the Red Army. Since German units discovered incidents from the first day of the campaign, before commissars and selected officers could have been carrying out an officially encouraged policy, it is tempting to generalize that the unprovoked mutilation and killing was an intrinsic characteristic of the Russian and the social conditions under which he lived.[47] Also, over-zealous commissars and some military officers directed the killings to encourage fanatical resistance, suggesting that the Germans were committing similar acts, and to incite similar, self-defeating German reaction.

Shortly after the war began, German combat units reported incidents that seemed staged for the brutalizing effects on the perpetrators, perhaps even as a psychological ploy to control the troops by threatening to reveal the killings to the Germans should they attemp to surrender under future German attacks.[48] On 30 June 1941 reconnaissance troops of the German 64th Motorized Rifle Regiment in the Ukraine found six "missing in action" from the regiment. The Soviets had maimed, mutilated, and then killed the Germans, and arranged the bodies in a circle about ten meters in diameter.[49] This and similar incidents indicate that some killings were staged for effect and had become part of a conscious Soviet policy to foment psychological conditions to keep their troops in the fight.

Soviet political commissars and officers told their troops from the start that the Germans would shoot all Soviet soldiers who either surrendered in battle or deserted later. The Soviets realized enormous effects from their conscious policy of claiming the Germans would shoot all their prisoners. The Germans interrogated large numbers of Soviet prisoners in Barbarossa and found that these factors virtually excluded all others addressing the tenacious resistance of the Russian soldier. Soviet political commissars and commanders commonly shot Russian soldiers unwilling or slow to move forward in attacks and those showing signs of surrender or desertion in defensive situations in bunkers and field fortifications.[50] The Russian soldier lived in an unenviable psychological state, knowing he would be shot if he hesitated to attack or wavered on defense, believing he would be shot by the Germans if he surrendered, and confronting death in combat as an uncomfortable third alternative.

The Germans achieved remarkable results with surrender passes dropped by air over and in the rear of the Soviet lines. The passes apparently nullified the intense fear of the Russian soldier that the Germans would shoot him. Once they had the surrender leaflets, the Russian troops tended to desert in large numbers[51] and shoot their commanders and commissars who attempted to force them to fight in hopeless situations.[52] The intelligence officer, German 6th Army in the Ukraine, noted in his report of 8 July 1941 that the previous day the army had taken "about 2300 prisoners, the greater part deserters coming across with air-dropped safe conduct passes."[53] The leaflets were a most effective antidote to the fear of immediate shooting that the Soviet soldier had been manipulated into believing awaited him at the hands of the Germans. Observing Soviet prisoners taken in the Ukraine after tenacious resistance, Germans noted—with intriguing insight—that the prisoners exhibited no sign of bitter disappointment or sullen anger at being prisoners, rather undisguised elation in escaping their own leaders and not being shot by the Germans.

Psychological research conducted in the First World War on the western front among soldiers immediately after they had been taken prisoner showed that, generally, they were euphoric at having been released from the fear of death in combat. Soviet prisoners probably showed the similar effect, intensified by their release from the additional fear of Draconian punishment. The observations on the deserters, as reported by the Germans in the Ukraine, go a long way toward explaining the apparent contradiction between verifiable, tenacious, Russian resistance and equally verifiable Russian prisoners in the millions.

The Russians also surrendered without air passes in great numbers out of the *Kesseln* created by the German advance as late as October 1941. In these encirclements and other engagements, the Russian soldier displayed definite levels of tolerance for German pressure, being particularly affected by simultaneous artillery fire and air attack.[54] Russian prisoners, from general officer to private soldier, also voiced respect for the great volume of fire the Germans generated with their bipod-mounted MG-34 light machine guns in the infantry squads.[55] The Germans also employed the guns mounted on tripods in machine gun battalions, an interesting holdover from the First World War for special defensive situations against the Russians. In the last great encirclement in Barbarossa—the double encirclement of Vyasma and Bryansk in October 1941—Army Group Center claimed in its summary of the completed battle that it had taken 673,098 prisoners.[56] Most of these prisoners surrendered under pressure of German gunfire and air attack, but only after tough resistance.

A German lieutenant commanding a light infantry gun platoon of the 67th Infantry Regiment, 23d Infantry Division, wrote an instructive account of the battle from the front line and the psychology of the Russian in combat.[57] Breaking through Soviet lines west of Vyasma, his division moved close to that city to join with other German divisions encircling vast Soviet forces cut off by the linkup of German panzer forces farther east. The lieutenant, with his infantry cannons, supported a German infantry company fighting against strong Soviet forces trapped in one of the large forests near Vyasma. He remembers vividly the fanatical resistance of the Russians in the forests, where great underground bunkers had been constructed. They refused to give up or to give much ground, and the Germans took virtually no prisoners in a battle that seemed endless. The lieutenant noted that in the early evening of the sixth day of battle, at the edge of the forest, the Russians suddenly began to surrender, inundating the single company he was supporting with the astonishing total of approximately 5,000 prisoners. Although the Germans were engulfed in Russians, the lieutenant remarked: "They had no fight left in them."[58]

This comment is particularly revealing of the strengths and weaknesses of the Russian soldier because the lieutenant referred to Soviet troops whom the Germans had allowed to regain their composure. In the earlier Bialystok-Minsk and Smolensk battles, the Germans established and maintained a pace that kept the Soviets off balance. The Russian soldiers fought tenaciously, especially in prepared positions, and attacked with determination, especially when given time to understand orders and rehearse the particulars of an assault. The Russian soldier rarely counterattacked at the tactical level, a style demanding initiative, and preferred to defend himself stubbornly from his individual position in accordance with orders to hold to the last round. In lower and intermediate commands, Soviet officers preferred to follow orders to the letter and adopt rigid formulas for their own operations. Major attacks by those commanders were carried out with great determination and even dash, including, for example, troops in trucks alongside tanks in the attack, firing from their vehicles, recorded by German units in the Ukraine on several occasions in June and July 1941. Thus, the Soviets found themselves at a severe disadvantage against the Germans in the Bialystok-Minsk and Smolensk battles. The Russian combat soldier was surprised by the speed and direction of the German advances, often surrendering when surprised tactically. Allowed to regain his composure, the Russian would often fight stubbornly to the death in improbable tactical situations in which the Germans took few casualties while inflicting disproportionally heavy losses on the Soviets.

In the great cauldrons, the Soviets were sometimes the attackers for significant periods. Under these desperate circumstances, the Soviet command ordered attacks carried out rigidly, with great determination by the Russian infantry, but often under frightfully adverse tactical conditions resulting in enormous casualties in killed and wounded. Even German private soldiers noted a frantic breakdown and panic in the Soviet attacks on the lines of encirclement. They also noted other ill-coordinated attacks launched from the march by newly arriving, newly raised Soviet formations. A German private soldier in the reconnaissance battalion of an infantry division in Army Group Center, holding a line of encirclement around Soviet forces near Gurki, recounts:

> Twigs were breaking on the ground ... [German] antitank guns, cavalry carbines, and machine guns went to the ready ... the Russians for their part were only 15 yards away ... machine gun and rifle fire hit directly into their ranks ... more and more Russians appeared out of the darkness storming forward into certain destruction. It was senseless dying.... The bodies of dead or dying Russians towered in heaps in front of the German positions ... But the Reds still would not quit from their insane purpose. They would break through under any circumstances. After about two hours it first became evident that there was no way out of the tightly closed German cauldron. Those of the Russians who were not lying dead or wounded began to ask for quarter.[59]

The German private rendered a clear, almost analytical account of the combat, in which he appears as a cool and thoughtful soldier and the Russians as tough and determined fighters but men with definite tolerances when balancing death against surrender. A Russian infantry regiment conducted the attempt recounted above, unable to escape after being pushed eastward from the Dvina River. It must have already been punished, harried, and largely off balance from the pace and violence of the German advance. This situation was repeated in varying levels of Soviet formations hundreds of times, with the Soviets fighting hard but pressed off balance and surrendering in the hundreds of thousands. It is important for understanding the German chances of success in Barbarossa that Hitler froze Army Group Center for the entire months of August and September 1941, giving the Soviet command time to regain its composure and form new divisions in the interior. The Russian soldier simultaneously recovered his equilibrium. Yet the Germans retained so much striking power that even after allowing the Soviets more than two months respite east of Smolensk, Army Group Center repeated the scenes of late July in October 1941.

In a forest, at a pine map table in White Russia, several of the more senior German commanders. Above from left to right, Fedor von Bock, Walter von Huenersdorff, Hermann Hoth, and Wolfram Baron von Richthofen. Field Marshal von Bock shows the direct and effective German combat command style, which involved few staff officers, executive assistants, and strap holders. (Bundesarchiv Bestand)

"I instructed my air force and flak generals to consider the wishes of the Army as my orders," said Field Marshal Albert Kesselring (left), Air Fleet I commander, shown below conferring with Panzer Group 3 commander, Colonel General Hermann Hoth. (Bundesarchiv Bestand)

Colonel General Hermann Hoth, at right, in a rare photo with Heinz Guderian. These two German leaders headed the panzer forces of Army Group Center and pulled along the conservative infantry army commanders in the center and the imaginative but erratic and nervous military dilettante, Adolf Hitler, to Smolensk and a hairsbreadth from final victory within twenty-four days of the opening of Barbarossa. (Bundesarchiv Bestand)

German offensive movement. German main battle tank, Pz.Kw. III, on the largest and finest highway in the Soviet Union, the road from Minsk to Moscow. The road is unpaved and has only light telephone and other electrical lines on one side. (Bundesarchiv Bestand)

Above, German concentration (*Aufmarsch*) for Barbarossa. A German ten-man infantry squad on 15 June 1941 in East Prussia. The squad leader is at left. The remaining nine men comprise, from right to left, the five-man rifle section and four-man machine gun section (note the two men with machine gun boxes and drums). Approximately 45,000 of these squads attacked the Soviet Union on Sunday morning, 22 June 1941. (Bundesarchiv Bestand)

Below, German infantry in the attack along a road in Lithuania in the opening days of Barbarossa. Note the bipods already opened on the machine guns. German infantry firepower was built around the MG-34, which the Germans felt could develop as much fire as twenty riflemen. (Bundesarchiv Bestand)

Above, Barbarossa combat. Two Soviet soldiers in the act of being captured by the German soldier at right center with pistol in hand. Opposite Army Group Center alone, from 22 June to 27 July 1941, the Soviets lost 634,000 men as prisoners. Note the soldier in the left foreground with grenade in hand. (Bundesarchiv Bestand)

Below, the Germans in Army Group Center inflicted tank losses of epic proportions on the Red Army formations on the Soviet western front. Two Soviet tank crewmen (first and third from right) immediately after capture being held by German tank crewmen at casual pistol point. (Bundesarchiv Bestand)

A Soviet prisoner-of-war laager near Minsk containing 25,000 prisoners. From 22 June to 8 July 1941, in the Bialystok and Minsk encirclements, the Germans took 324,000 Soviet prisoners. (Bundesarchiv Bestand)

During the first seventeen hours of the German advance into the Soviet Union, the Luftwaffe destroyed on the ground and shot down in the air approximately 2,050 Soviet aircraft. These four Soviet DB-2 medium bombers were destroyed on the ground while taxiing to take off. (Bundesarchiv Bestand)

Part III

The Defeat of the Soviets in Front of Moscow

Chapter Seven

Comparing the Fight in France with that in White Russia in June and July 1941

In the French campaign (1940), a blitzkrieg analogous to the opening stage of the Russian campaign, the actions and results help to understand Barbarossa. The Germans won the battle of France when spearheads of the main concentration of their tank force crossed the Meuse River near Sedan on the afternoon of 13 May 1940. It would be a long time before the French would ask for an armistice on 17 June 1940. There would be weeks during which the Germans would exploit the *Schwerpunkt* drive in the west. The essence of a modern blitzkrieg is such, however, that when the Germans crossed the Meuse with advanced elements of their mobile divisions, they had edged the threshold of victory. The German campaigns of 1939–1941 were not so much lighting wars as they were instant victories. An amazing characteristic of the six weeks' war—the title often given to the French campaign—is not so much that it lasted for only six weeks but that the Germans won it in only four days.

Conditions Leading to Victory in Blitzkriegs

Debate on whether four days is the exact time in which the Germans won is less important than understanding the following logic. Extraordinarily early in the French blitz, the Germans created circumstances that amounted to irreversible dislocation of the Allied armies and impending victory. What conditions did the Germans create in the French campaign, and how do they compare with those in Barbarossa? First, the Germans had the initiative in the blitz and concentrated their attack along a single axis of advance selected by them as decisive in the campaign—an important element in war. The Germans planned (optimistically) to encircle and destroy the French 1st Army Group (which included the British Expeditionary Force) by driving through its extreme eastern flank on its advance into Belgium. They would attempt this by suturing it off from the rest of France with an advance to the English Channel, then completing the encirclement by seizing the channel ports behind it. Success would lead to the destruction of the French, Belgian, and Dutch armies and the concomitant political collapse of the associated states.

In 1940, however, the western front included Belgium and the Netherlands and was so large and well-manned by Allied armies, which substantially outnumbered the Germans in personnel and tanks, that the Germans were forced to fight a two-stage campaign.[1] First, they encircled the French 1st Army Group, then paused and drove across the Somme River to defeat the French and British forces holding the defenses north of Paris. Notwithstanding the complex and spacious nature of the French campaign (see Map 1), the Germans had achieved a "set of conditions" by 13 May that ensured victory, culminating in the armistice of 22 June 1940.

How similar were the conditions on the evening of 13 May 1940 and those in the Soviet Union in the middle of July 1941? The essential conditions that caused French defeat by 13 May 1940 were movement, time, space, physical damage, and psychological equilibrium. These words describe the quick German victory in France and are useful to gauge German success in the Soviet Union in the analogous opening battle. In France, by 13 May the German 12th Army had quickly moved deep into French strategic space with the striking power to inflict mortal casualties and damage on opposing French forces. It disturbed the psychological equilibrium of both the French high command and the French combat soldier, and reduced their capability to survive under continued attack. The term *psychological equilibrium* conveys the idea that the French opposite the German *Schwerpunkt* army were thrown off balance psychologically by the unexpected pace of the Germans and the accompanying casualties and damage. The French command lost its capability to react to German moves, and French troops were overwhelmed by the same movement and the devastating effects of a formidable array of German weapons. As the

German 12th Army exploded into the rear of the French 1st Army Group, now well forward in Belgium, the Allied high command on the western front and the Allied field armies were similarly thrown off balance and began to disintegrate.

The Potential for German Defeat in France, 1940

The Germans won the French campaign but they were not preordained to win any more than they were preordained to lose the Russian campaign. Even as the French began to disintegrate, the Germans offered them opportunities to halt the German advance and win a stalemate in Belgium and northern France. The *Schwerpunkt* of the German 12th Army attack in the west was Panzer Group von Kleist, whose first wave was the 19th Panzer Corps. Although this panzer corps was followed by another panzer corps and a motorized infantry corps, it was the German unit whose success or failure would govern the success or failure of Germany in the battle of France. Franz Halder on 13 May 1940 brought the situation neatly into perspective:

> My estimate of the situation: In the area north of Namur we are now confronted with a completed enemy buildup comprising approximately 24 British and French and about 15 Belgian divisions. Against these forces [39 divisions] we can put up a total of 21. . . . South of Namur [i.e., around Sedan on the Meuse] we are faced with a weaker enemy, about half our strength. Outcome of the Meuse drive will decide if, when, and where we would be able to take advantage of the superiority.[2]

The 19th Panzer Corps and neighboring 15th began the Meuse drive.[3] They carried German hopes for a decisive success in the west on their sturdy shoulders. The German advance, like the advance in Barbarossa, was finely tuned and required forward movement along the *Schwerpunkt* axis of advance. That movement was necessary to keep the immediate enemy off balance and to drive into strategic space while destroying the opposing field armies. The 19th Panzer Corps moved great distances in a decisive direction with striking power to destroy the enemy forces in its path—thrown off balance by the advancing tank forces. In the German blitz it was anathema to let the opposition regain its psychological equilibrium and build up a coherent front. In retrospect, it is amazing that several levels of German command issued orders to 19th Panzer

Corps, which, had they had not been overruled immediately by the corps commander, would have slowed and probably paralyzed forward movement.

Guderian received orders on the following days that could have had fatal consequences in the battle of France. During the evening of 10 May 1940, the headquarters of Panzer Group von Kleist ordered the 10th Panzer Division, one-third the strength of 19th Panzer Corps, to move south to counter the threat of French cavalry imagined to be moving north from Longwy. Had the order been executed, Guderian's panzer corps would have advanced in divergent directions, with the mass of the corps weakened for the attack across the Meuse and possibly even halted to meet the threat from the south. It is difficult to believe that the attack across the Meuse, foreseen for 13 May 1940, would have taken place. As the hours ticked by, the French would be presented an increasing opportunity to discover the strength and purpose of the great German motorized force heading for the Meuse, but still to the east of it. In this hypothesized alternate past, the Germans might not have crossed the Meuse for days, or possibly a week or two later, against a physically reinforced and psychologically prepared enemy.

The Germans Attempt to Throw Away Victory in the French Campaign: The Pre-Dunkirk Orders to Halt on 15 and 17 May 1941

On 15 and 17 May 1940, after the Meuse crossing, Guderian's Panzer corps received orders to halt. These orders had potentially graver consequences than Hitler's later, better-known, and inadequately explained order to halt short of Dunkirk. Guderian sensed accurately and—though the word does not convey the importance of the consequence—fatefully that the *Schwerpunkt* force would never reach the channel and the offensive in the west would fail. In both cases largely alone, but with his prestige as architect of the armored force and its successful advance across the Meuse, Guderian kept the advance going and headed in the right direction. He fought more difficult battles with commanders above him in his own army than with the Belgian, French, and British field armies, probably a special characteristic of blitzkrieg-style operations. Although the data are limited and skewed—only two halt orders and another by the nervous military dilettante Adolf Hitler—they are weighty historical documents, important for understanding what makes a blitzkrieg stop or go. The higher in the chain of command and the farther from the front, the more likely the decision-maker would be to withdraw from the original daring purpose and deep drives of a blitz because of the diminished likelihood he would be in contact with the armored spearheads and sense the real possibilities in the battle.

In General der Kavallerie Ewald von Kleist's decision to halt on 15 May 1940, he appears to have been more concerned with securing the bridgehead across the Meuse than winning the war against France by continuing the drive to the channel coast. Kleist, who was not with the leading troops, was out of touch with the far-reaching dimensions of the rapid German victory developing with Guderian's tanks and motorized infantry. At the front of the armored wedge, Guderian, his subordinate commanders, and the combat soldiers sensed the impending collapse of the enemy and the necessity to keep him off balance. Kleist could not allow the French to regain psychological equilibrium enough to match the initiative, press, and quick reaction characterizing the forward movement of the German motorized force. His order to halt and defend the Meuse bridgehead was tantamount to breaking the pattern of initiative, press, and quick reaction of the Germans and presenting the French an opportunity of matchless operational magnanimity to stabilize their front. The French had lost the war on the Continent by the evening of 15 May 1940. Kleist by his single, discrete decision offered them the opportunity to rise from operational death and pack forces around Germans held in the Meuse bridgehead.

Several striking generalizations can be made about action, immediate effects, and outcome in blitzes by comparing the openings of the French and Russian campaigns. The current interpretation of the Second World War points out long-term, underlying reasons why the French lost the war in the west. These have come to include weak morale, a defeatist attitude in broad segments of the population, the defensive orientation of the armed forces as exemplified by the Maginot Line, and a relatively weak armaments effort compared with that of the German army. Writers similarly highlight the grand political and economic reasons why Germany lost its war in the east; the weakness of Germany's alliance partners, an ongoing war with Britain, and the marginal output of German industry in an extended two-front war.

The courses of the actual campaigns, however, do not support generalizations that any long-term or "underlying" factors were predominant in the German victory in France, or defeat in Russia. The British and French governments and Adolf Hitler were determined to continue their political policies by means of war—the realm of uncertainty and chance, in which the outcome depends on the armed violence and chance of battle. If no peacetime factor existed that can be shown to have doomed the Allies to defeat— and none can—then it follows that they were defeated according to the battles comprising the war. Rejecting the immediate postwar caricature of French defeat, I generalize that the French were defeated not because of some special political and social degeneracy acquired and matured in the interwar period but for the clear and cogent reason that they lost the battle of France.

Kleist's order to halt the *Schwerpunkt* force of the German advance in the west on 15 May 1940 supports a view that the Germans could have lost the battle of France by not breaking through to the channel. Inexplicably divorced from the necessity to push west, Kleist defended his order in heated argument with his subordinate, Guderian. He would agree to continue the advance for only another twenty-four hours to acquire sufficient space in the Meuse bridgehead for the following infantry corps of the remainder of the 12th Army. Had this order continued in effect, it would have slowed the pace of the battle, and the new pace could have been slow enough to allow a confused Allied command to recover and smother the German advance with slow-moving but tough-fighting infantry and tank forces. Kleist did not rescind his order, and on 17 May 1940, face to face and rather dramatically, ordered Guderian to halt. That order, however, originated with Hitler, who neared nervous collapse over perceived but unfounded danger south of the *Schwerpunkt*, and who raged and screamed[4] into the next day against continuing operations westward. Even in the restricted battle area of northwestern France and Belgium, the Germans could have lost enough momentum in only a few days to have let victory in the west slip away. Victory would have been lost, not because of special resistance by the Allied armed forces, Allied population strengths, or superior war production or numbers, but because the German command did not finish off the Allied armies when it could do so early in the battle.

Similarities Between the Opening Battles of the French and Russian Campaigns: Early German Attempts to Throw Away Victory in Barbarossa

In the Soviet Union in July 1941 the Germans faced a set of conditions analogous to those in France the year before. The fact that events developed in a strikingly similar pattern is not difficult to believe because the same Germans seized the initiative and fought battles similar to those in the offensive in France. In Barbarossa, both Hitler and the army high command agreed that the Soviet forces in Byelorussia would have to be destroyed as far west as possible to prevent their escape behind the Dvina and Dnieper rivers and the consequent buildup of a coherent Soviet front on the Smolensk land bridge, blocking the way to Moscow. As it was necessary in the French blitz to reach the channel coast and cut off and destroy the Allied forces in the lowlands, so it was necessary in Barbarossa to capture Smolensk quickly to prevent escape of the Soviet forces eastward and development of an effective resistance behind the Dnieper and Dvina rivers, centered on Smolensk. In France, after destroying the encircled Allied forces in the lowlands, the Germans intended to regroup on the Somme River and strike south on both sides of Paris. In the Soviet Union, after destroying Soviet forces to the west of Smolensk, the German army planned to regroup and strike east toward Moscow.

In the French campaign, from 15 to 18 May 1940, the Germans came close to paralyzing their own movement and never reaching the channel. In the battle of Russia, Guderian received an order to halt similar to that from Kleist in the earlier campaign. On 1 July 1941, Generalfeldmarschall Gunther von Kluge, commanding the 4th Panzer Army, into which Panzer Group 2 had just been placed, ordered Guderian to halt his movement to the Dnieper River to ensure tight lines of encirclement around Soviet forces trapped just west of Minsk. Because part of Guderian's 17th Panzer Division continued toward the Dnieper on 1 July 1941 under previous orders, Kluge called Guderian to his headquarters early on the morning of 2 July 1941 and berated him for not halting that movement. The next day, 3 July 1941, the last important Soviet forces surrendered in the Bialystok pocket, and the remnants in the Minsk pocket were tightly encircled and rapidly breaking up. By 3 July, Guderian had resumed his advance to the Dnieper and by 7 July was up against its right (west) bank with the Panzer Group.

Now, history repeated itself in several essential aspects. Hitler allowed his attention to become riveted by the Bialystok pocket, and, although he had ordered an ultra-quick thrust tc Smolensk to destroy even greater forces and exploit that into a more complete victory over the Soviets, he attempted to hold back the leading edges of the *Schwerpunkt*. Similarly, in France on 17 May 1940, Hitler drew back from the possible consequences of the enormous success of the *Schwerpunkt* far to the west of Sedan and ordered it to stop because he feared it would jeopardize the half-success of the Meuse bridgehead. In France, Hitler saw danger in the success of Guderian's 19th Panzer Corps, overestimating the strength of the French and their capability to crush the Meuse bridgehead by an attack into the southern flank of the German 12th Army. With little operational nerve, Hitler accepted securing the bridgehead as an end in itself, rather than as a means to destroying the Allied forces in Belgium. The Meuse bridgehead became an obsession of Hitler's for several crucial days—days that could have turned into weeks, acceptance of half-success in the opening battle, and loss of the following campaign.

There is a similar pattern in Barbarossa. Still, the campaign developed successfully because of the operational nerve of enough German military commanders to maintain the momentum of two panzer groups fast enough and far enough to defeat the Soviet Union. Curiously, opposing the existing interpretation that Hitler grossly underestimated the strength of the Soviet Union, Hitler substantially overestimated the Soviet armed forces in 1941 at virtually the only place that counted in the opening battle—opposite German Army Group Center. In the opening stages of Barbarossa, on 25 June 1941, Hitler badgered the high command of the army, questioning whether Army Group Center was already operating too deeply into the Soviet Union.[5] He demanded the two panzer groups be halted and turned around to ensure destruction of the Soviet forces trapped near and east of Bialystok. Like the case of the Meuse bridgehead, Hitler fixed his attention on the Bialystok pocket and nervously attempted to pace the whole campaign in Russia to his fears about the destruction of the Soviet forces there. From a day earlier, on 24 June, through about 5 July, Hitler exorbitantly underestimated the capabilities of Army Group Center to continue a full-blooded offensive toward Moscow while simultaneously destroying the Soviet forces in the Bialystok and Minsk *Kesseln.*

Had Hitler successfully halted the two panzer groups of Army Group Center on 25 June 1941 and manned lines of encirclement around the Bialystok pocket, Army Group Center might not have reached Minsk, let alone Smolensk, Vyasma, and Moscow in the battle for Russia. At this early crucial juncture in the battle, and the earlier the better in a genuine blitz, OKH had the courage on 30 June 1941 to order the combat units to advance to the Dnieper and Dvina rivers. The *OKH* could keep the battle moving on blitz schedule because of the superior combat performance of the German infantry divisions, the mobility and striking power of the mobile divisions, and the aggressive personalities of Guderian (Panzer Group 2) and Hoth (Panzer Group 3). The infantry divisions (horse-drawn and on foot) marched all the way to the area around Minsk, encircling two great pockets of Russians, extracting a significant percentage of the 324,000 prisoners taken, and crushing organized resistance in the second pocket west of Minsk by 7 July 1941. The mobile divisions (tanks, three-quarter tracks, and trucks) linked up south of Minsk on 27 June, setting the initial outer, loose lines encircling a force of some 500,000 Soviet army and air force personnel while severely disrupting command, control, and communications across the Soviet Special Western Military District. The aggressive and self-confident Guderian and Hoth continued the drive to the east, placing mobile forces of Panzer Group 2 against the Dnieper at Rogachev on 2 July 1941, and Panzer Group 3 on the Dvina near Polock the next day.

These details translate into the stunning debacle of Soviet armed forces and the Soviet state, which were on the brink of collapse on 3 July 1941. Politically, Hitler had ordered a war against the Soviet Union, beginning with a great surprise attack and ending in a lightning campaign. Masterfully, the army concentrated its forces, achieved surprise, and executed the opening *Schwerpunkt* drive to the Dnieper and Dvina rivers so well as to fatally disrupt Soviet forces opposite Army Group Center and fast enough to prevent Soviet mobilization of its full manpower and war production. In 1945, the Soviet Union would have eleven million men in its armed forces and produce tanks, aircraft, and artillery at an enormous yearly rate. In contrast, on 3 July 1941 the Germans were moving into the Soviet Union at a pace so fast that the fabled "inexhaustible" resources of manpower and the enormous productive capacities of the Soviet Union counted for little. The Germans had forced a blitz on the Soviet Union, and, in a blitz, the battle-winning capabilities of the present are decisive—not the promise of manpower and war production at some future date.

Influenced by the German loss of the Russian campaign, writers have researched and identified factors contributing to the German defeat rather than factors that, in the successful beginning of a blitz, could have led to German victory. The Germans lost the war after reaching the decisive turning point in the brief period from 22 June to 13 August 1941. At that time they had an overwhelming chance of winning, but later, as their strategic situation deteriorated, they had virtually none. Factors presented by the conventional wisdom to account for the German defeat include the time-honored numbers and stubborn toughness of the Russian soldier, and Russian space, winter, and mud. More modern factors include the fanatic, determined leadership of the Soviet Communists, their organizational abilities, and the resources and productive capacities of the Soviet state. All these factors contributed to the insuperable difficulties of fighting a long war in Russia in the painfully drawn-out, anticlimactic period from August 1941 to May 1945, but none contributed conclusively to the Germans' winning or losing the opening blitz.

The period from 22 June to 3 July 1941 highlights that generalization, for in that brief time the Germans achieved such great success with Army Group Center and the other armies on the wings of the advance that they established the immediate preconditions to defeat the Soviet armed forces. By doing so in approximately twelve days, the Germans largely negated the factors presented by the conventional wisdom as reasons for their defeat. Had the Germans continued the pace and destructiveness of their advance after 3 July 1941 (which they did), Russian numbers could not be decisive because they would never be brought to bear. The Russian winter would count for little because the Germans would be in Moscow at the end of August, and Russian mud would be reduced to subcritical proportions because the Germans would control the dense, higher-quality rail and road network radiating from Moscow and be fighting outflanked Soviet forces at Leningrad and in the Ukraine in relatively mud-free September weather.

The Soviet productive capacities similarly would count for little because the blitz would have caused irreversible damage to the Soviet armed forces. Meanwhile, the occupation of strategic terrain, as exemplified by the Moscow-Gorki space and Leningrad and the Ukraine, would doom effective Soviet resistance. Concerning the different, more immediate factors of stubborn tenacity of the Russian soldier and the organizational determination of the Communist party, the German field armies decisively overwhelmed the best the Soviets and the Russians could offer on the road to Moscow between 22 June and 3 July 1941. This schedule could be projected into defeat of the Soviet Union by the end of August 1941.

Chapter Eight

Reevaluating the German Advance Through White Russia in June and July 1941

Point: "The situation at the front is not even known by the higher leadership."
Interrogation of Soviet Generalmajor Dimitri Sakutny, commander 21st Army Corps.
U.S. National Archives, Records German Field Commands.

Point: "It would have to be reckoned that the German Army would take Moscow. The capital would fall despite further hard fighting."
Digest of Russian officer prisoner opinion.
U.S. National Archives, Records German Field Commands.

Counterpoint: On 22 July 1941 "Brauchitsch called and said the Führer has ordered that the further advance of the armor to the east is no longer a matter for discussion."
Fedor von Bock, *Tagebuchnotizen Osten I*, entry of 22 July 1941.

It is conceivable that the Germans had been mauled so badly in July 1941 by the Soviet defenders that they could not have advanced toward Moscow later in the summer. What had the Germans accomplished in July, and was it possible for them to attack in August? The answers lie in analysis of the German advance from 3 to 27 July 1941 on the front of Army Group Center.

On 3 July 1941, Bock and Army Group Center were so successful that they continued toward Moscow on a schedule calculated to win the war before the winter of 1941. Using curiously effective arguments, Bock assured Hitler that he would personally guarantee that the mobile divisions on the lines of encirclement on 2 July 1941 would stay until the Minsk-Novogrodek pocket was completely "burned out."[1] By exhibiting such concern for Hitler's fears over elimination of the pocket, Bock relaxed Hitler enough that he approved the earlier order of 30 June 1941 by OKH to advance on Smolensk.[2] Too early for Hitler, but too late for Bock, the panzer groups of Army Group Center set out to smash through the Soviet forces around Smolensk, then reorganize briefly for the attack on Moscow.[3]

The Germans Seize the Land Bridge to Moscow

At this juncture, Guderian noted that the Germans had to hurry to prevent the buildup of Soviet defenses on the Dnieper, which he intimates might have denied a German win in 1941. On his own initiative, with no encouragement from OKH or Bock, Guderian decided not to wait for the following horse-drawn infantry armies but to cross the Dnieper with his motorized infantry. Generalfeldmarschall Gunther von Kluge, commander of the 4th Panzer Army and Guderian's immediate superior, ordered Guderian not to cross the river but to await the following infantry. Despite this tough commander and the expected tenacious resistance[4] along the last great natural barrier to Moscow, Guderian attacked and successfully crossed the Dnieper by 11 July 1941.[5] He maintained the momentum of Army Group Center, and his successes in early July 1941 led toward the political and military collapse of Soviet Russia. At this moment, though, the German army was fighting two wars. As Guderian was defeating the main body of the Soviet armed forces, fighting on the Dnieper River for the immediate political and military survival of Soviet Russia,[6] Hitler launched an attack of his own that would accomplish what the Soviets were incapable of doing. He would halt and disperse Army Group Center. Halder notes in his diary of 13 July 1941: "1230 report to Führer . . . next objectives. We shall halt the dash towards Moscow by Armored Groups 2 and 3. . . . To this end Armored Groups 2 and 3 will be headed for the areas northeast and southeast of Smolensk," i.e., in roughly opposite directions and away from Moscow toward Velikie Luki in the north and the eastern Ukraine in the south.[7]

In the meantime the Germans in Army Group Center had achieved such great success that Halder could remark accurately that the war against the Russians—in contradistinction to the war with Hitler—had been won in the first two weeks. During this time the German armor had shown that it could move across the primitive Russian road system and through Russian resistance at a pace that would reach the Volga River at Gorki in a campaign extending through September 1941. Even more than previously suspected, the story is dominated by the advances and combat performance of the panzer groups. The 7th Panzer Division of Panzer Group Hoth reached the high road to Moscow at Smolevici, 40 km east of Minsk, on 25 June 1941. The panzer division penetrated approximately 275 km into the Soviet Union, only a little more than four days into the campaign. Two days later, on 28 June, the following German infantry armies would be close to locking the inner wings of the encirclement around major Soviet forces east of Bialystok. By the same day, the two panzer groups would have converged south of Minsk, and the 3d Panzer Division of Panzer Group Guderian would have advanced to Bobruisk, almost 400 km from where Panzer Group 2 entered Russia less than a week earlier.

The Pace of German Operations in White Russia

Few interpreters of the Russian campaign deny that the Germans moved at an extraordinary pace during these days and demolished any hopes the Soviets may have had of successfully defending White Russia. Amazingly, in less than five days, Army Group Center pushed the 7th Panzer Division into a position that not only ended the Russian defensive possibilities but also threatened to annihilate the Soviet forces deployed in the Special Western Military District—an immense force totalling approximately fifty-two rifle, armored, motorized-mechanized, and cavalry divisions.[8] By their linkup south of Minsk on 27 June 1941, Panzer Groups 2 and 3 had cut off almost this entire force from the rest of the Soviet Union. The Russians were in the panzer bag on 29 June, but could the tautly stretched German mobile divisions hold them there? The answer: largely yes, but partly no.

The situation was dangerous and complicated, particularly for Panzer Group 2, which lay directly east of the Soviet forces compressed around Bialystok by the 4th and 9th Infantry Armies. As early as 24 June, Panzer Group 2 found itself under attack from the west by badly coordinated but determined Soviet forces already cut off by its tanks half way to Minsk. Four days later, the German infantry armies completed a tight ring around a pocket of Russians stretching approximately 100 km from north of Bialystok to west of Volkowysk. During those four days, scores of thousands of Russians moved out of the open eastern end of the Bialystok-Volkowysk pocket and up against the outer lines of investment of German mobile divisions linking up at Minsk. Unsurprisingly, the Germans blocked the eastern end of the Bialystok pocket with one of Guderian's motorized infantry divisions. Then, as the horse-drawn infantry divisions and the 29th Motorized Infantry Division forced the surrender of the Russians in the first pocket, panzer forces blocked the escape of huge, shattered Russian forces streaming eastward, attempting to move through Minsk. The Germans formed a second great pocket west of Minsk around which they pressed horse-drawn infantry divisions freed from the Bialystok *Kessel*, liquidated by 1 July 1941.

Dual Role of the German Mobile Divisions in the Battles of Encirclement

As at the Bialystok cauldron, the German command at Army Group Center used precious mobile divisions to block the eastern end of the Minsk pocket. It was not enough for Guderian to advance to the Dnieper and keep the mass of the Soviet armed forces off balance and headed toward defeat on 5 July 1941. He had to leave behind his 29th Motorized Infantry Division, which shifted northeast from the Bialystok pocket to blocking positions at the eastern end of the Minsk pocket. Guderian also contributed his 5th Machine Gun Battalion and the Infantry Regiment Grossdeutschland. Army Group Center simultaneously ordered Hoth to keep his 12th Panzer Division, 14th Motorized Infantry Division, and 900th Panzer Brigade—the latter a unique force of tank warfare instructors getting practical experience of war—east of the Minsk pocket. The Russians made their strongest bids to break out of the Bialystok and Minsk encirclements toward the east. Mobile units of Panzer Groups Guderian and Hoth found themselves engaged in perhaps the lion's share of the short, intense, positional combat on the lines of encirclement. It was ironic and surprising that the panzer groups not only penetrated so deeply into White Russia that within five days they rendered the Soviet position untenable, but also that they did most of the fighting to hold the

Russians in the encircled areas.[9] The following data in Table 2 support this generalization.

Table 2. Soviet Prisoners and Booty, Bialystok-Minsk
(22 June–7 July 1941)[10]

German Unit	Prisoners	Tanks	Artillery	Aircraft
Panzer Group Guderian	157,176	1,233	384	0
Panzer Group Hoth	102,433	405	313	140
2d Army	40,003	90	87	90
9th Army	25,170	375	383	114
4th Army	2,210	1,085	663	0
Rear Area and Headquarters	5,019	0	0	0
Totals	332,111	3,188	1,830	344

The German infantry armies captured the considerable total of 67,483 Soviet prisoners, but the panzer groups dwarfed that figure with 259,609. Data are based on reports submitted by the various units of Army Group Center through the period of the fighting and can be considered accurate. The apparent misleading mathematical accuracy to six places, 259,609 rather than 260,000 in the panzer group numbers, reflects the system of consistently adding numbers exactly as reported from the combat units—staff officers did not tamper with reports by rounding numbers. The listing supports a view that the panzer groups did proportionately more fighting than the infantry armies. That must be handled with care because the 4th Army, which took only 2,210 prisoners, captured or destroyed the huge total of 1085 tanks. These data indicate that the foot infantry in the 4th Army fought violent engagements against powerful Soviet forces early in the fighting, especially to form the Bialystok pocket. The fighting took place when the Soviets were responding fiercely with local tank attacks and were not prepared to surrender.[11] Apparently, Russian soldiers surrendered in large numbers only when unable to force their way through German forces to obvious safety in the east. The mobile units of Panzer Groups 2 and 3, on the eastern lines of encirclement, and some infantry divisions under their operational control experienced the more desperate attacks by the greatest number of Soviet troops—those giving ground to the west, north, and south and compressed against the German mobile units on the eastern sides of the *Kesseln*.

The Complexity and Style of Fighting in the Russian Campaign

The complexity and style of the fighting are illustrated by the actions of 12th Corps, under Panzer Group 2, from 27 June to 1 July 1941. The corps was reinforced by the 29th Motorized Infantry Division in the fighting at the eastern end of the Bialystok pocket. The corps' two infantry divisions and the assigned mobile division blocked the most desperate attempts of the Soviets to break out eastward and experienced massive uncoordinated charges of Soviet troops. The fighting peaked on 30 June 1941, when the Soviets broke into German positions. The corps called on its last reserves and then took German troops, passing by on the great Minsk highway just to the east, and used those troops in the battle. In front of the 31st Infantry Division, the Russian infantry attacked in eight waves. "One wave after another was annihilated by light and heavy machine gun fire ... farther north the corps advanced detachment also fought against a superior enemy force." [12] Reporting on the combat results, corps headquarters gives the following numerical measure of the destruction caused the Soviet armies in White Russia (Table 3).

The corps did not estimate the number of Russian troops killed on its front during this intense combat. Because those were permanently lost to the Soviet command, it is important to estimate, at least generally, the number of Russians killed. This would provide a sense of the chances of Soviet survival at this crucial juncture of the initial, and possibly final, push of the German army into the Soviet Union. The corps reported annihilating eight "thick waves" of attacking Russian infantry by light and heavy machine gun fire within the sector of one German division.[14] This attack suggests similar ones throughout the brief period—but particularly towards the end—in a suicidal style characterized by masses of infantry attacking repeatedly at the same spot with little or no artillery support from the fragmented and uncoordinated Soviet commands.[15] Local Soviet commanders and commissars forced these senseless tactical charges, apparently fearing criticism and punishment. To this must be added a special fanaticism and fear of the consequences of capture by the commissars. Masses of docu-

Table 3. Representative Combat in the Opening Stages of Barbarossa,
White Russia, Bialystock Pocket (27 June–1 July 1941)[13]

12th German Corps	Losses Inflicted on Russians by German Unit		Total German Losses Men	Weapons
31st Infantry Division	5,900 Prisoners	35 Tanks		
34th Infantry Division	4,300 "	40 "		
Corps Advanced Detachment	4,500 "	30 "	359 killed	1 10.5cm Howitzer
610th Antiair Battalion	307 "	8 "	629 wounded 60 missing	1 15.0cm Infantry Gun
1st Antiair Battalion, 26th Antiair Regiment	200 "	4 "		
Corps Staff	204 "	0 "		
Totals	15,000 Prisoners	117 Tanks	1,028 Casualties	2 Guns

mentary evidence by Russian prisoners show that the Russian soldier was convinced that he would be shot immediately by the Germans, whether he surrendered or deserted. His fear of being shot probably counterbalanced all other motives together in his suicidal attacks and embittered defense of individual positions and bunkers.

The circumstances are curiously similar to those in the Pacific theater during World War II during ground combat between U.S. soldiers and marines and the Japanese imperial army, reflecting profound cultural differences. Although the Japanese never surrendered in significant numbers and fought in different terrain and tactical circumstances, they fought with similar tenacity and launched impressive but suicidal attacks when pressed at crucial battles. The casualty ratio showed approximately 10 Japanese killed for each American, a staggeringly high ratio in favor of the American forces but tempered by virtually no Japanese wounded or prisoners in the overall roster of casualties. Tenacious resistance and tactically inept attack against high-quality, high-firepower western armies, American and German, result in extremely high casualties for those unfortunate enough to be opponents. Regarding the German 12th Corps east of Bialystok, the American experience in the Pacific suggests that no one should be surprised by the extremely adverse ratios for the Russians killed in Barbarossa.

The Germans rarely presented figures on enemy killed. When they did, they seemed to illustrate exceptional cases. The figures in Table 4 support a view that exchange ratios would be extraordinarily adverse when Russian troops, jammed into pockets and fearful of being shot by their own officers and political commissars, were forced into tactically suicidal attacks against veteran German combat formations.

The single German infantry company, which counted 700 Russian dead in front of its position at Dubrowka (near Smolensk), had a strength of about 90 men. Had the company fought to total destruction, resisting desperate Russian attempts to break the encirclement, the German company could have suffered casualties in a pattern: 23 killed, 10 missing (presumed dead or captured), and 57 wounded. The company was not overrun by the Soviets but stood its ground and inflicted the Russian casualties with its own weapons and the help of powerful supporting arms. Had the German company been destroyed, as hypothesized above, to get the least adverse ratio of Russian casualties, the result is 30 Russians killed for each German. The German reconnaissance battalion engaged at Besenjata, Russia (north of Vitebsk) inflicted casualties in a ratio of 48 Russians killed for each German.

The exchange ratios at a higher operational level were also extremely adverse for the Russians, for example, in the Uman encirclement in the Ukraine in late July and August 1941. The Germans did most of the fighting in the Uman operations, especially the thinly stretched Panzer Group 1, blocking Russian attempts at breakout to the east. During the three weeks of the Uman encirclement, the Germans could not have suffered much more than 7,000

Table 4. German Reports of Russian Casualties (killed in action)

Type Combat	Location	Date	Russian Losses	German Losses
Soviet attacks [16]	Dobryn	4 July 41	c. 1,000 killed	30 killed
Soviet attacks	Dubrowka	17 July 41	700 killed	1 company engaged
Soviet attacks	Besenjata	20 July 41	95 killed	2 killed

killed based on established and verifiable German casualty figures for the eastern front and estimates of percentages for German units engaged around Uman. Halder estimated 200,000 Russians killed during the three weeks of combat, and the Germans thus inflicted losses in a ratio of approximately 29 Russians killed for each German.[17] Such ratios are associated with the cauldrons formed at Uman and six other locations on the eastern front by the Germans in 1941. The cauldrons characterized the operational style in Barbarossa and caused Russian casualties so great in killed and captured that the Germans could scarcely be accused of gross underestimation of their enemy.[18] While a tough Soviet dictatorship was willing and able to force Russian soldiers to absorb immense casualties, conversely, the veteran German combat formations were capable of inflicting them.

The German 12th Corps on the dangerous eastern encirclement of the Bialystok cauldron, taking 359 casualties killed, probably inflicted casualties in some high ratio, similar to those noted above. In the cauldron battles the Germans consistently observed inebriated Russian troops attacking, sometimes with arms locked together, without rifles. Such moves were observed in the cauldrons by Army Groups Center and South, along with motorized troops attacking in trucks and, in Army Group Center, cavalrymen charging with drawn sabers. Artillery support was lacking for Soviet troops unnerved by the fluid and dangerous escape from encirclement and for hastily mobilized units from the interior. It can reasonably be assumed that for the cauldron battles approximately 20 Russians were killed for each German. That ratio is extremely high and does not, of course, apply to noncauldron situations. These were proportionately more costly to the Germans, and included prepared positions of the "Stalin Line" attacks against fortresses such as Brest-Litovsk, and fighting in more stable conditions against psychologically composed Russian troops. Using the 20:1 ratio, the aftermath of a representative cauldron engagement should reflect the results shown in Table 5.

The Germans formed the cauldrons during fluid combat, in which German panzer and motorized infantry divisions drove through powerful but disintegrating Soviet forces. The Soviets were overrun by advancing German armor and motorized riflemen and suffered adverse ratios in casualties and damage similar to those noted by the Germans defending the lines of encirclement.

Table 5. Representative Cauldron Engagement (Barbarossa 1941),
Approximately One Week of Combat (rounded and generalized figures)

German Unit Engaged	Russian Losses	German Losses
Infantry corps with 2 Infantry Divisions	15,000 prisoners 7,000 killed 120 tanks	1,000 killed, wounded, and missing 2 guns

The German 4th Panzer Division reported that from 28 to 30 June,
it "destroyed in uninterrupted combat the mass of the Soviet IVth
Army Corps (with three divisions) and one cavalry brigade and 62
tanks of which eight were heavy."[19] The division based its report
on the statements of the captured Soviet commanding general, his
situation maps, statements by prisoners, and the "enormous figure
of 15,000 enemy dead and 12,000 wounded" abandoned along the
route of the German armor.[20] The division noted losses during the
same period of only 9 killed and 12 wounded,[21] figures that suggest
extraordinary loss ratios for the Soviets even if significant numbers
of their casualties were shared with other German spearhead formations sharing the same route.

The outlook for the Soviets was bleak. As long as the Germans
used this fighting style in operations, involving entire army groups,
they would defeat the opposing Soviet forces. If those Soviet forces
represented most of the armed forces available to defend the state
and were concentrated to defend terrain considered indispensable
for survival of the government and further prosecution of the war,
then the Germans would win the campaign in Russia and the war
in Europe. It should be noted that the 12th Corps had operational
control over the 29th Motorized Infantry Division and employed
it directly in the path of Russian attempts to break out. The 71st
Motorized Rifle Regiment of this division took 36,000 Russian prisoners during the same period, implying more violent fighting on
the front of the mobile division, greater casualties, and possibly a
more adverse ratio than 20–30 Russians to one German, suggested
previously.

The Breakdown of Soviet Command, Control, and Communications

In the first hours of the campaign, Soviet command and control
broke down, particularly at higher levels in the corps, army, and
district/front headquarters. The Germans shattered Soviet com-

mand and control by the general violence of the attack, not by some formula of operations targeted specifically at Soviet command-ers and technical instruments of communication.[22] The German mobile divisions advanced so rapidly that the Soviet command lost them on their operational maps. German infantry divisions moved proportionally even faster considering their movement largely on foot or by draft horse. The mobile divisions' deep penetrations and the infantry divisions' surge broke the Soviet telephone system and simultaneously displaced for days the Soviet field armies' headquarters and command posts. The Germans destroyed the phone system, displaced headquarters, and jostled Soviet units with particular effect opposite Army Group Center. Under interro-gation, captured Soviet Major General Jegorow, commander 4th Rifle Corps, stated that "right from the beginning," he and his staff had no further communication with their units and that "on the first day the formations of the corps . . . began to disintegrate."[23]

As Jegorow lost track of his divisions and regiments, Army headquarters lost track of Soviet corps and divisions.[24] Strain—indeed, disintegration—is shown on 25 June 1941, when "in the command net of the Western Military District Staff in Minsk around 0100 a lower level station reported that the IInd Rifle Corps could not be located." Not being able to locate a corps head-quarters or the divisions under its command was a considerable failure for the Soviet staff beginning to conduct the defense of Moscow, even under the impact of the opening stages of Barba-rossa. A German major serving as battalion commander in 3d Pan-zer Division, Panzer Group Guderian, observed that the "Russian troops seemed to have no communication among themselves." He and other officers in the division noticed that when a Russian unit found itself in the wrong place, hopelessly adrift from the tactical situation, it "took up an offensive stance and immediately attacked the Germans."[25] The German major linked the Russian behavior to ignorance of the German unit's location, associated surprise, and resultant "panic." He noted specifically that the Poles had better leadership and panicked later than the Russians in similar situations.[26]

The commanders of Panzer Groups 2 and 3 pushed their forces with such speed and élan that their mobile divisions fragmented the Soviet forces, inflicting casualties, occupying telephone ex-changes in the larger towns, cutting lines to interfere with Soviet communications, and physically overrunning headquarters in the field and in towns. When Hoth placed the 7th Panzer Division .astride the main highway between Moscow and Minsk on 25 June, he simultaneously cut the great rail line and telephone trunk line between those cities.[27] Hoth had thus physically severed the primary communications and transportation network between the capitals of White Russia and the Soviet Union approximately four days into the campaign. On the same day, from the south, Guderian cut most of the remaining roads, railroads, and telephone lines into the Bialystok area, where gigantic Soviet forces—most of the combat forces located in the Special Western Military District in June 1941—were already trapped. The Soviet forces, with little effective direction from the highest level command in Moscow during this time, and without effective control by the commander of the (Soviet) western front, moved instinctively eastward. They launched powerful but uncoordinated infantry and tank attacks against Guderian's forces. With impressive nerves, Guderian ignored the approximately 700,000 armed Russians streaming back toward his panzer group, anxious about getting to safety farther east. He felt that the infantry armies could pin down, intercept, and pen those Russians with help from a division or two of his own forces. He ordered the 24th Panzer Corps to continue east and, from the morning of 27 June to the morning of 28 June 1941, the 4th Panzer Division advanced a further 250 km into the Soviet Union.[28]

No historian can justify a claim that the Soviets were in control of events in White Russia in June 1941. The Germans not only overran the technical means and physical avenues of command and control of the Soviet leadership, but they also exceeded the capacity of the Soviets to cope psychologically with the advance. Without adequate historical style and capability to match the speed and violence of the German advance, the Soviet government and military leadership embraced a tactical formula for survival: All military formations were ordered by the Soviet command to resist to the death (or the "last cartridge")[29] in defensive positions and to attack in more fluid situations, notwithstanding tactical circumstance. Battlewise German troops at all levels observed that Soviet attacks came from illogical directions, repeated with mulish obstinacy at locations and times that made them self-destructive. German accounts of combat in the Ukraine, where they initially met larger, more powerful, confident Soviet forces, repeatedly describe violent attacks, sometimes involving coordinated divisions. Repeatedly, the accounts end with the words "bloody losses," euphemism in the south for enormous numbers of Russian dead and, until the great encirclement at Uman, modest numbers of prisoners taken by the Germans day to day, but which added up impressively as the weeks went by.[30]

Unable to match the speed of movement and command reaction of the Germans, the Soviet high command was clearly unable to match the Germans operationally, especially in large-scale maneuvers across an entire front. Almost forgotten today, the Soviets could not escape the Germans. It was soon apparent to the Soviets that the Germans could move so fast that there was not enough space between the German border and the most crucial terrain for survival, the Moscow-Gorki space. It followed that without effective control opposite Army Group Center, unable to match the Germans in operational level maneuver, and lacking space to trade for time against the fast-moving Germans, the Soviets made a virtue out of the necessity to hang on blindly everywhere. Still, the Soviets tried to maneuver out of several pockets created by the Germans near Bialystok, Minsk, Smolensk, and several subpockets around the latter city. The degree to which the Soviets lost control over events is illustrated by statements of captured Russians just after the heaviest fighting in the Bialystok cauldron: "Russian forces received the order on 29 June 1941 in Novogrodek [where another great pocket was forming] to retreat to Baranowicze. If Baranowicze were occupied by German troops, they were to go east to Stolpce and Minsk."[31] The order was remarkable for its especially presumptuous directions about what Russian troops would accept as a move into the punishing unknown and its sheer ignorance about the course of the war in White Russia. The Soviet command evidently was unaware that the Germans had already cut the main road out of Minsk 40 km farther east four days earlier, seized both Baranowicze and Stolpce on the same day, and taken Minsk by noon one day earlier. The Soviet command had totally lost control over events in central Russia and ordered forces around Novogrodek to retreat through cities already occupied by the Germans for several days to seek haven in the capital, which had fallen the previous day.

As the Germans pressed on in the great operational offensive of 3 July 1941, the Soviet command had not recovered its equilibrium. On 10 and 11 July, Guderian's divisions crossed the Dnieper at several locations with only light casualties. The successful crossing was a tour de force by Guderian on his mission to seize Moscow. He immediately ordered exploitation of the success by directing his 47th Panzer Corps to move against Smolensk. The familiar lack of Soviet command and control soon showed up, as air reconnaissance aircraft supporting the panzer corps reported a big Soviet column moving south through Gorodek (west of Smolensk) on the morning of 10 July, apparently intending to attack the German panzer force. By afternoon the same day, the corps intelligence officer observed that the column was "on its way back in a northeast direction towards Newel [and] the aimlessness of this movement leads to the conclusion that the Russian leadership is already confused."[32]

Guderian had impressed on the commander of his corp's 29th Motorized Infantry Division the necessity to reach Smolensk with all speed, and after the division crossed the Dnieper on the morning of 11 July it immediately exploited its success with a drive toward Smolensk. The Soviets were so surprised and confused that German motorized infantry of the division overran them conducting air operations at Sobowa air field, destroying or capturing twenty operational fighters on the ground. Later in the day, evidently out of touch with the operational situation, two Soviet staff officers, carrying maps of the headquarters 20th Army and the 23rd Air Division, landed on the field. German infantry disabled the aircraft, rushed it, and captured the crew, the staff officers, and the documents.[33] Soviet officers from the headquarters of a ground army and air division had lost contact with their own forces. Perhaps this is an overly harsh judgment; after all, the Soviet officers had found the unit and the air field they were looking for. As in Barbarossa, the Soviets had lost the German 15th Motorized Rifle Regiment and its parent division, which were wreaking havoc in the Soviet rear area.

The same German 29th Motorized Infantry Division had been the bane of Soviet field armies in White Russia from 22 June to 11 July, and its experience typifies Barbarossa. Moving fast, it arrived at Slonim on 25 June, where it stood in an ideal position with its strong (motorized) infantry to block the path of more than seventeen Soviet divisions attempting to escape east from Bialystok. Fortunately for the division, a web of German infantry divisions gripped the Soviet forces strongly enough to prevent the motorized rifle division from being overrun, while it inflicted immense casualties on the disintegrating Soviets. Assigned a blocking mission, the motorized division stood largely on the defensive from 25 June to 6 July, moving slowly northeastward to ensure the containment of the Soviet forces that slipped out of the Bialystok pocket only to be trapped again to the northeast in a second pocket between Novogrodek and Minsk. The 47th Panzer Corps, to which the 29th Motorized Infantry Division was assigned, took 7,600 prisoners on 28 June in the *Kesselschlacht* (the fighting on the lines of encirclement around a pocket)—an impressive achievement, but one that would become routine in the next few days.[34]

By 29 and 30 June 1941, the Germans noted fear and desperation in the Soviet forces. The independent 5th Machine Gun Battalion, fighting on the left flank of the motorized division, noted one Russian attack that penetrated to Rollbahn 2, the great road from Brest to Baranowicze and Minsk. In his combat report the battalion commander stated that the attack was contained: "The retreating Russian riflemen were almost annihilated by our machine guns [and] among the dead we found many Russians who had stabbed or shot each other to avoid being captured."[35] This astounding statement lends additional credence to a view that the embittered Russian resistance was based less on the traditional tenacity and sense of national patriotism of the peasant-based Russian soldier and more on a morbid, consuming fear of being shot by the Germans upon capture.[36] One must also suspect a monumental, primitive naivete in the belief of the Russian soldier that he would be shot. Yet in defense of his stubborn innocence, it must be reaffirmed that he was shot by his own officers, political commissars, and military police on straggler interception lines to keep him in the fight, and he could hardly expect better treatment from the enemy. The 5th Machine Gun Battalion nevertheless would take in 8,000 Russian prisoners on 4 July 1941 in the Minsk pocket, showing definite limits to naivete and fear among Russian troops.

In the meantime, the 29th Motorized Infantry Division in hard fighting along the Bialystok pocket from 26 June to 30 June had taken 36,000 prisoners, with a single regiment taking almost all of them. The division then held the main share of the front of Panzer Group Guderian on the eastern part of the Minsk pocket and, on 3 July, as the cauldron was rapidly burning out, took 11,000 more prisoners.[37] On 7 July, the division set off as rapidly as possible through Minsk to participate in the assault across the Dnieper, having taken 48,000 prisoners in the defensive combat of 26 June–6 July 1941. The flexibility of panzer group operations is exemplified by the 29th Motorized Infantry Division. After standing on the defensive for 11 days, the division nimbly shifted to the advance on 7 July and, after an extremely successful assault, crossed the Dnieper on 11 July and seized the city of Smolensk on 16 July. The division had to cross the Dnieper again to take Smolensk, in a daring coup involving the seizure intact of a peacetime bridge. By the latter date—16 July, a little over three weeks into the Russian campaign—the 29th Motorized Rifle Division had advanced 650 km through the heart of White Russia and taken Smolensk. From here strategic geography dictated that Army Group Center would attack directly toward Moscow. By 16 July, the division had captured 60,000 prisoners, an extraordinary accomplishment in modern war.

If there were a point or a lesson in Barbarossa, it would probably be that the successes of the 29th Motorized Infantry Division, against the brutally disciplined, hard-fighting, but continually collapsing Soviet field armies, were the rule rather than the exception. At the same time, in Panzer Group Hoth, the 7th Panzer Division had destabilized the Soviet military position in White Russia by its move to block the main road between Minsk and Moscow, only four days into the campaign. When the fighting began, Army Group Center advanced against four Soviet field armies deployed in the Special Western Military District, a grouping of forces under a single command equivalent to a German army group. The commander of the Soviet western front deployed three of his four armies well forward near Brest and into the Bialystok salient, projecting into German territory to the west. The Soviet armies in the west were well forward, centered roughly at the city of Bialystok, headquarters of the Soviet 10th Army. To grasp the war-winning mobility and casualty-inflicting power of the panzer groups, it is worth noting that the 7th Panzer Division stood 40 km east of the headquarters of the entire Soviet armed forces on the western, or Moscow, front only four days into the war. The same German division also stood 340 km east of where the center of mass of the Soviet armed forces had been only four days earlier. And on 26 June 1941, the other German forces, the unsung horse-drawn infantry divisions, and other mobile divisions, had formed a giant pocket between Bialystok and Volkowysk, whose center of gravity lay approximately 300 km behind the 7th Panzer Division.

In what condition was the panzer division after its four-day push to the train station at Smolevici? The answer is instructive for an accurate assessment of Barbarossa. The division was physically exhausted and mechanically strained by its accomplishment and had temporarily lost a significant number of tanks and trucks to the hazards of the primitive Soviet road system. In contrast, the division had suffered only light casualties and lost few tanks to Soviet gun fire. Four days later, after tough but relatively static combat around Minsk, in which the division took significant casualties but had time to repair and maintain its armor, it could report that it had 149 tanks ready for combat in the few days after its arrival near Minsk.[38]

The 7th Panzer Division fought from 26 June to 2 July 1941 to seize Minsk, effect the linkup with Panzer Group Guderian to the south, and block any Soviet attempts at relief of the encircled field armies. On 3 July, the division set off to the northeast, still in the 39th Panzer Corps and part of Panzer Group Hoth. The latter had the grand mission to join with Panzer Group Guderian in the heights around Jarcevo, northeast of Smolensk, to break up the last great Soviet defensive front before Moscow, encircle the Soviet divisions they hoped still lay to the west, and be prepared to continue to advance toward Moscow after a brief rest. Moving within this great stream of armed violence, the 7th Panzer Division now slipped south of Vitebsk on 10 July 1941 and projected itself onto the main road between Smolensk and Moscow on 15 July. As had occurred near Minsk nineteen days earlier, the 7th Panzer Division, now on the road and railroad between Smolensk and Moscow, destabilized the Soviet armed forces defending Moscow, most in disarray to the west of Smolensk. Unlike the earlier case near Minsk, the Germans were now 300 km closer to Moscow, and a psychological elation began to charge the German troops as they anticipated the decisive drive to Moscow. The Germans analyzed a host of interrogation statements by Soviet officer prisoners by mid-July 1941 and systematically asked the captured officers their opinions on the outcome of the war. The Soviet officers agreed, almost without exception, in June and July that the Germans would take Moscow—there would be a terrific battle, but the Germans would take the city and win the war.[39]

On 16 July, the day after the 7th Panzer Divisions arrived at Jarcevo, 50 km east of Smolensk, German motorized infantry of the 29th Motorized Infantry Division seized Smolensk. Army Group Center had trapped or partly trapped a huge number of Russian troops between the panzer groups and the following infantry armies moving up quickly using *Vorausabteilungen*, strong advanced detachments of battalion strength, the motorized elements of the largely horse-drawn German infantry divisions.[40] Although the German infantry division moved primarily at the speed of walking infantrymen and horses, pulling supply and equipment wagons, they contained motorized elements that could be used to form combat groups to close the great gap between the marching infantry and the panzer groups. These included a motorized pioneer company, armored car company, and antitank battalion (completely motorized). The Germans combined these elements into unlikely but strong combat teams that swept up enemy stragglers in the path of the armor and closed in on the more coherent Soviet units trapped in pockets. By 16 July 1941, Army Group Center had encircled or partly encircled vast Soviet forces west of Smolensk and, as occurred earlier at Minsk, would take approximately two weeks to get the advancing infantry around the several small cauldrons in the rear areas of Panzer Groups Guderian and Hoth and the great pocket on the boundary between them just north of Smolensk.

Faced with the destruction of three more armies in several small cauldrons and a super pocket near Smolensk as the Germans broke into Smolensk, the Soviets fought desperately. However, the best they had to offer was ferocious but blind resistance to the last cartridge in defensive positions and attack without regard to losses to escape through lines of encirclement. The Soviets had lost control of their own forces.[41] Aided, however, by the impressive toughness and stubbornness of the Russian soldier and his fear of being shot or "skinned alive"[42] by the Germans, the Soviet command managed to get scores of thousands of troops out of the eastern end of the Smolensk pocket. The chief of staff of the German 4th Panzer Army, Oberst Guenther Blumentritt, discouraged by the escape of many Russian troops at Smolensk, Minsk, and Bialystok through the thinly held lines of the mobile divisions, made the exaggerated statement that the Germans "did not succeed in seriously apprehending the enemy west of the Dnieper and

Duna, he always managed to evade swiftly and smoothly to the east . . . thus we had not gained much when we reached the Dnieper and the Duna."[43] This pessimism of a responsible high-level participant illustrates the misinformation that surrounds Barbarossa. For Blumentritt to write that the Russians always managed to evade swiftly and smoothly to the east is difficult to take seriously, considering the 634,000 prisoners, 5,537 tanks, and 4,929 guns left behind, and additional casualties in dead estimated at approximately 200,000 and a greater number of wounded evacuated. The relevant facts of the combat in front of Army Group Center in June and July 1941 are that the Russians swiftly lost well over one million men killed, wounded, and captured. They also lost staggering quantities of war material while being smoothly shoved back 700 km into the Soviet Union, directly toward Moscow.

The Soviets fought back stoutly in the several pockets around Smolensk and formed a coherent line of resistance approximately 80 km east of the city. Along that line, particularly around the road junction of Yelnya, they launched typical frenetic attacks to hold the Germans at any cost by profligate expenditure of lives traded for space and time. By 31 July 1941, the outlook was bleak for the Soviet government.[44] Except for the last part of the great Smolensk pocket, just north and east of the city, the Soviets had been cleared out of all encirclements. In despair, expecting the worst—that the Germans would gather themselves for the next great leap through Moscow—the Soviets could offer no more than a thin front. Behind that line they gathered virtually every reserve and new formation they could call to the colors, arm, and transport to the central front. The Germans rested and rehabilitated some of their formations for the anticipated push to Moscow, while several divisions cleared out the Smolensk pocket (by 4 August 1941). Other forces in Panzer Group Guderian and the 2d Army reorganized to assure potential German communications through Roslavl for the attack east and to eliminate any threat from a Soviet concentration around Gomel, farther south.

While German forces were regrouping, the Soviet command, desperately fearful of the next German move, used endless attacks as its tactical formula for survival against the German forces east of Smolensk, in positions to mount an attack against Moscow. As early as 30 July, the Soviets launched 13 ill-coordinated tank and infantry attacks against the German salient around the communications center of Yelnya. Although the attacks were badly led, the Russian troops advanced with determination, and, since the Germans remained static, the Soviet command developed impressive artillery support for its less impressive ground attacks. Halder made the extraordinary observation that "the German troops laugh off the tank and infantry attacks but are becoming concerned about the growing mass of artillery."[45] Several books on the Second World War interpret these attacks as "stiffening Soviet resistance," which forced the Germans to halt well short of Moscow and showed that they had severely underestimated the challenges of a campaign in Soviet Russia. The interpretation is a mistaken one. The Army Group Center forces halted, as planned and ordered by Bock, to reorganize briefly and launch the final attack on Moscow or advance south into the Ukraine.[46]

An important operational circumstance arose that demanded attention and would influence the timing of the final attack on Moscow. Army Group Center had driven from positions on the Polish border lying somewhat south of the latitude of Moscow. It had advanced not east, but east northeast, toward Moscow, and tended to block and ignore moderately strong Soviet formations in the southeast part of its sector. Those Soviet forces posed a latent threat to continued advance eastward and toward the end of July they still held Roslavl, the natural communications center for the advance of Panzer Group Guderian to Moscow. The Soviet command also maintained strong forces southwest of there, around Gomel. Bock faced a crucial operational decision that brings into focus the German war-winning dilemma in Barbarossa. The Germans unquestionably had the capabilities to reach Moscow and far beyond, but time was intuitively realized as the great dilemma (although never articulated in memoir or diary) by the army leaders from Halder (OKH) through Bock (army group), Hoth (panzer group), and even Generalmajor Walter Model (division). In a conversation with officers before Barbarossa, Hoth said that if the campaigns in the west had been blitzkriegs, then the campaign in the east would be a "blitz blitzkrieg."[47] Model had also remarked in preparations for Barbarossa that if the Germans were not in Moscow by Christmas, then they would never be and would lose the war.

Bock entertained similar thoughts and had already complained bitterly in his diary that the Minsk battle, swiftly as it had been completed, had taken too much time. Halder felt that Army Group Center would take until at least 5 July 1941 to continue the attack beyond Minsk and that the Germans would be ahead of themselves on that schedule. Bock managed to advance on the morning of 3 July, noting irascibly that the armor should have moved off two or three days earlier. Bock knew through a sixth sense, an extrasensory feel for military operations that helped select him as leader of the *Schwerpunkt* army group for the attack on the Soviet Union, that his command could defeat anything the Soviet government could put between him and Moscow. Yet he was aware that the accomplishment depended on ruthlessly continuing the drive into the forces defending Moscow. Bock and his panzer group leaders knew that the army group could not allow the Soviet command and the Russian soldier opposite it time to recover.[48] Bock penned the first sentence of the first paragraph of the directive for concentrating Army Group Center: "Every leader and soldier is to have hammered into him for this eastern campaign the foremost order: above everything else swiftly and ruthlessly forward!"[49] If one assumes that Bock meant this informative opening statement on Barbarossa, he is telling his troops (and the future world of historical interpretation) that the Soviets could be defeated in the summer of 1941. In the statement, there is not a hint of denigration or underestimation of the Russian soldier and the Red Army.

Chapter Nine

The German Capability to Advance on Moscow in August 1941: Possibilities Based on the August Situation and the Actual German Offensive of 2 October 1941

IN July 1941, with Army Group Center more than halfway to Moscow, Bock began to organize and time the final drive from around Smolensk. He encountered two challenges. First, he faced Adolf Hitler, desperately rent by some inner fear about fighting the great battle opposite Army Group Center necessary to defeat the Soviet Union. Next, he faced the mass of the Soviet armed forces, interposed between Army Group Center and Moscow—the point of no or, at least, improbable return for the Soviets.

Gripped by a Fixation on Leningrad, Hitler Vacillates over Strategic Objectives

Grasping at an incidental economic area, by December 1940 Hitler had come to consider Leningrad the primary operational target for the German armed forces attacking the Soviet Union.[1] On 13 July 1941, Hitler reiterated the idea of using Army Group Center to capture Leningrad, but toward the end of July decided instead that the army group should swing to the southeast to take the Ukraine. Bock and virtually every officer at higher levels of command, but not those immediately around Hitler in OKW, would fight this decision. This turmoil would keep Army Group Center halted east of Smolensk and delay its excursion into the Ukraine until almost September 1941. No Soviet armed forces action kept the Germans halted in August or delayed their aberrant move southward at month's end.[2]

As the German army stood immobilized by Hitler's concern for indecisive gains on the wings of the advance, a campaign and a war that could have been won in August 1941 irrevocably slipped away. At this moment, around the end of July 1941, the Germans came closer to defeating the Soviet Union and winning the Second World War in Europe than at any other time. These statements apply to the campaign begun in June, and without caveat about its delayed start caused by the severe winter of 1940–1941, a campaign in the Balkans, and allegations of motor transport shortages. Hermann Hoth correctly predicted that the Russian campaign would be won as a blitz blitzkrieg (or blitz²); and Fedor von Bock agreed wholeheartedly as he voiced his demand: swiftly and ruthlessly forward! Time, perhaps more than any other factor, provides a focus for the realities of the eastern campaign. Surely, had the Germans reached Moscow in August 1941 they would have won the campaign and war. Almost as surely, when Hitler delayed the final strike for Moscow until October 1941, the Germans had little chance of winning. Finally, had the Germans not captured Moscow by Christmas 1941, then Walter Model's prophecy of defeat would have been valid. The reversed scene above—the Germans at Moscow in August rather than short of Moscow in December—is paramount. It leads to a fundamental reinterpretation of the war, which posits that had the Germans taken Moscow in August they would have won and, conversely, had they faltered then, they would have been constrained by time and the strategic circumstances to suffer certain defeat—all in the space of a single month. To make this argument it must be proved that Bock had the capabilities in Army Group Center to defeat the main concentration of the Soviet armed forces, roughly handled but continuously reinforced, between him and Moscow.

The Turning Point in World War II and a Possible Alternate

With a timely order in late July 1941 to seize Moscow, Bock would have directed Guderian, with infantry support, to seize the communications center of Roslavl and used the great road through it to Moscow. Bock actually ordered Guderian in late July 1941 to seize Roslavl, and Guderian attacked on 1 August with a small part of his armor and a large infantry force comprising two corps. The operation had an unusually complex scheme of maneuver,³ and Guderian led it personally to a victory, taking 38,000 Russian prisoners and clearing the area around Roslavl and to the southeast toward Bryansk.[4] According to the senior infantry corps commander, by 8 August the Germans ended the battle, even cleaning up the numerous enemy stragglers.[5] Bock then prepared for the attack against Moscow with the attack timed after needed rest, maintenance of weapons and vehicles, and stockpiling of fuel, ammunition, and rations. General Hermann Geyer, commanding the 9th Infantry Corps in the Roslavl battle, remarked: "The decision for battle was from the Panzer Group. It was bold, but correct. The success was morally and materially very great. We hoped with it that we would move out quickly in the direction of Moscow."[6]

Bock had shown great determination in the June and July battles and the earlier preparations for the campaign. He visualized striking immediately for Smolensk, had kept the campaign on schedule by breaking the armor free of the Minsk encirclement, and, as early as 27 July, ordered the Roslavl attack to seize forward positions for the advance against Moscow. During the crucial period from 15 July to 27 July, during which Army Group Center had partly encircled, broken up, and largely destroyed the Soviet field armies between it and Moscow, Bock resisted the temptation to permit operations to become eccentric, veering south toward Gomel and north to Velikie Luke.[7] Determined to destroy the Soviet field armies opposite him and seize Moscow, he kept Army Group Center concentrated at Smolensk in July 1941. Assuming that Bock had been ordered in late July 1941 to press on to Moscow, it appears reasonable that the holy fire of Kustrin[8] would have eschewed eccentric operations and accepted the risks of maintaining his army group concentrated and moving toward Moscow.

Supposing that the German high command (OKW and OKH) had decided on seizing Moscow, and arguing that Bock would have been free of the Roslavl battle by 8 August 1941, it must be shown that the Germans had the military capabilities to capture Moscow. They proved so strong in 1941 that one can convincingly argue they were virtually assured of reaching Moscow in August, based on their performance in the actual delayed offensive of October. In that offensive, after preliminary moves by Panzer Group Guderian south of Bryansk, the Germans launched Operation Typhoon on 2 October 1941, an autumn attack intended to take Moscow. The Soviet high command had been presented with an exceptional period of two months, from roughly 1 August to 1 October 1941, to compose itself and mass forces to defend Moscow uninhibited by any German advance eastward. Under those self-imposed adverse circumstances, the Germans could be expected to make slow progress toward Moscow. This assumption is supported by the fact that, two months later, the Germans ground to a halt on the doorstep of Moscow in the week of 30 November–5 December 1941.

Whereas Army Group Center faced four Soviet armies in its advance into White Russia in June 1941 and took advantage of complete tactical and virtually complete operational surprise in its attack against them, it confronted an entirely different situation in October. Thanks to Hitler's diffusion of the campaign into military sideshows, Bock and his three infantry and three panzer armies[9] now faced no fewer than nine Soviet armies amply warned and waiting. These armies had been formed bit by bit and thrown forward in desperation to slow down the German drive for Moscow. That the Soviets raised, armed, and transported a large part of nine armies to the collapsing front can be attributed less to the strengths of the Soviet Union in men and weapons and the organizing energy of the Communist party than to the paradox that Adolf Hitler personally had presented the Soviet government with two months to raise those forces and regain its composure.

The German Halt in the Advance on Moscow

The enormity of this situation is difficult to exaggerate and can be illustrated by an analogue in the French campaign. The modish interpretation of the Second World War in Europe would have us believe that the Germans won easily in the lowlands and France against limited Allied manpower, weapons, and space. The same wisdom emphasizes that the Germans faltered gradually during a great surge into the Soviet Union, in which they underestimated the men, weapons, and space of the Russians and were overcome by numbers and space in 1941 and thereafter. Considering these campaigns together, one might ask: What if the Germans had sat in the bridgehead over the Meuse for two months while Hitler accepted the half-success of merely forcing the Allies out of Belgium, then kept the armies halted until he had seized the industrial and mining region of Alsace and Lorraine? The answer is that the badly defeated British, French (and probably Belgian) forces would have reformed on the Somme, joined by additional forces raised by the British and French governments, having been given an almost incredible two additional months to regain their composure and dip into a population base of eighty-six millions in Europe and additional millions in their empires. The exact details of that are conjectural, of course, but it cannot be denied that two months' grace for the Western Allies would have secured their political and military survival on the Continent. Such analysis shows not only that the Germans might have been defeated under western strategical circumstances by Hitler's nervous concern over extraneous targets, but also that the self-imposed German halt at Smolensk was of immense significance, and a similar halt would almost certainly have led to defeat in the west. The analysis supports a reinterpretation of the Second World War in which the Soviet Union survived Barbarossa not because of the fanatical determination of Communist bureaucracy, or the courageous stubbornness of the Russian soldier, or even Russian space and weather, but by the quixotic procrastination and perverse mentality of Adolf Hitler when the Germans were on the strategic offensive.

Other Problems for the Germans in an Autumn Advance

On further analysis, the German autumn offensive can be seen as even more advantageous for the Soviets. Before the two months' period noted above, which is keyed to the beginning of the Roslavl battle on 1 August 1941, the Germans reached positions from which the offensive would eventually take place, thus adding to the self-imposed delay. Elements of Panzer Group Guderian seized Yelnya earlier on 20 July 1941, and units of Hoth's panzer group were also ranged in the positions from which they would attack Moscow seventy-two days later. The Soviets had more than two months to prepare for the attack against Moscow. The German 7th Panzer Division, however, actually reached its attack positions around Jarcevo, east of Smolensk, even earlier, on 15 July 1941, and was still in positions close by seventy-eight days later. With the main concentration of the Soviet armed forces lying just to the east of its positions, unattacked for seventy-eight days, it is difficult to imagine that this panzer division would make much progress toward Moscow in mid-autumn 1941.

In contrast to the hour of 0305 on 22 June 1941, when the Germans northwest of Bialystok had attacked the Soviet Union, the Germans now attacked at 0615 on 2 October 1941, adding another damage factor stemming from Hitler's procrastination: The Germans had six fewer hours of daylight in which to fight each day in mid-autumn. Russian Octobers also included more days with overcast skies and low ceilings, which reduce the effectiveness of air attack against ground targets. The Luftwaffe was a special trump in Barbarossa; it not only destroyed over 2,000 Soviet aircraft in the first day of the campaign but also concentrated its attacks in support of the panzer wedges. Despite its relatively small numbers, it attained important effects against the Soviet field armies.[10] Criticized from irrelevant premises for not conducting strategic bombing in the campaign, the Luftwaffe was an extremely potent tactical air force, maintaining air superiority over the advancing Germans and providing fire support for the ground armies similar to that provided by artillery. The Luftwaffe also conducted air attacks against Soviet rail and highway communications that could be characterized more as battlefield interdiction and less as close air support. The Luftwaffe provided powerful support for the German armies in Barbarossa but was severely restricted by the adverse weather conditions of October—less sunlight, less daylight, and more clouds and ground fog.[11]

The Germans Destroy Eight of Nine Soviet Field Armies Massed for the Defense of Moscow

Despite adverse conditions of season and weather and the lack of strategic surprise, Army Group Center attacked the consolidated defenses of the main concentration of the Soviet armed forces. Unlike the operations against the Bialystok and Kiev salients, jutting into German-held ground, the army group advanced against Soviet defenses with no seriously exposed flanks along their approximate 450-km length. The Germans created "artificial" pockets where few natural possibilities existed, under unfavorable climatic conditions, and with less air support against nine Soviet field armies. They faced adverse strategic circumstances compared with a possible earlier advance, and could expect to stall along an arc about 300 km from Moscow. Confounding the sophistry behind the strategic posture in which Hitler through procrastination and concern had placed it, Army Group Center won the quickest and most decisive victory of the Second World War. With only modest losses but great exertion by the troops and strain on weapons and equipment, the army group destroyed the Soviet armed forces— those between it and Moscow. With exceptional luck, a drought in

October 1941 in European Russia, the German army might even have seized Moscow and the surrounding area, giving the Germans an excellent chance of defeating the Soviet Union the following summer.

The Germans completed the battles comprising Operation Typhoon in the brief period of 2–14 October 1941. Although preliminary operations began on the southern front on 30 September and the Germans would comb the battlefield until 17 September, Typhoon ran its course in approximately thirteen days. The operation contained substantial elements of operational deja vu. The 7th Panzer Division, 46th Panzer Corps, Panzer Group Hoth, cut the main highway to Moscow, the supply and escape route behind huge Soviet forces, for the third time in the campaign with remarkable speed. Attacking north of the highway, as it had done at Minsk and Smolensk, the 7th Panzer Division advanced at 0615 on 2 October into the area north of Vyasma. Elements of the division's 6th Motorized Rifle Regiment cut the main highway to Moscow 2 km north of Vyasma at 1700 on 6 October, only 107 hours later. The same day, the division joined the 10th Panzer Division advancing about 100 km from the south of Vyasma, encircling approximately fifty-five Soviet divisions in a great *Kessel* to the west of that city. Farther south, panzer columns of the 17th and 18th Panzer Divisions, 47th Panzer Corps, Panzer Group Guderian, moving almost twice the distance, would encircle vast Soviet forces totalling approximately twenty-six divisions in two pockets, north and south of Bryansk. German infantry divisions moved up rapidly to spawn lines of encirclement on which violent fighting would fall. Up to about 11 October, the Germans took few prisoners, and many Russians escaped from the southernmost pocket. Then, almost suddenly, between 11 and 14 October, the Soviets collapsed. As commander of Army Group Center, Bock notes that his forces "demolished" eight Russian armies comprising numerous rifle and cavalry divisions and thirteen panzer divisions or brigades, yielding from 2 to 17 October 1941 the booty shown in Table 6.[12]

Had the Germans retained their mobility after this singular victory and advanced toward Moscow, they probably would have overcome remaining Soviet strategic reserves massed around the capital, and any "Siberian" forces from the east, and taken Moscow. That would have changed the future course of the war, but it is doubtful that the Germans would have won because time had

Table 6. Soviet Collapse at Vyasma and Bryansk
(losses largely incurred from 7 to 14 October 1941)

Personnel captured 673,098
Tanks captured or destroyed 1,277
Artillery cannon captured or destroyed 4,378
Flak and Pak captured or destroyed* 1,009

---

*Flak = antiaircraft cannon; Pak = antitank cannon

slipped away to the Soviets' advantage. Actually, rains began about 10 October 1941 and continued for the rest of the month, paralyzing German movement on the unpaved roads of the Soviet Union and offering the Soviets another chance at salvation. With greater cloud cover, shorter days, and longer nights, the Russian roads and countryside were saturated and became permanently impassable until the first heavy frosts of mid-November. The Soviet high command received yet another month to build defenses around Moscow and call up forces from the interior, and the Germans irretrievably lost the Second World War in Europe.

Except for the vague possibility of a record drought in autumn 1941, Typhoon was foredoomed to be a strategical dead end for the Germans. Nevertheless, Army Group Center won an operational victory of the first magnitude. Had it consolidated its positions after the victory, a scant 150 km from Moscow, the army high command would have had a reasonable chance of converting Hitler to the campaign-winning course of defeating the Soviet armies defending Moscow in 1942, and then securing the eccentric objectives so dear to his heart in the Caucasus. Far more important than this conjecture, which projects possible events into 1942, is the observation that Typhoon was an operational success at the right place but the wrong time! It is difficult to avoid the conclusion that Army Group Center would have destroyed the far weaker Soviet forces defending the capital two months earlier in August 1941. The Germans could not exploit the Typhoon victory into the seizure of Moscow and the collapse of the Soviet armed forces because autumn rains paralyzed German movement on the unpaved roads of European Russia. It is equally difficult to avoid concluding that the same army group, moving across the same roads under the summer skies of August 1941, would have destroyed the main concentration of the Soviet armed forces, taken the capital, and collapsed effective military resistance.

The Timing of a German Summer Advance on Moscow and Defeat of the Soviet Union

Could the Germans have launched Typhoon on or about 13 August 1941? If the answer were yes, then clearly it espouses an interpretation of the Second World War in which the Germans could have taken Moscow in late August. And if that were not enough, it also suggests the corollary that the Germans would have continued operations in September 1941, forcing the Soviet government to withdraw Soviet armed forces in European Russia east of the Volga River. It is doubtful that the Soviet government could have survived such a blow to its prestige. It is also questionable whether the high command could have retrieved the forces in the Baltic and Ukraine, and doubtful that an adequate base for credible resistance existed in the east.

The timing of the attack is possibly the most important question that can be asked about the Second World War because it pinpoints the possible German victory. Before Barbarossa, the German victory in the battle of France and defeat in the aerial bombardment of England neither ensured nor prevented a German victory in the war. After Barbarossa, the Alamein battle in Africa and the struggle around Kursk did little to determine victory in the war, merely confirming the predetermined German defeat after the turning point of Barbarossa. Had the Germans won these battles, temporarily holding the British in North Africa and stabilizing the eastern front for the remainder of 1943, they still did not have a significantly greater chance of victory. German style and skill won campaigns quickly or not at all, and in Barbarossa, victory in the campaign translated into victory in the war in Europe.

German Army-Level Attacks Before the Seizure of Moscow

Army Group Center could have successfully captured Moscow based on the historical fact that one of its significant elements made a strong preparatory attack between 1 and 8 August at Roslavl for the final advance on Moscow. The attack showed that Panzer Group Guderian and the 2d Army had completed the Smolensk operations so long before the end of July that they could plan, logistically prepare, and launch an army-sized attack (approximately eleven divisions) on 1 August 1941. Its intent was to widen the front and secure more effective communications for the coming advance against Moscow. Hitler's psychological compulsion to secure the resources of the Ukraine before seizing Moscow and defeating the Red Army slowed the Germans advance out of Roslavl by a month, and then in the wrong direction. The resistance of men like Halder, Bock, and Guderian to the eccentric drive of part of Army Group Center toward the south caused Hitler to hesitate and procrastinate through much of August, finally ordering the attack to the south on 21 August. Army Group Center executed the attack on 25 August 1941 with the bulk of Panzer Group Guderian and the 2d Army (approximately fourteen divisions) and advanced successfully 450 km into the Ukraine. The move was coordinated with corresponding advances by Army Group South and netted the Germans the destruction of the Soviet field armies in the central Ukraine and the taking of 660,000 prisoners. The battle has been called by at least one authority "the greatest battle of encirclement in history."[13] It was similar in dimensions to the Vyasma-Bryansk battle fought approximately a month later in October 1941.

Army Group Center began the Kiev battle on 25 August. The timing and scale of fighting showed that it could make a strategical push against the main mass of Soviet armed forces. During the preceding period, from 1 to 20 August 1941, Panzer Group Guderian, the 2d Army, and the remainder of Army Group Center were not permitted to launch a concentrated attack in a direction decisive for winning the campaign. They stood strategically paralyzed by the struggle between Hitler and OKH. Army Group Center, nevertheless, had the capability to advance in August 1941, as shown in the unfocused operations of 1–20 August, in which the forces of Guderian and *Generaloberst Freiherr* von Weichs (commanding the 2d Army) launched attacks resulting in the capture of 132,000 Soviet prisoners and the destruction or capture of 344 tanks and 976 guns. The attacks were unfocused because no one could be certain of the direction of the next strategic advance on the eastern front until the end of the struggle between Hitler and OKH, from 21 to 23 August 1941. Guderian's and Weichs's forces were scarcely exhausted by their attacks either logistically or mechanically because on 25 August they began the great oblique advance away from Moscow into the Ukraine.

These details—the major attacks of Army Group Center between 1 and 20 August 1941 and the strategic advance of its southern half into the Ukraine on 25 August 1941—support my contention that the Germans were capable of advancing against Moscow in August 1941. The same details show that had the Germans focused Army Group Center on the seizure of Moscow toward the end of the Smolensk battle in the last half of July 1941, they would probably have started the advance on Moscow about 13 August, but no later than about 20 August. The earlier date is based on the assumption that Guderian and his supporting infantry would require five days to recover from the Roslavl battle. It also assumes that farther north, Hoth and the infantry fighting with him, pressed by Bock to move on Moscow as soon as possible, would have finished off the main Smolensk pocket, checked Soviet spoiling attacks, and advanced by the same date. It is hard to escape the conclusion that a German advance on 13 August would have reached Moscow before the end of August and, by the location and timing of the result, given Germany victory in the Second World War in Europe.

Part IV

German Casualties, Tank Losses, and Logistics

Chapter Ten

German Casualties and Tank Losses: Did the Germans Have the Combat Strength to Seize Moscow in the Summer of 1941?

HISTORICAL convention avers that the Germans suffered severe casualties from the beginning of the Russian campaign and faced lengthy rest and reorganization by the end of July 1941, before continuing the advance into the Soviet Union. Contrary to this view, the Germans suffered relatively light casualties, especially considering that during Barbarossa violent fighting took place along the entire front as the Germans advanced everywhere to bring the war to a quick end. German forces on the eastern front stood at a strength higher than any other time in the war and, according to all accounts, the Russian infantry fought stubbornly in defensive positions and counterattacked fiercely, often in wave after wave. Thus, the convention has maintained without adequate verification that the Germans attacking along the entire front must have suffered crippling casualties.

It is evident today that either the Soviets had been surprised and adopted a makeshift strategy to attack the Germans as far west as possible with all reserves, or they had been caught in the middle of an offensive deployment of their own. As a German observer pointed out, however, "In pursuing this policy they evidently grossly overestimated German losses."[1] This acute observation—largely accurate—might also have read, "In pursuing a policy of defense to the last man and counterattack without regard to tactical reality or losses, the Soviets evidently felt that the Germans were suffering severe losses similar to their own." By 3 July 1941, the Germans

Table 7. German and Soviet Casualties Compared
(22 June–3 July 1941, entire front)

German (documented)		Soviet (estimated)	
Killed	— 11,822	Killed	— 200,000
Wounded	— 39,109	Wounded	— 400,000
Missing	— 3,961*	Captured	— 335,000
Total	— 54,892	Total	— 935,000

*Comprised of captured and killed, with some of the former also wounded.

had completed the first phase of Barbarossa—Army Group North had broken out of the Dvina bridgeheads and moved north in a late but great rush toward Leningrad, and Army Group Center had moved away from the large pocket near Minsk and moved east toward Smolensk. That date is a reasonable one to check German casualties and gauge the possibilities of a push for Moscow in the immediate future. Table 7 compares German and Soviet casualties during this period.

The Germans attacked with close to 3,000,000 personnel, and the Soviets initially had approximately 2,500,000 men committed in western Soviet Russia. German forces would be drawn down gradually during Barbarossa, while the Soviets would be immensely reinforced by mobilization. Soviet mobilization, however, was counterbalanced by the tactical and operational superiority of the German field armies, reflected in catastrophic Soviet casualties, particularly in captured and killed. The result is that at any single moment during Barbarossa, with one notable exception, one could expect to find approximately 3,000,000 Germans engaged in combat with a similar number of Russians. The exception is early in August, when Army Group Center was so successful that the Soviet forces opposed to it, according to German intelligence estimates, appeared to have been reduced to roughly half the strength of Army Group Center. To grasp whether or not German casualties in the first phase of Barbarossa were leading toward a German collapse in August, one should note that the campaign involved approximately 6,000,000 men who could be engaged in combat at any time. German casualties totalling 54,892 in the first twelve days of combat, involving some 6,000,000 men, can be described as moderate. German casualties compared with Soviet losses during the same period show an overall exchange ratio of approximately 1 German casualty for every 15 Soviet casualties. The Germans suffered so few casualties and managed to extract so uneven a ratio in their favor that any analysis of casualties supports the view that the Soviets were losing on 3 July 1941 and had little time left to survive if the Germans continued their pace.

They did. By 16 July 1941, when they seized Smolensk, they had lost only 102,488 men, and by 2 August they had taken 179,500 casualties. On the latter date, had they been operating under the hypothetical case of a direct advance on Moscow from Smolensk, where they were at that moment, they would have been less than two weeks from a final offensive on Moscow and scarcely deterred by the casualties incurred up to 2 August. The casualties were small for the results achieved, the sizes of the German and Soviet armies engaged, and the closeness of the Germans to victory in the entire campaign.

Not surprisingly, the Germans had anticipated casualties in the war they had planned, and they had providentially taken steps to be prepared for them. They estimated their losses in the great "border" battles, anticipated to last from June to August 1941, would be 275,000 and felt that they might incur another 200,000 in the month of September.[2] For an army so often accused of grossly underestimating the challenges of war in the Soviet Union, the Germans anticipated casualties, one of the challenges of war, with uncanny accuracy. The army anticipated 275,000 casualties for June–August 1941 and had that number available in its field replacement battalions and the Field Replacement Army to replenish the forecasted losses. Actually, the army slightly overestimated the casualties it would take under the army scheme of maneuver (as opposed to Hitler's eventual procrastinated maneuver) in Barbarossa, suffering roughly 257,000 casualties during that period. Hence, it can scarcely be claimed that the Germans were surprised and thrown off stride by the severity of their losses, which were less than they had anticipated, or that they were inhibited significantly by casualties in launching a great strategic offensive toward Moscow on 13 August 1941.

Other Means of Gauging German Casualties: The Situation in the Divisions

Other ways of gauging German losses can be used to sense how close the Germans were to victory in the opening stages of the campaign. The Germans attacked with approximately 141 divisions reinforced by "army troops." The latter troops were held by corps, army, and army group commanders and assigned as required to support the operations of the divisions. The army troops comprised powerful forces, particularly of artillery, pioneer, chemical mortar (smoke), and self-propelled storm gun units. They fit into the picture of combat in Barbarossa and the other campaigns largely by the way they were used to reinforce operations by the German divisions. The divisions were the largest self-contained maneuver elements used by the Germans, and they can be used to gauge casualties in Barbarossa. On 22 June 1941, the attacking German divisions were powerful combat organizations averaging approximately 15,745 men among the infantry, panzer, and motorized infantry types.[3] On 23 August, approximately when it would have been closing in on Moscow under the hypothetical direct advance, and after fighting a series of hard battles (Roslavl, Rogachev, and Gomel) to open the way south, Panzer Group Guderian controlled eight divisions averaging 12,543 men, each at "engagement strength."[4] The divisions had additional men in unevacuated, lightly wounded, and temporarily sick. The German divisions of the heavily engaged Panzer Group Guderian of Army Group Center were operating at 80-percent personnel strength compared with their numbers at the beginning of the war.[5] That strength shows that Army Group Center would not have been prevented from taking Moscow because of casualties.

Contrasting Numbers and Qualities of the Opposing Tank Forces, 1941

The German army was not inhibited on 2 August 1941 by casualties, but it still could have been crippled by losses in its single most important weapon during the advance—the battle tank. In 1941, the German battle tanks, in contrast to reconnaissance types, were relatively light vehicles that could have suffered heavy losses at the hands of the numerically large Soviet tank and antitank forces. The Germans held the tanks shown in Table 8.

The German Pz.Kw. II was scarcely suitable for tank-versus-tank combat or infantry support. A weak tank production effort in serious battle tanks had forced the Germans to use the Pz.Kw. II alongside battle tanks in combat. The Germans used them judiciously, emphasizing their value in reconnaissance and coups de main, but the tank could be expected to suffer heavy losses. The

Table 8. German Battle Tanks, Barbarossa, 1941 Specifications*

German Tank	Tons	Armor**	Gun	Road Range (km)	Maximum Speed (km/hr)
Pz. Kw. II A–E[6]	10	15mm	2.0cm	260	48
TNHP 38 (Czech)[7]	10	25mm	3.7cm	230	42
Pz.Kw. II A–H[6]	20	30mm	5.0cm L42	175	40
Pz. Kw. IV A–E[6]	21	30mm	7.5cm L24	200	40

*The German tanks include numerous letter variants complicated in turn by retrofitted material, but the specifications are predominately as shown.
**Max armor at a few frontal locations.

Czech-manufactured TNHP 38 tank was no heavier but had thicker armor in several frontal locations and a much more potent 3.7cm long-barreled, high-velocity cannon. The German tank was a light reconnaissance vehicle used to play a presumptuous role as a battle tank. By the standards of the day, the Czech-manufactured TNHP 38 was at least a marginal battle tank, comparable to the Soviet BT cavalry tanks and T-26 infantry support tanks available in huge numbers to the Red Army. At the beginning of the war, the Soviets had approximately 17,000 of the BT and T-26 tanks, compared with 746 German Pz.Kw. II and 812 TNHP 38 tanks in the invading field armies. In similar types of marginal battle tanks, therefore, the Soviet tanks outnumbered the Germans numerically by more than an order of magnitude. A more complete picture of Soviet battle tanks is given in Table 9.[8]

The more credible German battle tanks—Pz.Kw. III and IV—were overmatched by the Soviet T-34, KV-1, and KV-2 vehicles, especially in the tank-versus-tank combat qualities of armor protection and main armament. In a curious turnabout in the campaign, high-quality Soviet tanks in small numbers faced German tanks in larger numbers with similar missions but inferior qualities. In the first months of the war, the Soviets probably used approximately 500 of these vehicles. The Germans, in contrast, entered the Soviet Union in the first days of the war with 1,065 combat-model (as distinguished from command-vehicle) Pz.Kw. III and 489 Pz.Kw. IV tanks. It is only fair to note that these German tanks would have their hands full with the immense numbers of

Table 9. Soviet Battle Tanks, Barbarossa, 1941 Specifications*

Soviet Tank	Tons	Armor**	Gun	Range (km)	Speed (km/hr)
T-26 A–C	10	15mm	4.5cm	225	28
BT-2, 5, 7	12	13mm	4.5cm	375	52
T-34 A, B	26	65mm	7.62cm	400	52
KV-1 A–C	48	120mm	7.62cm	335	35
KV-2	52	110mm	15.0cm	250	26

* The Soviet tanks include different letter variants, but the specifications are predominately as shown.
** Max armor over wide areas at front of hulls and turrets.

BT and T-26 vehicles, almost all of which were armed with the Soviet 4.5cm tank cannon—quite capable of penetrating the armor of most larger German tanks at realistic combat ranges. These same German tanks would also have their hands full with the larger Soviet tanks, whose armor was impervious to the projectiles fired by the German 5.0cm L42 and 7.5cm L24 tank cannon. The Germans were saved in this almost incredible technical mismatch by the flexible use of other weapons to support the tanks, including the 10.5cm light field howitzer, 10.0cm field gun, and 8.8cm flak (antiaircraft cannon).[9] The German tanks could knock out a few of the Soviet T-34, KV-1, and KV-2 tanks only because of their high rates of fire and impacts best described as statistical outliers—unlikely impacts, or combinations of impacts against gun tubes, drive sprockets, and the junctions between turrets and hulls.[10]

The Importance of Tanks in the German Blitzkrieg

The Germans depended for success in Barbarossa largely on aggressive, self-confident panzer leaders and the qualities and numbers of their tanks. Tanks were so important to them that a shorthand way of comprehending the strategic possibilities would be to compare the numbers of tanks available at any stage in Barbarossa. The Germans, of course, had combined tanks with other combat arms, such as motorized and eventually mechanized infantry (i.e., armored, tracked vehicles to carry riflemen), motorized artillery, pioneers, antitank guns, and special communications, repair, and supply detachments. Tanks could not perform effectively in combat without the support of the other combat arms and service units. The synthesis of these weapons in panzer divisions represented a unique achievement of the Germans in the interwar period.

Many military officers in other states—especially Britain, France, and the Soviet Union—emphasized the development of tanks and tank divisions, but none combined tanks and the other combat arms so effectively into balanced combat organizations capable of strategic movement and swift campaigns. In counterpoint to this concept of combined arms, although tanks could not move effectively without the complex organized support of other arms and service units, blitzkriegs in turn stopped without the tanks. The Germans executed the ultrablitz into the Soviet Union with panzer divisions in the lead. The striking power of the divisions and, in turn, the strategic possibilities for the Germans therefore can be represented by the number of tanks available at any time for German panzer leaders to deploy over the Russian countryside.

An analysis of the value of tanks can be made by summarizing the numbers (Table 10), then showing whether or not the Germans had enough to do the job required in Barbarossa.

Table 10. Russo-German Tank Balance, Barbarossa, 1941

Russians		Germans[11]	
T-26 A–C	c. 12,000[12]	Pz.Kw. II	746
BT 2, 5, 7	c. 5,000[12]	TNHP 38	812*
T-34 A, B	c. 1,200[13]	Pz.Kw. III	1,065
KV-1, 2	c. 582[13]	Pz.Kw. IV	479
	c. 18,782		3,102

*Number includes some older TNHS 35 vehicles.

The balance supports a number of important generalizations about Barbarossa, some old and well known, others new and inadequately explored. To the Germans, tanks were so important that the qualities and numbers of Soviet vehicles were debated at all levels. Hitler, with his penchant for detail, was concerned about Soviet tanks. He underestimated their numbers, lending support to the thesis that the Germans fatally underestimated the numbers and qualities of Soviet weapons. Guderian, however, who led the largest panzer group into the Soviet Union and fought against a large share of the Soviet tank force, seems to have had no illusions about the numbers (even 18,000 to as many as 22,000).[14] With respect to the qualities of the enemy tanks, Guderian was seriously discomfited by the appearance of significant numbers of Soviet T-34 tanks in October 1941, but he was not surprised by their qualities. The German army had been roughly handled by Allied tanks at the end of the First World War. As a direct result, the infantry and mobile divisions built in the 1930s had many antitank guns, anticipating the threat of great numbers of Allied infantry support tanks in any war.[15] This anticipation carried into the war against the Soviet Union, and a large percentage of the extraordinary numbers of Soviet tanks destroyed in Barbarossa was accounted for by the German infantry divisions' antitank guns.

The Soviets had so many tanks they could deploy huge numbers in battalion-level organizations to support their infantry divisions. They could also place large numbers in motorized-mechanized brigades and tank divisions before the German attack. The Soviets employed so many tanks and deployed them so extensively that the German infantry divisions met huge numbers and knocked out virtually all with the 3.7cm and 5.0cm antitank guns of the antitank battalions and regimental antitank companies (the fourteenth company of each German infantry regiment).[16] In the opening days of the war the German 256th Infantry Division, advancing from the northwest toward Bialystok, was forced to stop and defend itself against Soviet tank attacks from 24 to 26 June at Kuznica. The infantry division antitank guns and attached self-propelled storm artillery destroyed 250 Soviet tanks in this engagement[17] and contributed to pinning down and encircling huge Soviet forces in the Bialystok pocket.[18]

The panzer groups, particularly in Army Groups Center and South, faced similar powerful counterattacks. The panzer divisions of the groups averaged approximately 164 battle tanks each and could advance against strong Soviet tank forces. Even the panzer divisions and their accompanying motorized infantry divisions ran into powerful Soviet mechanized formations, which could be neither bypassed nor ignored and forced major tank battles from the first day of the war. Such battles lasted from several hours to a full day in Army Groups North and Center, and even longer in Army Group South. The German panzer and motorized rifle divisions would drive into a mass of at least 8,000 and possibly as many as 12,000 tanks as the Soviet tank forces were attracted to the more dangerous, deeply penetrating mobile divisions. Considering the numbers, one wonders how the Germans advanced at all against such a mass of Soviet tanks.

Hitler and the Balance Between the Soviet and German Tank Forces

In a conversation with Guderian in July 1941, knowing that his field armies were wrestling with vast Soviet tank forces, Hitler remarked that he would not have attacked the Soviet Union had he believed Guderian's earlier estimate of 10,000 Soviet tanks in the late 1930s. The remark shows that Hitler had underestimated the number of Soviet tanks and leads to an interpretation of the campaign in which the masses of Soviet tanks had slowed, then stopped, the Germans. The Germans were surprised by the appearance of extremely high quality T-34 A and B and KV-1 and 2 tanks in and among the more numerous lighter vehicles.[19] The conventional wisdom gathers impressive support in the thesis that the Germans were halted by the numbers and quality of the Red Army, particularly its tanks. In short, the masses of moderate-quality lighter vehicles slowed the Germans, while enough of the superior quality T-34s halted the Germans short of Moscow by December 1941.

Hitler probably underestimated the size of the Soviet tank force and the special qualities of a small but important part of it. Yet the German tank force—tanks combined entirely in the four panzer groups—advanced so swiftly against the defending Soviets in June and July 1941 that it established the preconditions for defeat of the Soviet Union. Hitler's underestimation of the size and certain qualities of the Soviet tank force is accurate but irrelevant to the Russian campaign because the German panzer groups advanced against the Red Army and its tanks on a schedule that could be projected in June–July 1941 into the defeat of the Soviet Union. If Hitler underestimated the Soviet tank force, and yet the German panzer groups advanced swiftly through it, logic demands that Hitler must have underestimated the striking power of his panzer forces. The intriguing generalization supported by such argument is that the underestimations cancel themselves. The underestimated Red Army and its tanks found themselves all but eliminated by the pace, destructive power, and territorial gains of the underestimated German army and its panzer groups by the first of August 1941.

German Tank Losses in the Great Opening Battles of the Russian Campaign

By that time, in Army Group Center, Panzer Groups Guderian and Hoth had destroyed or captured 1,638 Soviet tanks in the Bialystok-Minsk battles and, assuming a similar percentage of Soviet losses in the Dvina-Dnieper and Smolensk battles, an additional 1,635 vehicles. While maintaining a blitz pace and positioning themselves east of Smolensk much earlier on 15 July 1941, the panzer groups had "knocked out" approximately 3,273 Soviet tanks.[20] This astounding achievement in so brief a time along the high road to Moscow is a convincing argument to support the thesis that the Germans had the capability to defeat the Soviet Union in the summer of 1941. We know the Soviet tank losses, and they could be characterized as fatal if the Germans had the strength to push on immediately toward Moscow. The question has been posed, however: Did the Germans lose so many tanks in fighting their way through massed Soviet vehicles along hundreds of kilometers of unpaved Russian roads that they were checked by the beginning of August 1941?

The striking power of the German panzer forces attacking the Soviet Union on 22 June 1941 is equatable with their 3,102 battle tanks. By early August, to win the campaign, Army Group Center had to begin the attack on Moscow soon and depend for success largely on the number of tanks available. OKH data for August show the Germans early in the month had approximately 85 percent of their tank strength available for combat and only 15 percent as total losses. The Germans still had most of the tanks with which they had begun the campaign, but a significant fraction of these could not advance because of needed repairs. Preparing for an advance as important as that on Moscow, the Germans would make a strong effort to effect those repairs and in Army Group Center would have had approximately 65 percent of their original strength in tanks available to advance on 13 August 1941 and some 20 percent in the work shops.[21] Having started the campaign with 1,780 battle tanks in Army Group Center, the Germans still had approximately 1,157 tanks running and 356 in repair. This impressive number of tanks would have been with the field armies in August for an advance on Moscow and probably augmented by approximately 390 additional tanks from Army Group North.

On 4 August, when it appeared possible that Hitler had changed his mind and decided in favor of an advance on Moscow, Guderian and Hoth estimated for OKH that their combat strength for the next offensive, against Moscow, would be 50 percent and 60 percent, respectively.[22] The panzer leaders based their estimates largely on tanks available for the advance. The two panzer groups of Army Group Center were similar in size. Thus the estimates show approximately 55 percent of the original total of tanks in the army group ready for a hypothetical advance on Moscow on about 13 August. The 65 percent estimate in the listing above, applied to Army Group Center, is more optimistic but probably also more accurate than those made by the panzer group leaders for a projected offensive hedged in by Hitler's reservations, excursions, and ancillary tasks. Had they known before the end of July that they would be called on to drive singlemindedly for Moscow, they probably would have achieved the tank percentage suggested above.

German Tanks Available for the Advance on Moscow in August 1941

The figure of 65 percent of the original German tank strength gives a realistic picture of the numbers of tanks the Germans would have used in an offensive against Moscow in the first half of August 1941. The percentage is pessimistic with respect to the remaining striking power of the panzer groups. When the Germans attacked the Soviet Union on 22 June 1941 with 3,102 battle tanks, a significant percentage would have been under repair for the attrition associated with the assembly for Barbarossa. This was particularly true among the panzer divisions concentrated at the last moment in Wave 4b for the offensive.[23] Tanks under repair on 22 June can be estimated at 10 percent, but the important point is that the striking power of the German panzer force was not 3,102 battle tanks but approximately 90 percent of that figure. All German estimates of tank strength after 22 June 1941 use percentages of an original strength of 3,102. This strength was never available because the Germans attacked on 22 June with about 2,792 combat-ready tanks (and 310 in repair). Thus, the Germans on 13 August would have been attacking with an estimated 65 percent of the tanks available on 22 June, but approximately 72 percent of their striking power on the first day of the war. Actual percentages would be slightly different, but the percentages used by the Germans to measure remaining striking power would have to be adjusted upward.

By about 13 August 1941, the Germans had suffered Soviet combat action losses of approximately 12 percent of their original tanks. For Army Group Center, with 1,780 battle tanks in its divisions when it attacked earlier in June, this translates into 214 German battle tanks "knocked out" by Soviet combat action on the eve of the hypothetical German advance on Moscow. During the same period the German tanks of Panzer Groups 2 and 3 destroyed and captured 3,273 Soviet tanks. Although German tanks did not damage all of the Soviet tanks that were destroyed in the Soviet totals, the exchange ratios in tank losses were 1 German tank lost to 15 Soviet. By early August 1941, the German tank formations and infantry divisions had inflicted fearsome tank losses on the Soviets, and the panzer units unquestionably had enough striking power to advance to Moscow and beyond.

The Soviet T-34 Tank: Reality, Myth, and Irony

One of the great myths of the Russian campaign is that the Soviet T-34 tank appeared as a miracle of Soviet technology to produce an element of superiority over the Germans, which turned the tide in favor of the Soviets in October–December 1941, especially at the gates of Moscow in November and December. Myths are difficult to analyze and dispose of because of their combination of truth and fiction. The T-34 tank was superior to any German tank deployed in Barbarossa in gun power, armor thickness and slope, and cross-country mobility—major factors in tank-versus-tank combat. Yet it is rarely mentioned that the Soviet T-34 A and B tanks had poor observation out of the vehicles, had virtually no radios for effective command and control, and, incredibly, were designed with inefficient two-man turrets. Despite their frustration at seeing their tank gun projectiles having little effect on the thick, sloped armor of the T-34 hulls and the well-shaped turrets, German tank crews were amazed that they would fire two, three, or four rounds against the T-34s to every round they received. In the Soviet two-man turrets, the tank commander had to double as gunner, thus reducing dramatically the rate of fire and the ability to acquire new targets—particularly in fluid operations and sudden, meeting engagements.

The Germans faced a severe technical inferiority: German tank cannon projectiles would not penetrate the Soviet T-34 tank. Soviet tank cannon on the T-34 penetrated the armor of all German tanks in the east in 1941, at extended ranges for the day of approximately 1,000 m. Fortunately for the Germans, the Soviets had only a few T-34 tanks available for combat in June and July 1941. Obligingly they distributed them across the entire Russian front, singly or in groups of two or three, among other tanks, including the similarly shaped BT cavalry tanks. With their combined arms teams, including 5.0cm antitank guns, antiaircraft guns, and artillery, the Germans could handle the T-34s comfortably in June and July. It was not until October 1941 that the T-34 tanks menaced the Germans so greatly that the tanks have been identified as one of the most significant causes of the German defeat in the battle for Moscow.[24] By then, the Soviets had shifted production toward the T-34s, which appeared in more significant numbers (with the same superior qualities) in packs of twelve to twenty tanks capable of slowing the thinned German panzer divisions of October–December 1941.

In June, July, and August, however, the Soviets lacked enough T-34s to form big concentrations and affect the campaign. The Germans were not menaced by the T-34s until the first week of October 1941, when Guderian's tanks near Orel in Operation Typhoon were two months behind schedule on the road to Moscow and unable to advance against them as they appeared in medium-sized packs. The T-34s show the potential fatal nature of time delay in a blitz against a strong opponent. Had the Germans attacked Moscow on the army schedule of about 13 August 1941, they would not have met the T-34s on the road to Moscow. Those tanks could not have been there in significant quantities to produce any noticeable effect on the advance of Army Group Center.

From another viewpoint the situation was also ironic. Hitler perceptively insisted on a campaign against Soviet Russia as early as possible, sensing correctly that every moment counted to prevent the Soviets from growing stronger and more dangerous by their armaments production. Once the campaign began, he who had been in a rush to end the Soviet armaments menace in 1941 procrastinated and by his dilatory and indecisive conduct of military operations gave the Soviets the opportunity to employ T-34 tanks. The T-34 myth emerged from an area that would have fallen to the Germans about 18 August 1941, and the tanks were manufactured largely in facilities in Moscow that would have been captured by approximately 28 August.

Chapter Eleven

German Logistics: Could the Germans Support an Advance into the Moscow-Gorki Space in the Summer of 1941?

IN the campaigns of 1939–1941, the Germans emphasized numbers and logistics differently from the characteristic extremes of western and Soviet operations. The German high regard for numbers was illustrated in the attack on Poland, when they stripped the western front—with impressive operational nerve—to achieve decisive numbers for success.[1] The Germans had an equally high regard for logistics. Yet their style would not allow logistics, in the subtle ways developed in the west, to set the spirit, style, and pace of military operations. Western writers contributed to misinterpretation of the course and possibilities of the war in Russia by criticizing the German logistical system from the Allied attrition viewpoint. In a recent (1977) well-documented study, which includes German operations on the eastern front, the writer posits that the German logistical system was inherently incapable of supporting successful military operations in the east.[2] That thesis is tenable, and original, applied to the period from September 1941 to May 1945, but it obscures the point that the Germans intended to win the campaign by August 1941 with a logistic plan and system capable of supporting the victory.

A Logistical System for Victory in Summer 1941

The German army did not lose in the east because of its logistical system, developed to support the attack on the Soviet Union. Halted, then misdirected for two months of late summer campaign weather, the German field armies relinquished virtually certain victory to almost certain defeat through recovery time presented the Soviets while German physical strength and psychological dominance were frittered away. What is important about the German logistical system is how it was designed so successfully to support Barbarossa in June, July, and August 1941, not its irrelevant (to victory in the Russian campaign) frailties from September 1941 to May 1945. The statement's validity depends on the thesis that the Germans won the Russian campaign by August 1941. For analysts disturbed that the Germans went on to lose the Russian campaign and the Second World War by May 1945, the author suggests that the June–August 1941 German victories were so decisive that the issue is not so much that the Soviets came close to defeat but that the Soviet recovery must be regarded as a resurrection from operational death. It is more important to understand the logistical system that came so close to supporting victory in August 1941 than the one that supported defeat in May 1945.

Accepting the thesis that the Germans subjected themselves to certain defeat from the moment they attacked the Soviet Union because they could not cope with the demographic, psychological, and economic dimensions of the country and its people, one could seek and accept evidence that the German armed forces logistical system was incapable of supporting the war. From the alternative viewpoint, that the Germans had won the struggle by August 1941, having calculated the logistical capabilities required to support successful attacks toward Leningrad and Kiev, and Moscow late in the summer of 1941, it is not surprising that the Germans constructed 14,000 miles of German-gauge railways and repaired 10,000 additional miles for use by their armed forces in Barbarossa. The Germans were aware of the challenges and necessities of a campaign in the Soviet Union, performed this rarely noted achievement, and did so by imaginative use of the Reich Labor Service and the Todt Organization. The lesson appears to be that the Germans, who launched Barbarossa to defeat the Soviets by a series of successful great, opening battles, had constructed a logistical system adequate to support the planned military operations. Further, these actually proved to be ahead of schedule at several crucial junctures in June and July 1941 in a schedule that most commentators have denigrated as hopelessly optimistic.

Winter Clothing and Supplies for the Germans in 1941

Winter clothing for the German field armies is a useful topic for considering the realities of the opening stages of the Russian campaign. Commentaries, both primary and secondary, note ad infinitum that the Germans were ill prepared for the Russian winter of 1941–1942. Commentators point out accurately that the Germans possessed neither adequate winter clothing and footwear for the troops nor suitable lubricants and fluids for the weapons and equipment of the ground forces and Luftwaffe. They illustrate the inadequate preparations for cold weather with examples, particularly during the onset of the extreme cold of late November–December 1941. They note the failure to fire of the German family of light and heavy machine guns (the famed MG-34 series), not too surprising for automatic weapons. They also note large-scale functional failures in the German standard service rifle (the also famed Gewehr 98, or Rifle Model 1898), very surprising for a proven, bolt-action rifle. German artillery pieces with hydraulic recuperators and/or recoil mechanisms also failed in the extreme cold. The engines of motor vehicles and aircraft could not be started or were damaged because of thickened lubricating oils and frozen liquid coolants. In extreme cases, caused by collective embrittlement of rifle firing pins, lubricant-seized bolts, and "frozen" machine guns and artillery, the Germans engaged in combat with hand grenades, entrenching tools, and rifle butts.[3] These practical details tend to focus attention on German underestimation of the Russian theater of operations and can also be seen as harbingers of the defeat of the Germans in the east. They support, of course, the conventional interpretation of Moscow (December 1941), Stalingrad, and Kursk as turning points in a war characterized by the gradual decline of the Germans.

Such details of winter warfare in the Soviet Union and effusive German self-criticism obscure the combat style of the German phase of the war and hence the course and turning point of the Second World War. What is important is not that the Germans naively underestimated the strength of Soviet Russia and found themselves without socks in summer jackboots, wearing cold-transmitting hobnails and using kerosene with some imagination to lubricate machine guns and rifles in and around Moscow (e.g., the northwest suburb of Khimki and at Skopin, 150 km to the east), but that Moscow had not fallen months earlier in the warm and relatively dry August of 1941. The lack of winter clothing and cold-weather lubricants and fluids for weapons and engines focuses attention on the situation around Moscow in late November–December 1941 and away from the truly epic German possibilities of the summer of 1941. In the winter of 1941–1942, the battle for Moscow was the first of a long, drawn-out series of anticlimactic battles incidental to the summer of Barbarossa—in which the Germans fought with the near certainty of victory and immediately afterward faced the near certainty of defeat, something for which they had neither planned nor prepared.

German Logistics in Barbarossa: Rail Lines, Rail Heads, and Truck Columns

In June and July 1941, the Germans suffered neither personnel casualties nor tank losses that could inhibit their further advance on a like scale toward Moscow in August. In that brief time the Germans had proven unstoppable with the logistical system they had developed for war in the Soviet Union. But what kind of system did the Germans have? Was it capable of supporting the German drive into the Moscow-Gorki space in August 1941? It is likely that the same Germans who played numerous operational war games to calculate the chances of success in a campaign would have worked just as soberly to assess their capabilities to supply a blitz in the east. But the thought must nag at many interested in sorting out the turning point of the war in Europe: Did the operationally oriented Germans neglect logistics in some way that would prevent them from taking Moscow in August 1941?

In 1941, German industry and inter-European imports would supply enough food, fuel, and ammunition to support a partly motorized army of about three million men in a great field campaign, planned to last about seventeen weeks. The German armaments effort had been thin in many ways because it was geared by Hitler more or less instinctively to support his preferred style of relatively heavy consumer production. With almost a year to prepare, produce, and stockpile for Barbarossa, the Germans had enough fundamental materials of war to win in the Soviet Union in 1941. The German logistical problem was how to transport material from adequate stockpiles to an army operating under difficult circumstances in a large country without normal-gauge railways and with unpaved roads. The Germans would center logistics on the construction of rail lines and station installations. They would also organize great truck forces to move materials from stockpiles on the frontier until the new rail lines could be completed and rail heads (i.e., train stations where supplies were stockpiled) could be established in the Soviet Union.

In essence, the German logistical system in the east could be likened to a rail line at the end of which was a station with facilities for unloading and areas for stockpiling materiel. The field armies sent trucks to pick up supplies and carry them closer to the corps and divisions, which, in turn, picked them up at smaller and more advanced stockpiles. In the fluid operations the Germans had to build a railroad system quickly into European Russia to maintain rail heads at satisfactory distances from the advancing field armies. On 22 June 1941, the German rail heads stood at the German border in East Prussia and the so-called Government General of Poland. The Germans organized great logistical truck forces behind each army group to pick up supplies from the frontier rail heads and deliver them into truck dumps as close as possible to the advancing field armies. The truck forces, broken down into flexible 60-ton-capacity columns of vehicles to move supplies, would operate back and forth from the frontier stockpiles until the new train stations and German-gauge rail lines could support traffic into the Soviet Union to forward rail heads.

The German Concentration of Forces Against the Soviet Border

From the moment Hitler alerted the armed forces in late July 1940 for an attack on Soviet Russia, the army general staff thought in terms of rail schedules to execute the *Aufmarsch* (concentration) for Barbarossa and regauging or rebuilding the Soviet rail system for logistical support of the advance. Generalleutnant Rudolf Gercke, chief of German army transportation, began to oversee the railroad tasks under the first important OKW order for Barbarossa, the Ausbau Ost (Eastern Buildup) order of 9 August 1940, directing the improvement and expansion of eastern Poland's rail system. The Reichsbahn (State Rail Service) and the Ostbahn (Eastern Rail Service) began to build up the eastern rail facilities under the codeword, Program Otto. Concomitantly, Gercke was largely responsible for coordinating the transfer of thirty-five German infantry divisions from France to Poland and East Prussia, using existing facilities, at a leisurely pace from July to October 1940. By 17 January 1941, Gercke informed OKW that of the 8,500 km of rail lines to be improved or rebuilt to concentrate forces for Barbarossa, 60 percent had been completed, most double track.[4] On 2 February 1941, Brauchitsch and Halder began the concentration of forces for Barbarossa, intended to be in four waves of rail movement lasting through 15 May 1941.

Due to unexpected circumstances, including the Balkan campaign and the severe winter of 1940–1941, the German concentration of forces continued until 22 June. Amazingly, the OKH moved some 17,000 trains over and above the normal traffic in the east after the battle of France.[5] Through secrecy and deception, the German command achieved almost complete tactical and operational surprise against the Soviet armed forces and a large measure of strategic surprise against the high political leadership. Stalin and his advisors received warnings of German aggressive intent months before, but they reasonably discounted most of such warnings based on alternate explanations and the vast deceptive circumstance that Germany was at war with Britain. The Soviets must also have had aggressive intentions of their own. Retrospectively, it appears possible that they were preparing to attack Germany or client states of Germany possibly as early as autumn 1941, and probably no later than summer 1942. Finally, although Stalin was prepared for German political pressure in the summer of 1941, and possibly even military incidents, he was caught totally off guard by a full-blooded military invasion with the Olympian mission to defeat the Soviet state immediately. The unobtrusive movement of 17,000 extra trains to the east and the deceptive explanation of unconcealable activity associated with the concentration of forces made possible the surprise on 22 June 1941, which could have translated into the defeat of Soviet Russia.

Gercke executed the eastern movement in waves beginning with the more innocuous infantry divisions and only a few mobile divisions at a maximum of twelve trains daily along each of the six main rail lines established under Program Otto. The chief of army transportation moved seven infantry and two mobile divisions in the first wave (relatively few), among which it was possible to disguise one panzer and one motorized infantry division. The Germans were extremely sensitive about transferring mobile divisions to the east. They were operating according to the doctrine that panzer divisions and closely associated motorized infan-

Table 11. Barbarossa Concentration of Forces (Aufmarsch)*

Wave and Time	German Divisions	Trains
Wave 1, 2 February–14 March 1941	9	c. 14,000 trains for
Wave 2, March 1941	18	divisions
Wave 3, 8 April–20 May 1941	17	c. 3,000 trains for
Wave 4a, 23 May–2 June 1941	9	Luftwaffe, army
Wave 4b, 3 June–23 June 1941	24	troops, supply and
Beginning 21 June–24 July 1941	24	reserve forces
Totals	101	17,000 trains

*Prior to the concentration, the Germans had 47 divisions in the east that eventually took part in the invasion: 12 divisions from the Polish campaign and 35 divisions emplaced between July and October after the French campaign.

try divisions were to be employed exclusively for deep strategic offensive missions. The Germans assumed with a mirror-image mentality that the Soviets would immediately recognize danger regarding the excessive number of panzer divisions in the east. Accordingly, they left the overwhelming mass of the mobile divisions until the last possible moment for movement eastward. Table 11 illustrates the German sensitivity to ensuring surprise and the magnitude of the Aufmarsch for Barbarossa:

In Wave 4b, the last wave of the divisions that launched the attack across the frontier on 22 June 1941 (a day later in a few cases because of the relatively narrow attack fronts), the Germans moved twenty-four panzer and motorized infantry divisions. These, with their tracked and wheeled motor vehicles, were difficult to move and even more of a challenge to conceal. The Germans took major precautions to screen the movement of these divisions, then make them disappear into the countryside after offloading. Once this movement began, they considered it would have significant chances of being detected, and it could not be explained by any subterfuge. The Germans also delivered to the border by train an additional twenty-four divisions, which would not take part in the initial attacks but would move into former Soviet territory toward the front from 26 June 1941 onward.

German Rail Lines, Rail Heads, and Truck Columns in the Soviet Union

The trains that moved the German army and the Luftwaffe ground organization to the border could not deliver the armed forces farther east. The Germans would have to move tactically from the frontier and depend for support on the distance between their rail heads and the infantry divisions in the front lines. For the mobile divisions, it was the distance between the German railway system and the finger-like projections deep into Soviet territory. In Barbarossa, the Germans advanced rapidly into territory having no normal-gauge railroads. Logistics would depend on the German capabilities to advance their own rail system into the Soviet Union while simultaneously connecting German rail heads with their troops, disappearing over the horizon into Soviet Russia. An untold, unusual situation almost immediately after Barbarossa began supports a view that, logistically, the Germans had the capability to defeat the Soviet Union. In Army Group Center, seventeen German panzer and motorized infantry divisions did everything in their power to distance themselves from the German railheads. By 26 June 1941, the 7th Panzer Division was 300 km into the Soviet Union from its start on the Lithuanian border, and on the following day the 3d Panzer Division reached Glusa, 350 km into Russia. Current literature has not asked how the Germans could resupply two panzer divisions at that distance from rail heads in German territory. Obviously, they successfully organized truck columns with enormous capacities to run the supplies from the German border to the advancing armies.

By 26 April 1941, the quartermaster general of the German army and the chief of transportation had collected 25,020 tons (freight capacity) of trucks for Army Group Center and smaller amounts for the remaining two army groups.[6] When the campaign opened, the high command of the army provided Army Group Center with approximately 45,000 tons of trucks to deliver supplies from the rail heads on the border to the advancing armies. After a complex transition, their new rail heads were at various distances from the border in Soviet territory.[7] The Germans considered that the 60-ton (freight capacity) truck columns could bridge approximately 400 km between rail heads and the advancing field armies.[8] As the normal-gauge rail lines were constructed along the most important logistics routes into White Russia from Brest to Minsk, the Germans expected on 17 July to take off most of the 60-ton truck columns from the frontier to Minsk between 20 and 30 July 1941. The columns continued to run from the border in decreasing numbers until finally stopped on 5 August 1941.[9] By then, the rail lines were completed beyond Minsk, and the Germans would be operating from rail heads approaching Smolensk.

German Logistics: Quantity of Material and Mode of Operations Required to Reach the Moscow-Gorki Space

To advance on Moscow in August 1941, the Germans depended logistically on the capacity and location of the rail system they had built by that time. The army high command massed strong forces of railway pioneer troops, battalions of the Reich Labor Service (Reich Arbeits Dienst, or RAD), and Organization Todt (OT) immediately behind the field armies to ensure construction of the normal-gauge rail lines, train stations, and marshalling yards. In Army Group North, the high command inserted 18,219 men for railway construction during June–August 1941.[10] The construction troops were organized along military lines, armed with rifles, pistols, and light machine guns, and advanced so aggressively behind the German combat formations that they reported 84 combat incidents with scattered Soviet troops. These resulted in 162 combat casualties to themselves. The Germans placed similar construction troops and special railway reconnaissance detachments with the panzer group spearheads to estimate damage and help pull the construction process forward. The details of German-gauge railway construction into the Soviet Union and the exploitation of undamaged Russian-gauge lines, locomotives, and rail cars support a conclusion that the Germans accurately forecast the logistical necessities for Barbarossa and effectively executed the operations.

Gercke, chief of German army transportation, estimated that one railway battalion could change tracks from Russian to German gauge at a rate of 20 km per day.[11] Railway pioneer units also quickly employed Russian-gauge lines to help bring supplies forward even before they completed the German lines. They used both simultaneously, as long as Russian locomotives and rolling stock held out. On 24 June 1941, Railway Operations Company 203 took over the intact Soviet wide-gauge rail line from Brest to Zabinka, 30 km from the border. The company observed that the Russian-gauge line was intact for an additional 25 km eastward to the station at Tevli. The company began to reduce the haul of the 60-ton truck columns, already running far to the east to support Guderian's panzers, now 220 km on the road to the upper Dnieper at Rogachev.

The German railway pioneer and other construction troops simultaneously built normal-gauge rail lines at a fierce pace, advancing by 25 June some 80 km toward Minsk.[12] By 29 June, they extended normal-gauge track from the frontier at Brest to Oranczyce and, by 1 July, onto Baranovice.[13] As Gercke commented, a German railway pioneer battalion could replace wide-gauge line with normal at 20 km per day. The distance from Brest to Baranovice is 210 km, a little longer using the rail line. The Germans took eleven days to construct the new line, uncannily close to Gercke's estimate despite violent fighting on the southeastern lines of encirclement around the Bialystok pocket. Contrary to conventional interpretation of underestimating the challenges of a campaign in the Soviet Union, the Germans mastered logistics and built their own rail system into the Soviet Union.

Blitz Logistics: Normal Gauge Rail, Brest to Minsk

To operate the rail lines, the Germans had to regauge rail sidings and marshalling areas and, depending on battle damage, to repair buildings and equipment at the train stations.[14] On the most important rail line in Barbarossa, the tracks from Brest directly toward Moscow, the Germans completed the line from Brest to Oranczyce by 29 June 1941 and began to move German trains on normal-gauge track on 30 June. That day, four supply trains arrived at Oranczyce, 85 km into the Soviet Union, with approximately 2,000 tons of supplies. Meantime, regauging of Russian lines continued with work being completed to Baranovice junction by 2000, 1 July, and three trains reaching that city, 210 km into the Soviet Union. The Germans continued their impressive pace of building a normal-gauge rail system into White Russia and completed regauging from Brest to the capital, Minsk, at noon on 5 July. Army Group Center ran four supply trains there the same day, more than 330 km into the Soviet Union.[15] By 5 July, the Germans began to develop a great rail head at Minsk, which capably supported the lightning panzer advance to Smolensk that overran the city on 16 July. In a historic performance, the Germans regauged the Russian rail system from Brest to Minsk by early July and extended construction to Smolensk before the end of the same month. Their performance established a logistical system able to support an offensive toward Moscow before the middle of August 1941 and bridge the gap between Smolensk and Moscow in a single offensive, similar in style to the earlier leaps to Minsk and Smolensk.

That generalization derives from the actions of Army Group Center from the middle of July to early August 1941. On 15 July 1941, the quartermaster general reviewed the supply status of Army Group Center in terms of its capabilities to continue offensive operations. He made it clear that the great rail head for continuing operations lay in the cities of Minsk and Molodecno, no longer on the prewar frontier. The army group then had 45,450 tons of 60-ton truck columns and, deducting one-third as inoperable at any time and in repair, still had approximately 30,700 tons available for continuous operations.[16] In mid-July 1941 the German army transportation chief guaranteed the substantial total of fourteen trains and 6,300 tons of supplies daily for the Minsk-Molodecno base. The quartermaster general averred that, based on the logistical situation of 15 July 1941, Army Group Center could conduct an offensive on Moscow with four panzer, three motorized infantry, and ten infantry divisions with appropriate army reserves, maintaining the remainder of the army group in static fighting around Smolensk. This logistical feat was moderately impressive for the middle of July, with enough trains arriving at the Minsk-Molodecno railroad and more than enough trucks to move a panzer group and an infantry army to Moscow. Meanwhile, the Germans were fighting the battle of Smolensk and would take two more weeks to finish the job and another week to tidy up operationally. The Germans used this time to build up logistic stockpiles at the rail head in the center of White Russia and regauge the main rail line from Minsk through Orsha into Smolensk.[17]

By the second week of August 1941, Army Group Center regained operational freedom of movement. If the army group had been directed by Hitler and OKH at the end of July 1941 to continue operations toward Moscow as soon as possible, it would have eliminated remnants of Soviet forces in the great pocket just north of Smolensk and cleared the communications zone of Panzer Group Guderian to the south. Unhampered by Hitler's stubborn attempt to diffuse the combat strength of Army Group Center about the Russian countryside, and the battle between the Führer and OKH over one decisive objective rather than many indecisive ones, Army Group Center would have entered a period of rest, rehabilitation, and stockpiling on approximately 5 August 1941. Regarding the logistical possibilities for an advance a little over a week later, on 13 August 1941, Army Group Center would receive almost double the number of trains daily it had received a month earlier [18]—approximately twenty-four trains rather than fourteen. With time to establish larger stockpiles, and with rail heads advanced to Orsha and Smolensk, Army Group Center obviously had the logistical system to support its advance on Moscow with its entire strength. [19]

Part V

Examining the Possibilities of August 1941

Chapter Twelve

Constructing an Alternate Historical Past: Taking Moscow and Defeating the Soviet Union, August – October 1941

BY 5 August 1941, Army Group Center on the road to Moscow had beaten the Soviets and faced weak Soviet field armies, estimated earlier by the Germans at "parts and remnants" of fifty divisions and a combat strength of thirty-five divisions, compared with sixty intact, individually superior German divisions.[1] The crucial element was time. Although the Soviets stood helpless east of Smolensk, the Germans knew they had put together a total of twenty-eight new divisions, moderately well armed although badly trained. The Soviets massed them with a no-nonsense, survival instinct almost entirely around Moscow. That the Soviets concentrated their strategic reserve around the capital does more to buttress the theme that they had lost the war by early August than perhaps any other argument.

In past wars, the Russians had shown an ingrained mentality, always keeping a substantial reserve even in the most desperate situations.[2] It is not surprising therefore that the Soviet high command shrewdly held back large forces from the doomed front, seeking salvation in some unlikely but possible weakening or error by the Germans. The Soviet high command may also have felt that it had no time to set up additional effective defenses in the area just east of Smolensk. During the first days of August 1941 they would have to have reasoned that the Germans would soon launch yet another inimitable 300–400-km leap forward on the central front. Bordering on collapse, the Soviet high command had few options other than to concentrate the twenty-eight newly raised divisions at Moscow, in defenses before the capital. Soviet forces blocking the way to Moscow between Smolensk and Vyasma might have slowed the Germans enough to allow yet more forces to be concentrated around Moscow. Perhaps the Germans had been weakened by the stubborn defenses and profligate attacks of the Russian soldiers in June and July 1941. Yet the Soviet high command must also have thought that the Germans would dispose of the shaken Soviet forces opposite them in record time, even for Army Group Center. The twenty-eight untrained but moderately well-equipped Soviet divisions deployed around the capital would face, toward the end of August, most of sixty veteran, victorious German divisions. The Soviets faced a challenging situation bordering on a nightmare.

How Would the Germans Reach Moscow in August 1941?

Assuming that the alternate past is about to unfold, how would the Germans have reached Moscow in August? Since the Germans did get to Moscow in late November and early December 1941, placing troops in the Moscow suburb of Khimki, it is tempting to take the discrete, reproducible advances of October-November and back them into August. One problem is that the actual advance was discontinuous. The Germans won an immense victory in the double encirclement of Vyasma-Bryansk in the first half of October, then were mired in the mud of the unpaved Russian road system until the last half of November.[3] Recalling that a German offensive on 13 August 1941 would have met warm, dry summer weather, one could make a convincing case that a German summer offensive would have covered more or less the same ground of October-November 1941 in a much shorter time. The case is convincing because the weather would be better, mud would disappear from the equation, and the Soviet armies would be far weaker in front of Moscow. One could say, reasonably, that if the Germans broke through, encircled, and largely eliminated the forces in front of them in a battle from approximately 2 to 14 October 1941, they would take less time against far weaker forces in better weather and longer daylight. With the surrender or near-surrender of the *Kesseln* in the initial advances, they would also be prepared to move on to Moscow almost immediately.

When the Germans moved on Moscow early in October, OKH

reinforced Army Group Center with the two high command reserve panzer divisions (2d and 5th Panzer Divisions) and armor
from Army Group North including the 1st, 6th, and 8th Panzer
Divisions. In the hypothetical advance of 13 August 1941 it is reasonable to assume that OKH would have similarly reinforced Army
Group Center, especially since Halder insisted in July and August
that Army Group North was fighting against a relatively weak
opponent in difficult tank country.[4] Army Group Center can be
assumed to have an extremely strong mobile force leading the advance. The army group would have held five more panzer divisions
than it had in the attacks at Minsk and Smolensk, and it would
have attacked its weakest opponent in Barbarossa to that date.
The Germans would advance directly east toward Moscow, avoiding significant Soviet strength, dangerous but dangling, to the
south around Gomel and similar forces around Toropets to the
north. Bock notes that those forces would have been pinned down
with similarly sized or even slightly smaller German infantry
forces. The result: Army Group Center would have opened its attack east with a mass of twenty panzer and motorized infantry
divisions and approximately twenty-five infantry divisions against
a severely shaken Soviet force equivalent to about sixteen numerically intact divisions. The Germans would have fought along a
broad front with overwhelming numerical superiority and would
have achieved, as attackers (with the initiative), far greater local
superiorities. This astonishing situation highlights and underlines
the fundamental reality of the German invasion of the Soviet
Union: The Germans, who had planned to win quickly, could have
done so in August.

The Advance of Army Group Center into Moscow and Beyond

It is reasonable to reconstruct an advance of Army Group Center
in August and to assume that the Army Group would attack with
forty-five divisions, almost half of them mobile. It is also reasonable
to project the advance from the same positions used by the Germans in the attack of October 1941, except for the southern part
of the army group. In the hypothetical August battle, Guderian
would have commenced the advance on Moscow farther north,
although he probably would have traced an advance similar to the
actual October battle. The Germans would have advanced on a
narrower front at the start of the attack, so it would be reasonable

to assume that Panzer Groups Hoth and Hoepner would have linked up near Vyasma, shaken free of the lines of encirclement in eight days, then advanced on approximately 21 August 1941 for objectives around Moscow. Guderian would not have been involved in an encirclement near Bryansk. He would have advanced instead directly through that city in a wide swing to the south of Moscow, probably seizing Tula, the great munitions center, about the same time Hoth and Hoepner were moving out from around Vyasma, about 190 km to the west.

Unlike in mid-October 1941, when they were halted by autumn rain and mud on an unpaved road system,[5] the Germans would have driven immediately into the Soviet strategic reserve around Moscow and the defenses being put up before the city. They would have enjoyed late summer weather, with long days and strong support from the Luftwaffe. They would also advance into reserve forces without combat experience, with only a scattering of T-34 tanks. In August 1941, the mobile forces of Hoth and Hoepner would have to be projected within a few days into an area that they had reached later, after Hitler's strategic delay and the twin disasters of mud and record cold. Within approximately five days, Hoth and Hoepner could be projected as moving to Kalinin and Klin, northwest of Moscow, and Podosk to the south. As Guderian converged on Minsk and Smolensk earlier in the campaign, he would now be converging to the east of Moscow and across the Oka River at Kolomna. On 26 August 1941, the Germans would have been near the locations reached in the campaign interrupted by Hitler, then delayed into October and November 1941.

Three days later, on 29 August, the three panzer groups would have converged on Moscow: Hoth's troops across the Moscow-Volga canal at Dimitrov to seize Zagorsk, Hoepner's forces into suburbs from the south, and Guderian's troops cutting the great highway between Moscow and Gorki at Noginsk, 50 km east of the capital. The Soviets appear not to have had any intention to fight in Moscow; the city had no citadel comparable with that at Brest, nor seacoast and great lake as at Leningrad, nor favorable strategic circumstance as in Stalingrad. The Soviets intended to evacuate the place, then begin to trade space for time to somehow survive east of the Volga. With powerful German forces all around a relatively indefensible city, it is tempting to conclude that the Germans would have possessed the capital in the next day or so, approximately 31 August 1941, in the middle stages of eliminating the pockets formed to the west and south of Moscow.

The Final Leap: Early Autumn Drive to Gorki, September 1941, and the Destabilization of the Soviet Strategic Position West of the Volga

Assuming that Army Group Center would take approximately six additional days to capture the Soviets in the pockets around Moscow, it would then face five days of reorganization, rest, and maintenance of equipment in Moscow, in a great arc around it. Then, on approximately 11 September 1941, Army Group Center would have one more great pounce in it before the winter paralysis of large-scale offensive military operations. Seizing Moscow, Army Group Center would, in one stroke, have destabilized the Leningrad and Kiev fronts. The Soviets at Leningrad would have been automatically and immediately cut off from all the supply fundamentals— food from the greater food-producing areas of the state, ammunition, and fuel. Army Group Center in Moscow stood astride the rail, telephone, and road communications between Leningrad and the remainder of the Soviet Union. Only two moderate-capacity, tortuous connections would exist between the Baltic and the rest of Russia, and both would soon be cut by the Germans. A fixed strategic relationship existed between Leningrad and Moscow in the event of an attack by an enemy from the west. The fall of Moscow would lead automatically to the fall of Leningrad, whereas the fall of Leningrad leads only 650 km farther to the southeast to Moscow.

Seizing Moscow, the Germans predetermined the fall of Leningrad, but they had not entered into the same strategic equation with Kiev and the eastern Ukraine. In the south, Soviet forces in the Ukraine faced strategic disaster, but they could with difficulty be resupplied by rail and retreat from that vast theater of operations on the same rail lines. The Soviets had come under heavy pressure in the Ukraine between 13 August and 11 September. Army Group South fought the great encirclement battle at Uman, completing it by 8 August, and pressed on to eliminate the Soviet forces west of the Dnieper, including those in the great eastward bend of the river. Resisting the temptation to diffuse its strength in side excursions and to expect too much of its willing but weak allies, Army Group South gave the fourteen-division Romanian army and the smaller Hungarian and Italian forces the safe southern

sector of the Ukraine. The Allied forces, totalling twenty division-
and brigade-level formations, were to seal off the Soviet forces in
the Crimea and advance on a moderate-width front directly east
along the Sea of Azov. With a secure flank on the sea, the Allied
forces would advance into the Don Basin against potentially strong
Soviet forces. They would be accompanied to the north by powerful German force attacking with deadly final purpose in the Ukraine.
The Allies would tie up important Soviet forces.

The Great Battle Southeast of Moscow

By 31 August 1941, the same day that Army Group Center seized
Moscow and an immense arc around it, Army Group South concentrated the bulk of its forces—the 17th Army, Panzer Group
Kleist, and the 11th Army (disentangled from the allies in the
south)—in the great bend of the Dnieper. Generalfeldmarschall
Gerd von Rundstedt, a skilled commander and forceful and determined like Bock, resisted the lure of heading east into the Don
Basin and southeast to Rostov, seeking instead a showdown with
his stubborn and skillful opponent in the Ukraine. As the Germans
closed on Moscow in the last week of August, it was apparent that
the Soviet position at Kiev—and virtually the entire Ukraine—
would be untenable, then encircled, if the Germans used their last
two pounces in the campaign season of 1941. To develop a picture
of the hypothetical defeat of the Soviet Union, a "pounce" is a
useful term to describe a German panzer drive of about 400 km,
lasting from two to three weeks, and causing great carnage and
disarray within the opponent's forces. On 31 August 1941, OKH
knew that Bock had one more pounce in Army Group Center,
probably to start about 11 September. Simultaneously, OKH concentrated Army Group South in the great bend of the Dnieper
against a shaken opponent.

About a week earlier, the Soviet command in the Ukraine faced
the impending fall of Moscow and knew it would be left to fend
for itself. The Soviet southern command knew that the supreme
command was determined to defend Moscow and that the capital's
fall would result in the destruction of the weakened but powerful
forces defending it and annihilation of the Soviet strategic reserve.
The mere presence of Germans in Moscow was a deadly danger to
communications on the Soviet Ukrainian front, demanding an im-

mediate withdrawal to the east out of range of the German capability in space (Moscow) and time (late August) to exploit the situation into a grand encirclement. With the collapse at Moscow, and while displacing itself far to the east across the Volga, the Soviet high command ordered the Ukrainian front forces to withdraw.

The German high command had won Hitler over to continuation of the offensive toward Moscow by guaranteeing that the fall of Moscow would lead immediately to seizing Leningrad and the Ukraine. Army Group South detected signs of a Soviet withdrawal in the last days of August and began to press OKH for a decision on the time, direction, and objective of a concentrated drive out of the great bend of the Dnieper. Brauchitsch, Halder, Bock, and Rundstedt had to make an immense, coordinated decision. They had won the war—exemplified by the seizure of Moscow—on 31 August 1941, but they still could lose it. For military leadership as decisively oriented as the German, the decision was a choice between turning about and destroying the Soviet forces around Leningrad and Kiev, or continuing the drive to the east.

Faced with lingering Soviet recuperative powers by the government and people and the necessity to finish the bypassed Soviets on the wings of the advance, the German leaders faced a cruel choice between being decisive in one direction or another. They were also forced by Hitler's nervous fears to halt the drive to the east to ensure the half-successes so dear to the heart, mind, and style of the supreme commander. The Soviet collapse at Moscow, however, opened new possibilities in the war; opposite Army Group Center, destruction of the Soviet strategic reserve forced Soviet armed forces remnants on the central front to escape—not trade space for time, but essentially escape—to the Volga. There, a remote chance existed that a discredited government might mobilize forces farther east and stay in the war at about half strength or less. In the first week of September 1941, considering the Soviets weakness, the Germans could perhaps have their cake and eat it too—they could advance to the east while destroying the most important target on the wings.

Late in August 1941, OKH anticipated the fall of Moscow about 31 August. The high command also observed signs of disengagement on the southern front. A crucial juncture had arrived in the Second World War in Europe, compelling OKH to issue the following orders on the last day of August 1941 to bring the war to an end in 1941:

1. *General:* Enemy confused and in disarray at Moscow. Signs of general withdrawal in Ukraine. Situation must be exploited immediately to destroy enemy forces still resisting and to seize territory east of Moscow crippling further mobilization and ending war in this year.

2. *Missions: Army Group Center* exploits enemy disorganization to advance to area Jaroslav, Gorki, Penza and organize winter positions. Center links up with Army Group South in area southwest of Yelets to encircle and destroy enemy Ukrainian front armies. *Army Group South* attacks northward immediately from great bend in Dnieper toward Kursk to encircle enemy in Ukraine. *Army Group North* pins down and destroys enemy in place exploiting new axis of advance from Kalinin.

3. *Tasks:*

a. *Army Group Center: Pz. Gp. Hoth* sends flying columns of one mobile division each to secure Jaroslow and Gorki prior to arrival of infantry. Mass of group concentrates at Murom and advances to Penza. *Pz. Gp. Hoepner* concentrates at Kashira and advances south to vicinity of Yelets to link up with *Pz. Gp. Kleist* and ensure destruction of enemy in Ukraine. *9th Army* secures winter positions along front Gorki-Yurievets-Kostroma and seizes Volgda to block enemy communications to Leningrad. Army transfers three divisions to Kalinin for attack toward Leningrad under operational control of Army Group North. *2d Army* advances east behind *Pz. Gp. Hoth* to set up winter positions along Sura and Uza Rivers to Pensk. Army transfers one division to Kalinin for attack towards Leningrad.

b. *Army Group South: Pz. Gp. Kleist, 17th Army,* and *11th Army* advance across Dnieper between Kremenchug and Dnepropetrovsk. *Pz. Gp. Kleist* advances through Kharkov to Kursk to link up with Panzer Group Hoepner southwest of Yelets and destroy enemy trapped to west. Army Group takes over operational control of *Pz. Gps. Guderian* and *Hoepner* in area south of Yelets and coordinates entire battle of encirclement. *llth Army* follows behind *Pz. Gp. Kleist* providing security for east flank and reinforcement as required on lines of encirclement. *17th Army* advances inside (west) of *Pz. Gp. Kleist* intercepting enemy force withdrawing from Kiev and sets lines of encirclement. *6th Army* engages enemy around Kiev and slows withdrawal movements to east. Army takes operational control over Army Group Center forces opposite enemy group at Gomel. Army Group follows destruction of enemy forces with move east into winter positions along line Penza-Rtischev-Novo Khopersi and a line farther south to assure occupation of the Donets Basin and Rostov.

c. *Army Group North: 18th Army* attacks enemy around Leningrad to break up and prevent withdrawal eastward. *16th Army* attacks enemy west of Lake Ilmen to break up and prevent withdrawal eastward. Army takes operational control of four divisions at Kalinin and drives westward into flank and rear of enemy.

Attacked and pursued under the above order in September 1941, Soviet armed forces on the central front, which had collapsed with the seizure of Moscow on 31 August, were forced to trade space for time and withdraw precipitously east of the Volga. Army Group Center executed the pursuit to the Volga and Sura rivers with the determination characteristic of its commander and, at the end of September, had deployed the twenty-one divisions of the 9th, 4th and 2d Armies along an extended, discontinuous front backed in depth by a mobile reserve comprising the eight panzer and motorized infantry divisions of Panzer Group Hoth. With German troops of Army Center in Kalinin (26 August) and Jaroslaw (3 September), OKH now found Army Group North essentially behind Army Group Center. OKH had encircled the Soviet forces on the Leningrad front by seizing Moscow and moving the 9th Army east and northeast beyond the capital. Soviet forces on the Baltic front were the weakest enemy during the campaign, and evidence exists to show that the Soviet high command sensed that of three critical areas—Moscow, Leningrad, and the Ukraine— that might have to be given up, Leningrad was the most expendable. Cut off entirely from the east with the accompanying fear and panic, bombarded by the air-delivered German surrender leaflets, and attacked from a decisive new direction by the Germans from the south-east, Soviet forces on the northern front disintegrated. *OKH* pressed Army Group North and the Finns to finish this battle quickly, then transferred the army group east during October and November 1941 to Moscow to serve as a great strategic reserve for the eastern front and a counterbalance to any Soviet attempt at revival during the winter of 1941–1942.

OKH faced its greatest danger and opportunity in the south. The seizure of Moscow had made the Ukraine untenable, forcing Soviet forces to withdraw to the east. These extremely powerful forces could not be followed east, for if they made it back to the Don and Donets intact they would represent a concentration of "unbeaten" strength, a catalyst to revive a discredited government and a beaten armed forces. Certainly, few doubted by the end of September 1941 that the Soviets had been soundly defeated at Leningrad and Moscow.

OKH ordered a decisive drive of Panzer Group Kleist into the area around Tim (east of Kursk) to intercept Soviet forces in the Ukraine and force them to fight with their front reversed. The 11th and 17th Armies attacked, with the mobile force to the northeast, echeloning their divisions behind Panzer Group Kleist to intercept the Soviet forces attempting to return through Sumy and Kursk to the east. Ten days after the advance started, mobile divisions of Panzer Group Kleist were in Belgorod, with an advanced detachment halted by strong Soviet resistance at Obojan, 70 km farther north. The Soviets, closely pursued by the 6th Army and nine divisions of Army Group Center from the Gomel area, were determined to keep open a wide escape corridor north and south of Kursk. Checked at Obojan on 9 September 1941, Kleist shifted two of his following divisions farther east to seize Tim, on the great road east out of Kursk, and block Soviet forces attempting to break out south of the city.

On 8 September 1941, the six divisions of Panzer Group Hoepner advanced southward along two axes to link up with Army Group South. Shortage of fuel forced Army Group Center to start the operation with only Hoepner's divisions and order Guderian to advance about 10 September, when army group supply and transportation would have relieved the temporary shortage. Hoepner's lead divisions advanced very fast through terrain partly cleared of Soviets by the earlier advance to Moscow. They entered terrain only lightly held by an enemy withdrawing southeast to the Volga, unable to be redirected by a disrupted Soviet command to hold up the panzer group. The leading division seized Yelets and the bridge across the Sosna River in a coup de main during the early morning of 11 September 1941. Hoepner moved two divisions through Yelets, to the east and southeast, to block the terrain north of Kleist's units at Tim. By 12 September, strong Soviet forces moved through the unoccupied space between the two German mobile division, but by evening two more German divisions were in position, and by noon next day a total of six German divisions blocked the Soviet retreat north of Tim. The battle was centered just east of Kursk in relatively open terrain, favorable to the encircling Germans. The violent battle continued until 19 September, when the pattern of mass surrender in the other great pockets repeated itself, and the Russians surrendered in droves. By 23 September 1941, Army Group South had largely eliminated the Kursk pocket and gave its formations five days for rest and maintenance prior to moving to winter lines for the year.

Based on the encirclement of Soviet forces at Kursk, OKH redirected Panzer Group Hoepner to the operational control of Army Group Center and ordered it to move through Yelets and Lipeck to Tambov. Earlier, on 10 September 1941, OKH ordered Guderian (minus one panzer corps released to Hoepner for the Kursk encirclement) to move southeast to Tambov, where he now stood, limited by supply from the rail heads of late September 1941, behind Army Group Center at Moscow and behind Army Group South through Kursk and Voronezh. OKH directed Hoepner to concentrate behind Guderian, with the implied possibility of a possible winter advance during clear weather, frozen ground, and light snow conditions. OKH further directed Panzer Group Kleist into the area around Borisoglebsk, south of Tambov, and ordered the 17th Army to follow and assume winter positions along the Khoper River from Borisoglebsk south to the Don. The 6th Army was ordered forward into the infantry-free gap between Borisoglebsk and Penza. Army Group South began to execute these orders on 28 September 1941. Panzer Group Hoepner had reached Tambov by 1 October 1941, when the muddy season had become a fixture. Advanced elements of Panzer Group Kleist were at Borisoglebsk. The 6th and 17th Armies advanced to the Don but were then slowed by mud in the move east to the Khoper River.

By 10 October, the Germans commanded most Soviet territory up to the Volga River. The seizure of Moscow, the advance beyond it, and the destruction of the Baltic and Ukrainian armies had changed the physical and psychological balances of the campaign. The Germans not only inflicted four million permanent casualties killed and captured, but they also seized the Soviet troop mobilization base by taking the central region around Moscow and the area to the southeast, between the Don and the Volga rivers. The

Germans also took most of the industrial region of the U.S.S.R. and with the impending drive of the reinforced 11th Army to Rostov, the entire Ukraine. These areas represented some 45 percent of the total industrial capacity of the Soviet Union. The Germans also had taken that area in which approximately 42 percent of the Soviet population lived on 22 June 1941. By October, the Soviets had inducted many military-age males into the armed forces and transferred others east as part of the shift of industry toward the Urals. The Germans, nevertheless, would occupy an area with vast populations representing crippling losses in manpower. The casualties hypothesized above are based on the estimates in Table 12.

The casualties, estimated at almost five million, must be added to the German occupation of the mobilization center of Soviet Russia between Moscow and the Volga. The Germans had inflicted so many casualties and occupied so much of the heavily populated area of Soviet Russia that they had fundamentally changed the strategic balance in the war. They had accomplished a similar result by seizing a large percentage of the industrial capacity of the Soviet state, illustrated in Table 13.

Table 12. Soviet Casualties (22 June–10 October 1941)

Actual (22 June–13 August)*		Hypothesized (13 August–10 October)**	
Baltic	150,000	Baltic	450,000
Bialystok-Minsk	324,000	Vyasma	200,000
Lvov	150,000	Moscow	300,000
Uman	103,000	Kursk	650,000
Dnieper	144,000		
Smolensk	310,000		
Roslavl	38,000		
West of Kiev	18,000		

Totals 1,237,000 captured   1,600,000 captured
Grand Total 2,837,000 captured plus approximately 1,500,000 killed***
and 1,500,000 severely wounded.*

*Based on primary German sources.
**Estimated but in reasonable accord with casualties in similar-style battles in same area in 1941.
***Rough approximation, probably conservative, based on formula of two significant wounded to one killed, and, in turn, 50 percent of significant wounded characterized as severely wounded, i.e., out of action for more than thirty days.

Table 13. Soviet Industrial Capacity Seized by Germans
(22 June–10 October 1941)

Industrial Output of Cities Seized (%)[6]		Industrial Output of Region Seized (%)[7]	
13 cities (Moscow through Krivoy Rog)	25.05	European north	1.9
13 cities (Voronezh through Rybinsk)	5.80	European west	6.2
14 cities (Shakhty through Volvzdn)	3.60	Center	16.8*
Plus smaller cities (*estimated*)	4.55	Ukraine	20.2
		White Russia	1.6
		Baltic republics	2.0
Totals	39.00%		48.7%

* Reduced percentage to take acount of reduced area of German occupation.
See Paul E. Lydolph, *Geography of the U.S.S.R.* (New York: John Wiley, 1964),
p. 330, from Lindsdale and Thompson, "A Map of the U.S.S.R.'s Manufacturing,"
Economic Geography (January 1960), facing p. 36. The 1955 data show percentages reflecting a significant shift eastward in industry from the western-oriented condition of June 1941. The Soviet shift of industries from June to August 1941 out of the path of the advancing Germans tends to make the percentages lie somewhat closer to those of September 1941.

The data are for the year 1955. They show that depending on the analysis by city or by region, the Germans occupied in the hypothetical advance by 10 October 1941 between 39 and 49 percent of the industrial capacity of the Soviet Union as distributed geographically in 1955. The distribution, however, was different in October 1941, concentrated farther west, even considering the frantic and effective Soviet transfer of industrial plant toward the Urals. A reasonable estimate of the percentage of Soviet industrial plant seized by the Germans by 10 October 1941 would be greater than 39 percent—the minimum possible using 1955 data for output by cities—and is estimated higher, at approximately 45 percent of the industrial capacity of the Soviet Union in 1941. The percentages for industrial output by regions indicate that the industrial output seized by the Germans in the hypothetical case could be somewhat higher.

How do the casualties inflicted, the populated area seized, and the industrial capacity taken affect the issue of the Germans' winning the Russian campaign? The figures are so overwhelming that they support a conclusion that, even if the Soviets managed to suborn the Russians into continuing the war, the result was foregone by October 1941. In 1941 the Soviet Union was European Russia, a vast area stretching from the old Polish border to the Urals. That Russia represented a special synthesis of Russian people (largely Russian Slavic), Russian space, Russian resources, Russian strategic relationships, and a special half-Russian bureaucracy. By October 1941, that synthesis, which represented so much political and military strength, had been changed greatly—bent to the point that it could be considered broken. Otto von Bismarck, unifier of modern Germany and a tough realist, described Russia as an elemental force, rather like the weather, and essentially bigger than life. By October 1941, the German army had seized half of European Russia, including Moscow, Leningrad, Kiev, Gorki, and Kharkov, the five most populous cities in the state,[8] and reduced Bismarck's Russia to less than "elemental" proportions. A relatively unscathed German army, though admittedly tired and impressed with its accomplishments, controlled half of European Russia and, perhaps more important, did so with a psychological superiority reflected in the words of a Russian officer prisoner: "The Germans will take Moscow. It will be a tough fight but the Germans will take Moscow." This psychologically accurate statement says it all: The Russian officer perceived that the war would end with the capture of the region around the capital because the Russians would have neither the physical strength nor the will to continue the fight.

It is not known if in the German advance to the Volga in October 1941 the Soviet Communists could have kept the Russians fighting determinedly in the war. From an analysis of casualties, population base, and industrial plant, even if the Communist leadership had managed to keep resistance alive, it could not have been sustained by the reduced amount of support. This generalization about Soviet resistance seems true, particularly against a physically intact and psychologically supreme invading army. From it stems the interpretation of the Second World War in Europe that the Soviet Union would likely have been defeated, despite coherent and determined resistance in the spring of 1942. It is also possible to visualize a disintegration of Communist control in the east, reflected in a Communist retreat with a small cadre of forces to a remote corner of the Soviet Union. Then, the war would have been largely over by 1941 instead of clearly and irrevocably won.

The Germans, by taking Moscow relatively easily in August 1941, would have won the war based on another factor not yet discussed. In 1941 Moscow was the center of the European Russian rail, automobile highway, and telephone systems. That year, strategic movement in European Russia was almost entirely by railroad. The unpaved automobile road system, impassable in autumn and spring and difficult during heavy snowfall in winter, made it subordinate to the rail system for shifting troops and moving supplies and industrial production. The Soviet defense of Leningrad and the Ukraine depended on controlling the rail lines and vast marshalling and storage facilities of Moscow. When the Germans seized the great Soviet rail system hub on 31 August 1941, they controlled all of Soviet Russia to the north, west, and south of the hub. The Soviet field armies west of Moscow were cut off strategically from the remainder of the state and would be forced to withdraw or be destroyed.

The Germans had taken Moscow with light losses and moved well to the east before being halted by a combination of muddy roads and outrunning the supply system. Then, the Germans needed time to push the rail heads forward into the Soviet Union, particularly Moscow, and then expand to the east and southeast. Curiously, the timing of events was almost ideal from the German viewpoint. Forced to halt by the unpaved roads, they decided to winter close to their positions and had the opportunity to extend the German normal-gauge rail lines to rail heads close by. As Army Group Center moved out from Moscow in the second week of September 1941, the railway pioneers and supporting labor service battalions had connected Smolensk with Moscow by one normal-gauge double-track line. With a rail head at Moscow and significant numbers of captured Soviet vehicles, the Germans survived the attrition of their supply services trucks from the rail heads to the advancing troops. The German rail head at Moscow assured Army Group Center of logistic supply to continue the advance eastward until the autumn mud. The Germans aggressively regauged the Russian rail system radiating from Moscow to the east and assured themselves of the logistical capability to maintain the initiative should they encounter strong Soviet resistance along the Volga.

For the Soviet high command, German seizure of the Moscow

rail hub splintered the existing front into three pieces, each isolated from the other. Those to the northwest, around Leningrad, and southwest, around Kiev, faced quick destruction. When the Germans entered Moscow, they reduced the fighting quickly to a single, compact central front. The north was immediately sealed off and the Soviet forces trapped there quickly destroyed. The south was half isolated, and strong Soviet forces in the Ukraine would be intercepted and destroyed. The remaining territory in the Caucasus was outflanked strategically by the Germans, more than 1,200 km away at Moscow, but in command of the Soviet rail net.

When the Soviets gave up Moscow on 31 August 1941 and began to trade space for time to reach the Volga, they lost the strategic center in European Russia and any traditional focus for continuing serious resistance. A fair question is, where would the Soviet government set up its new capital, and how would that capital reflect Soviet chances of winning the campaign? Kazan and Kubyshyev were too close to the Volga, and Perm or Sverdlovsk, in the central Urals, so distant as to highlight the Soviet defeat. With the Germans in Moscow and Gorki, what credibility resided in the Soviet Communists, and how could they coordinate a war from, for example, Sverdlovsk? Even at Perm, the Soviet government would be fighting for its own legitimacy and credibility. The relocation of the capital to a location as far east as Perm (modern Molotov) not only focuses the fundamentally changed strategic relationships but also portends the likely collapse of the Soviet government.

However, the great unknown in the hypothetical events of August–October 1941 is not whether the Germans won the campaign against the Soviet Union. The casualties inflicted, mobilization base seized, industrial output denied, and the special transportation and communications advantages acquired by taking Moscow point with certainty to a German victory by October 1941. The most important unknown is whether the Germans could finish the campaign, occupying most of European Russia and keeping the Soviets by bay with an occupying force. The occupation forces would be impressive, even including a strong operational mobile element to conduct panzer forays from a kind of *Militargrenze* (a military frontier, with implications of fluctuation and dispute) in the Urals. The panzer forays would resemble the Mongol golden horde against Muscovite Russia on a previous occasion, using flying columns of superior steppe cavalry to penetrate the forest country, extracting tribute, ensuring obedience, and then departing.

Under the favorable strategic calculus of November 1941, the Germans could have taken advantage of the frozen ground from mid-month onward to launch panzer raids eastward.[9] These would keep the operational situation fluid and, in one or two areas, seize and hold territory. Hypothetically, operations resulting in a German advance to the Volga would permit the advancing field armies to winter on a line between Penza and Balashov, about 150 km northwest of Saratov. This was an industrial center on the Volga in the center of a transportation network, the last effective link between the Soviet rump area to the east and the Caucasus. By 10 October 1941, the Germans concentrated most of Panzer Groups Guderian and Hoepner facing Saratov. They could have taken that city and the surrounding area after the ground-hardening freezing weather with the assistance of the 6th Army, which moved into the area after September operations in the Ukraine. That move would reduce the possibilities of successful Soviet resistance in the Caucasus and kept the Soviets off balance on the Volga.

This discussion represents, of course, the worst case for the Germans. In this case, the Germans have won the war by maintaining their strength intact and fundamentally changing the strategic balance in their favor. The Germans cannot lose; the question is when the campaign can be considered finished. The Soviets have denied reality and are determined to bring down the state with them in a continued, bloody, conventional war. At the end of the war, the Soviets would attempt to conduct protracted guerrilla warfare in the Urals. Then, the Germans would probably have ended the conventional war by mid-summer 1942, occupying the Caucasus and territory east of the Moscow-Gorki area close to the Urals.

In contrast to that analysis, which highlights the worst case for the Germans, it is probably as reasonable to consider a course in which the Soviet Communist government collapses after revealing its incapacity to secure the capital of Soviet Russia. Even by imperial Russian standards of centralized bureaucratic excess and local landlord severity, the Communist dictatorship had been harsh. As in the past, the Russians had suffered such treatment because of a pervasive national fear of the outside world, but once the brutal, familiar dictatorship could not keep the enemy out of its own capital, they had cause and opportunity to rid themselves of a dictatorship tainted by its emphasis on nonnational urban workers of the world in a state dominated by peasantry with roots in a different past. The opportunistic call of the Soviet government on 3 July 1941 for a patriotic war was flexible but desperate and transparent. If the Soviet Communists could provide evidence that they would win, the Russians peasantry would continue resistance in a unique national brotherhood—Communist with Russian.

With the attack of Army Group Center on 13 August 1941 and the fall of Moscow on 31 August 1941, one must consider that the Soviet government could have lost its capability to mobilize the peasants and would have disintegrated politically. Strong anticommunist currents survived in Russia, which could have combined to end the war in late autumn 1941 with mass support of a peasantry unwilling any longer to be shot either by Soviet commissar or German combat soldier. Then, the campaign could have ended with "negotiations" between a Russian government and the National Socialists, while the German army advanced eastward against a small, rump Communist government and forces loyal to it. Regarding the potential for collapse of the Communist government, these possibilities are summed up effectively in the words of a Russian prisoner in July 1941 to his captors: "Where have you been; we have been waiting for you for 23 years."

Part VI

Reinterpreting World War II

Chapter Thirteen

Hitler: The German Führer Driven by a Siege Mentality

ADOLF Hitler has strong claim to being the paramount political figure of the twentieth century. That judgment is obviously not on a moral plane but based on the historical capability of one man almost single-handedly to win the Second World War in Europe. A National Socialist German victory would have had consequences at once incalculable and vast—indeed, epoch making. To win, Hitler had only to order Army Group Center to continue its attack in reinforced strength toward Moscow on or about 13 August 1941. Every German army officer outside of OKW supported an uninterrupted drive toward Moscow and continuation of the offensive beyond, as appropriate to the developing campaign. Even in OKW, virtually every officer who voiced his views on continuing operations in July and August 1941 favored the drive to seize Moscow immediately. The exception, Generalfeldmarschall Wilhelm Keitel, chief of OKW, is clear in his memoirs that he intended to be only a conduit for Hitler's concepts and not give his professional opinion on a military topic, even if asked.[1] Hitler made the most important decision of his life—and the most important judgment for the political shape of the twentieth century world—against the professional judgment of virtually every German soldier who had an opportunity to comment.[2]

Hitler and the Most Important Political Military Decision of the 20th Century

Curiously, Hitler's great decision was a military one, albeit within the framework of a politically inspired war. That a military decision could be so important is jarring in a modern world obsessed with social forces, economics, the "masses," and the concomitant decline in emphasis on "kings and battles" in history. Modern historians portraying political history tend to bridge the gap between kings and battles and social forces by emphasizing political history rich in economic and social inputs. So it is curious that despite contemporary historical style, Hitler, a king in the sense of an important individual leader—the Hero in history—made the great decision of the twentieth century. The decision narrowed even further from the conceptual perspective inspiring proponents of mass social forces because it concerned fighting only the next battle in a military campaign. Yet the German failure to seize Moscow in August 1941 was the turning point in the Russian campaign. After that, the Germans faced certain defeat in the Second World War, an outcome that altered fundamentally the course of events in this century.

How could Hitler have made such a decision, and how can it be explained? If it can be explained, does the result further an understanding of the man and his judgments? So important a decision would provide clues to the man. The more important judgments should reflect the same fears, doubts, and strengths of others, only with such factors magnified because of greater importance. Another question is: Did Hitler know he was making his supreme decision? It is easy for the historian to make such a claim and buttress it with supporting argument from the commanding heights of retrospection. Making history is different from writing it, and Hitler may not have realized that he had reached the pinnacle of his career and a turning point for the world. It is hard to imagine that he knew he was making his most significant decision, particularly since it was fatally deficient and must lead to certain defeat. It is likely, though, that Hitler knew his decision was extraordinarily important, perhaps the most significant he would ever make. This explanation permits claims to a better understanding of the man through an understanding of his aberration before Moscow.

Hitler's Decision-making Pattern

Hitler revealed an uncannily similar behavior pattern in planning and executing the earlier French campaign. He approved a modified, seemingly more decisive plan to conquer France in late February 1940. But a closer examination of the operation plan controversy shows Hitler approving a new scheme of maneuver not because it was decisive but because something new was demanded by the compromise of the original plan on 10 January 1941 in Belgium and the excessive delay in the attack.[3] Hitler had little faith in the Manstein plan to produce a decisive victory over France. His planning for an offensive in the heavily fortified Rhine area and emphasis on the taking of the Lorraine ore fields show preoccupation with extraneous economic targets in France analogous to the Donets Basin in the Ukraine during the Russian campaign. Day after day, in the Halder diaries the hardworking German chief of staff notes discussion and preparation for a Rhine offensive and, astoundingly, shows Hitler in June 1940 holding up attacks to the south and southwest of Paris because of his concern over the certainty of seizing Lorraine.

In contrast to his irresolute dispersal of effort in a military campaign and his peculiar disregard for the time element in war, Hitler reached his great foreign policy decisions with a special, almost unique resolution and corresponding swiftness. Events from March 1935, with the announcement of conscription in Germany, through the decision in July 1940 to attack the Soviet Union reflect a relatively young man—Hitler was forty-six in 1935—in an almost incredible hurry. He exceeded even Bismarck by bringing Austria, admittedly a rump state but nevertheless German Austria, into the Reich in February 1938. He could have retired in March 1938, among the most distinguished German statesmen of all time, having recovered the Rhineland for Germany and added Austria to it. After the rearmament of Germany in 1935, remilitarization of the Rhineland in March 1936, and the annexation of Austria in March 1938, how could he have pressed on so aggressively in the spring of 1938 as to be on the verge of war with Britain, France, and Czechoslovakia in May of the same year? What happened to his retirement plans? From 1935 to 1940 he carried out a veritable *Blitzaussenpolitik* (lightning foreign policy) in addition to the so-called blitzkriegs of 1939–1941.

Hitler's *Blitzaussenpolitik* advances and apparent lightning wars complemented one another and led with ice-cold logic toward the conquest of Europe. Regarding his decision to attack the Soviet Union, one marvels at the consistency of pattern, the fanatical sense of urgency, and the sensitivity of the policy to time. With a genius for effective timing, Hitler determined to attack the Soviet Union as quickly as possible after the French campaign, notwithstanding the potentially embarrassing war with Britain. Although claiming consistently that an attack on the Soviet Union was necessary to defeat Britain, Hitler must be seen as attacking the Soviets to achieve the National Socialist *Weltanschauung* (world view) and end the war in Europe by seizing European Russia and smashing Soviet communism. Hitler concealed his fundamental purpose, using the tortuous, half-believable argument that Britain could be defeated only if it denied Soviet Russia as an ally. The argument was both convenient and necessary because of the time element in any attack against the Soviets. Alongside his British argument, Hitler repeated with equal consistency his more substantial fears that Stalin was planning an attack against Germany; and every day that passed decreased Germany's 1940 advantage in the balance in armaments and mobilized personnel. In June 1941, Hitler seems barely to have beaten Stalin to the punch and was correct in his general strategic assessment that delaying an attack against the Soviet Union until 1942 would give the Soviets improved armaments and mobilization, decreasing German chances of success in any attack.

Soviet Intentions in the Summer of 1941

Recently, published evidence and particularly effective arguments show that Stalin began a massive deployment of Soviet forces to the western frontier early in June 1941.[4] The evidence supports a view that Stalin intended to use the forces concentrated in the west as quickly as possible—probably about mid-July 1941—for a Soviet Barbarossa. Statements of Soviet prisoners also support a view that the Soviets intended an attack on Germany in 1941.[5] The extraordinary deployment of the Soviet forces on the western frontier is best explained as an offensive deployment for an attack without full mobilization by extremely powerful forces massed there for that purpose.

An extraordinary element in Barbarossa is the utter disbelief by Germans like Major Peter von der Groeben, thirty-nine years after the event,[6] and the similar disbelief of others like Bock and Halder about the Soviet strategy to fight for every inch of Soviet territory. That strategy made no sense to the German command and could never make sense so long as it was based on the premise that Stalin and the Soviet government were surprised in a defensive stance and fearful of a German attack. If, however, the Soviets were deployed for an attack of their own and were not surprised, then such a situation would demand the Red Army reaction— furious attacks by masses of men and materiel and the appearance of a surprised defender deciding on a strategy of holding every inch of Russian (and other people's) territory. A subtlety in this interpretation is that the Soviet command was perhaps surprised by the timing and violence of Barbarossa, although not surprised that Soviet forces soon would be in combat. For the first time, then, the Soviet decision to fight on the border, a decision that was wrong and would have ensured a German victory but for Hitler's mid-Barbarossa procrastination and diffusion of German strength, comes into focus as the only one possible, given the Soviet deployment for offensive operations at the harvest end in 1941.

Hitler's Aggressiveness During German Initiatives in Foreign Policy and War, 1935-1941

It is unlikely that Hitler anticipated the offensive Soviet deployment in June 1941 because Stalin probably ordered the deployment, reacting to his knowledge of a German military buildup. It is likely that Hitler accurately forecast that Stalin could not resist taking advantage of Germany's preoccupation with Britain to launch an attack in the immediate future, no later than the summer of 1942. With his inimitable foreign policy forcefulness, Hitler pressed for an attack as soon as possible after the fall of France, the earliest serious campaigning weather being late spring 1941. Hitler's political forcefulness and sense of timing to get things done quickly to reach his foreign policy goals were important elements in his remarkable string of foreign policy and war successes from 1935 to 1940.

By an attack on the Soviet Union in the spring of 1941, Hitler accentuated the scale and pace of an already savagely dynamic foreign policy. The term "foreign policy" does not explain what Hitler was about, for he was literally conducting a lightning foreign policy war (*Blitzaussenpolitikskrieg*). Hitler cannot be faulted for lack of forcefulness or pace in his foreign policy; rather, he was a paragon of concentration, force, and speed. While making his foreign policy decisions he was assailed by fears, doubts, and procrastination, but he always overcame them. He impressed his decisive will on his foreign policy opponents from 1935 to August 1939 and achieved every goal without recourse to war. When finally forced by the crisis of summer 1939 to attack, he was fully prepared not only to fight a war with Poland but also to win it before any opponent could exploit the dangerous situation into which Germany was projected. When Hitler reached his greatest decision, it was with the same forcefulness and sense of urgency that characterized the past. The decision to attack the Soviet Union was the correct decision for Germany in July 1940, for whether or not Britain was defeated in the autumn of 1940, Russia would have to be attacked in the campaign season of 1941.

Once in a war with Britain and France, Hitler continued his decisive political actions, sending German armed forces into successful military campaigns in Denmark and Norway, Belgium, Luxembourg, the Netherlands, France, Yugoslavia, and Greece, apparently with a fine sense of the strategic demands and the importance of time. With Germany at war, the German high command achieved even greater prominence than the leadership of the National Socialist movement, forcing Hitler to assume his role as supreme commander of the armed forces and wield control over them. As supreme commander, Hitler showed devastating weaknesses, based on characteristics muted during his rise to national political power in Germany and to international political influence in Europe.

Examining the challenging, complex problems that Hitler successfully mastered in bringing a political movement to power in Germany, it is possible to understand and define the singular qualities of the man. The same qualities served Hitler well in the challenging period during which he raised Germany to predominant influence in Europe. He was intense, distant, personally withdrawn—a lone fanatic. Simultaneously he sensed what disturbed every German over losing the First World War and the associated trauma. He was a German's German, the most average of all Germans, a gregarious sponge appealing to the greatest number. He has been described as both banal and terrible; disastrously disorganized in personal and public life but a great organizer based on his development of a mass political movement from a tiny, sterile debating club. These contrary appraisals, each with substantial elements of truth, are not particularly helpful in gauging what Hitler would do in a given situation. He prided himself on a fanatical will to surmount difficult times and situations—"walls may break but not our hearts." It was to be expected, therefore, that he would be fanatical when faced with challenging situations. But how does a fanatic be fanatical? Does he fanatically attack or defend, concentrate on his great mission, or run off in pursuit of the tactical details of the moment?

Once at war, in 1939, Hitler was faced with pursuing "politics by other means," essentially Clausewitz's ominously couched "armed violence." Hitler was used to brawling and action in his rise to power (brawl) and execution of dramatic foreign policy (action). Unlike the other senior statesmen of his day, Hitler even had experienced war as a private soldier in the First World War. In 1939, however, Hitler faced the challenge of continuing German foreign policy by armed violence. The street brawls and pistol of the (fanatically) courageous messenger of an infantry regiment in Flanders would be replaced by the thunder of artillery and the roaring engines of panzer formations with distant strategic targets. Hitler faced the self-imposed task of providing strategic political direction for Germany in war while in operational command of the armed forces. This two-faceted situation quickly highlighted the strengths and weaknesses of the man and enable us to understand him—the strategic vision, the operational fears, and the tactical compulsions that drove him.

Adolf Hitler Revealed by Barbarossa's Challenges

In Barbarossa, Hitler had the initiative to win the war and was more clearly revealed than at any other time. With almost unique perversity, he revealed his greatest strength, a thinly developed sense of proportion. His many detractors point to his decision to attack the Soviet Union. They also note the hyperbole in his designating the Volga as the goal to be reached in the campaign as evidence of a man divorced from reality. They might as well have pointed to his decision to become the seventh active member of a blue-collar political club in Munich and his declared goal to take over Germany with it as evidence of similar hyperbole. The conventional view of Hitler belabors the point that he was a man without a sense of proportion but links the characteristic almost exclusively with the period from 1939 to 1945. Further, they show how it contributed to his fall and intimate that it was his most significant weakness.

Had Hitler exhibited a reasonable, normal, or balanced sense of proportion, he would not have become one of the most important political figures of the twentieth century. Had he possessed a sense

of proportion, he would not have presumed to start a mass political movement from an inconceivably small base. However, without
that sense of proportion, by 1932 he became leader of the most
successful political party in Germany. Had he a sense of proportion
he would not have refused the vice chancellorship in August 1932.
However, without it he refused and became chancellor in January
1933. With a sense of proportion he would not have ordered German troops into the demilitarized Rhineland in March 1936,
putting Strassburg within range of German cannon and plunging
Germany into war with France and Britain. Without a sense of
proportion, Hitler won a historically unsurpassed string of internal
political, foreign policy, and military victories from 1920 to 1941.

Lacking that sense of proportion, Hitler made the correct decision at the right time to attack the Soviet Union as early as prac-
ticable in 1941. It was the most significant move in his political
career. Making that decision in July 1940, he gave Germany a clear
chance to win the Second World War in Europe. Attacking the
Soviet Union while violating the August 1939 nonaggression pact,
he added an element of special brazenness. Historically, the action
was almost unparalled and shows him as a man lacking an ordinary sense of proportion. Yet the decision was no bolder than
many Hitler had made in the past with less chance of success. He
had a greater chance to defeat the Soviet Union in 1941 with the
formidable blitz potential of the German army than he had to take
over Germany in 1920 with a handful of disgruntled Munich beer
drinkers. Hitler's missing sense of proportion probably resulted
from some perception of personal destiny, mission, and messianic
self-assurance. Rather than causing him failure, it was an important reason for his success.

Were There Two Hitlers?

Hitler showed an almost infinite capacity to make grand and dangerous political decisions. Once within the framework of his greatest political decision, however, his obsessive concern about economic details and opportunities in a military campaign against the
Soviet Union showed a sense of proportion that ran contrary to
the overwhelming boldness of the decision and contradicts the
logic of a lightning war. Hitler, the master political strategist in
Germany and Europe in the interwar period, appears in retrospect
to have been unstoppable in his impossibly bold decisions. He

demonstrated a breathtaking disregard for practical necessities in his greatest decisions, leaving the observer mystified as to how he believed they could be carried out. For example, in a political crisis only twenty-four hours old, at approximately 1330 on 9 March 1938, Hitler informed Generaloberst Ludwig Beck, army chief of staff, and Generalmajor Erich von Manstein, casual visitor to the chief's office, that he required a military option for the crisis rapidly developing in Austria. He demanded that the two generals prepare to move the German army into that state no later than 0900 on 11 March. It would be difficult to find a high-level decision made with greater decisiveness but less sense of proportion about the possibilities of success. Hitler got his just deserts in this case because the German army moved into Austria thirty minutes late, at 0930 on that fateful Saturday morning. The army's massed presence, nevertheless, ignited overwhelming national support for the unification of the two German peoples and paralyzed effective counteraction by neighbors.

Unlike his boldness and lack of sense of proportion in political and military decisions up to July 1940, Hitler was concerned over seizing economic targets in the Soviet Union during Barbarossa. With an impressive sense of proportion about Germany's economic capabilities to win a European war, he determined to pace Barbarossa to the seizure of Leningrad, the eastern Ukraine, and the Crimea for economic reasons. It is the supreme irony of his bold and unrestrained foreign policy from 1935 to 1941 that he was defeated by his restrained and realistically proportioned concern over the seizure of economic targets in Russia. How it is possible that in his boldest political decision he determined a timorous war plan designed to assure the seizure of economic terrain rather than defeat of the Soviet Union?

Were there two Adolf Hitlers: one capable of deciding to attack the largest state in the world while simultaneously at war with an even larger Athenian-style empire, the other incapable of taking risks in war? Hitler has been described as a compulsive gambler, a political leader with an urge to self-destruction, a man with a death wish. He made decision after decision from 1924 (i.e., after the November 1923 *Putsch*) through 1941, decisions so daring and fraught with peril that they seem almost calculated to fail. Almost every important decision he made during that period was successful. Thus, he was an improbable gambler. Gambling—wagering on uncertain events—demands a result in which the gambler loses about as many times as he wins in his gambling. In uncertain situations during those years, Hitler won almost every important political wager and can scarcely be described as a gambler except in a misleading, pejorative sense. He was an extraordinarily skillful and daring political leader whose focus on a single distant goal added system to his skill and daring. Yet the same man was incapable of entertaining risks in the ultimate military execution of his vast political decisions in 1939–1941.

Hitler's Leningrad Fixation in Barbarossa

The role of the individual Hero in history has rarely been more important than in the German loss of the Second World War in Europe. Germany could not have won that war by virtue of superior population and productive resources. It could not engage in a struggle simultaneously with France, Britain, and the Soviet Union with any prospect of success. Germany could have won the war through Hitler's political skill and daring and the battle-winning capabilities of the German army. Hitler had the time to intervene in the military planning for the advance into the Soviet Union, but his boldness faltered during the military campaign. In essence, he diverted the campaign in Soviet Russia into an attack against Leningrad, then confounded the apparent illogic of that limited outlook by changing his mind during the campaign and ordering instead an attack into the Ukraine by Army Group Center. Hitler pursued the Leningrad decision from August 1940 through approximately 13 July 1941, then veered toward a different target but one just as indecisive as Leningrad. The Leningrad decision and the final belated Ukrainian version of it was Hitler's most important mistake. Executed at the end of August 1941, the decision wiped out his successes prior to the planned diversion; all of his accumulating failures after it—Alamein, Stalingrad, Kursk, and others—were anticlimactic, inconsequential to the issue of victory or defeat in the war. The decision must provide the most significant insight possible into what drove Hitler.

The Leningrad diversion seemed senseless, including its hasty conception by Hitler within days after he announced his decision to attack the Soviet Union. How could he have concluded by August 1940 that the most important element in Barbarossa was to take Leningrad at once? Is it possible that in his mind he saw

Leningrad as the key to securing the Baltic route of Swedish iron ore to Germany? If so, Hitler may have ordered the attack against the Soviet Union to secure the Swedish ore resources. In that case, however, the means to secure a given end are exaggerated to the point of incredibility—an attack against the Soviet Union to secure the summer route of Swedish ore shipments to Germany! Yet conventional wisdom demands acceptance of a similarly exaggerated means to a given end—an attack on the Soviet Union to secure the successful end to war with Britain. This approach is not convincing. There was a fanatical sense of mission in Hitler's political strategy, driving him toward a final showdown not with Britain but rather with international Jewish bolshevism, exemplified by the Soviet Communist party. It is unlikely that Hitler would plan a confrontation with Soviet Russia as an incidental part of a war with Britain. It is likely that he would be forced to consider tactical details in such a strategic showdown, and these could provide us with probing insights into his thought processes.

In planning for Barbarossa, Hitler redirected the energy of the decision to attack and overthrow the Soviet Union into a wholly different plane of consideration, the seizure of several economic objectives. He lost sight almost immediately of the strategic purpose of the invasion—the quick overthrow of the Soviet government. In the actual execution of Barbarossa starting on 22 June 1941, he redirected the energy that he had planned to seize several vast economic objectives into mastering myriad (for the supreme commander) local combat crises. Through a process and style difficult to fathom, he saw the campaign he had ordered with decisive strategic energy only in terms of the parts and the pieces. Surely there were two Adolf Hitlers: one going his way with the assurance of a sleepwalker through one gigantic political decision after another, the other wringing his hands and raging over local crises and self-manufactured fear, doubt, and concern.

Reversing the analysis gets at the Barbarossa Hitler. Reaching for the part (Leningrad), the parts (Leningrad, Ukraine, and the Crimea), and the pieces (local war fighting crises and self-inflicted fears in every battle on every front), Hitler reveals the mentality that drove him. He was a popular dictator, extraordinarily concerned about his personal popularity and the potential strain on it from the economic rigors of a war. He was an uncompromising idealist who saw Germany secure as a great power only by the acquisition of enough contiguous space to ensure economic autarky. He was a romantic propaganda genius who combined the spoken word with brilliantly staged visual pageantry to convert millions to National Socialism and overawe others with impressions of irresistible energy. He suggested to German audiences a manifest destiny for Germany in line with the words, "tomorrow belongs to me," sung by a German youth in the successful modern play, *Cabaret.* These facts are well known. They are important because they bring into focus the Hitler who conducted the planning for Barbarossa. Standing alongside the Hitler with the sure touch and incredible self-assurance in the grand decision, the other Hitler was immediately fearful of the economic impact of the war on Germany. The lower-case Hitler, concerned for his popular image and fanatically determined not to stress the German population with either the substance or the appearance of wartime austerity, fastened on the economic necessities of war. With insight regarding the relationship between war and economics, he fussed that his generals did not understand economics and politics in war. With some far-reaching insight into mass psychology, he conducted the war against the Soviet Union in a rather sophisticated way—assuring stability on the home front while adding Leningrad, the Ukraine, and the Crimea[7] to the economic base of an expanded Germany.

Hitler's : Earlier Fixations in Norway and France

Deeply concerned about the possibility of a British attack on Scandinavia and the seizure of Narvik or the Swedish iron ore fields, Hitler had ordered an invasion of Norway, carried out successfully in April–June 1940. He was prepared to embark on an extremely challenging amphibious campaign to secure the Swedish ore and conceived the campaign almost entirely on his own. Grossamiral Erich Raeder, commander of the German navy, had suggested such an operation earlier but for entirely different reasons, and the suggestion had fallen on deaf ears. Later, however, with exceptional sensitivity about the loss of the ore resources, Hitler seems to have been personally responsible for a campaign of great strategic boldness and operational imagination. He used OKW to plan and execute the campaign, employing OKH only as a source of ground combat units. The Norwegian campaign and its determined, successful execution are powerful arguments supporting a view that

Hitler was driven significantly by economic considerations during the war. With that mind set, one could suspect him of fastening immediately on the economic ramifications of Barbarossa, and a pattern can be seen developing.

Even earlier, in the more important development of a plan of attack against France, Hitler showed extreme concern about his "economic popularity"—the concern of a modern popular dictator for his image and mass support, dependent upon the state's economic conditions. Hitler emphasized visual effect in the great propaganda triumphs that characterized him—the party day rallies, the Potsdam garrison church ceremony in 1933, and his compulsive interest in the Olympian, heroic, neoclassical architecture for a new Berlin: "Will we Germans be remembered for our department stores and banks or our great government buildings and triumphal arches?"[8] As long as he had power, he appeared set on assuming the appearance (and substance) of economic solvency. German economic solvency, in the first part of war, combined an armaments effort strong enough to support the campaigns initiated by Hitler with surprisingly full consumer production. Concerned about his political popularity, and linking it decisively with economic conditions, he faced a little-known situation in October 1939 that drove the entire French campaign.

The large body of literature on the French campaign presents excruciating detail on its planning and execution but little explanation for the actions of the man with the strategic initiative and personal authority to launch an attack. A distinguished British authority describes in italics on a single page how Hitler had to reach Belgium first, before the Allies, and was stimulated by fears in early October 1939 that the Allies in Belgium would constitute an increased danger to Germany's Ruhr.[9] A distinguished German participant in the war does not even mention the basic, initial stimulation for *Fall Gelb*, the plan for an all-out German attack in the west.[10] That the Germans would seriously consider a winter offensive at all simply disappears in the literature.

Virtually every work on the war in the west notes that the Germans called off *Fall Gelb* approximately fourteen times because of bad weather, which would restrict air and motorized ground operations in the opening attacks. Not one work on the subject makes the point that even had the weather been good enough to launch the attack, any advance would have been largely paralyzed by the following bad weather, characteristic of northwestern Europe in winter.

Hitler knew these points because he aborted the attack on the occasions noted above, using forecasted bad weather as the reason. He also knew through experience of combat in Flanders in the First World War that the German armed forces would have only a few days of good weather during which they could attack. He was convinced that the time would suffice to assure keeping the Allies out of Belgium and away from the Ruhr. Hitler probably felt that he would have a reasonable chance of taking the Belgian coastline and conducting more effective sea and air operations against Britain. He must have had an important reason to order the illogically circumscribed attack planned—a winter attack by the concentrated German army with the limited objective of seizing Belgium. In the original *Fall Gelb*, Hitler overreacted to potential Allied initiatives against Belgium, seeing adverse effects on his political image and popularity and damage to political stability in Germany in the event of a successful Allied coup. He saw danger to the Ruhr and economic trauma in Germany that he determined to avoid because of similar adverse effects on his political image. He linked his popularity and prestige with the political stability of the National Socialist state and was willing to pace the war to prevent perceived adverse economic and political effects in Germany.

When conditions changed in January and February 1940 with the assumed compromise of the original *Fall Gelb*, the lack of Allied interest in a preemptive move into Belgium, and demands for a decisive plan of operations by the commander and staff of Army Group A, Hitler shifted toward a new plan. It was inspired largely by Manstein, apparently unaware of Hitler's conservative mentality that had shaped the original plan, who bombarded OKH with suggestions for a decisive war-winning offensive in the west. OKH fashioned a new plan intended to defeat the Allied armies on the continent in a lightning campaign. Hitler had little confidence in a victory over France and made decisions that held up the army. If Hitler had confidence in Manstein's plan, or understood it, he would not have issued the nervous barrage of orders slowing and finally halting the advancing German armies to secure various half-successes disconnected from any reasonable intention to defeat France quickly.

Even more importantly (and largely missed in interpretations of the campaign), Hitler ordered another great offensive into the heavily fortified area of northeastern France opposite the Rhineland, near the main Maginot defensive works. That operation seems calculated to disrupt the decisive operations at Sedan and in Belgium at the other end of the front. This offensive drained resources and command energy from the main effort and makes little sense in a blitz campaign or achieving a quick military victory. Uninfluenced by any other person, Hitler personally ordered the attack, considering it necessary to assure seizing the French iron ore resources in Lorraine to buttress the German economy. As with the Swedish ore and Norway, Hitler was not only aware in a conventional sense of the importance of iron ore and steel to the German wartime economy of 1940, but he was also diligently assuring his popular political authority. Ordering the attack into northeastern France, he proved he had no confidence in a quick victory over France. It is just as possible, however, that in a subtle way he never really appreciated the decisive nature of the panzer attack through Sedan. In the role he played as an inspired messianic figure, keeping to himself psychologically, he may have still considered Manstein's ideas and the OKH plan realistically only a means to seize Belgium. Under such circumstances, Hitler would require the northeastern offensive to secure Lorraine iron ore and the industrial belt around it to reinforce Germany economically for a longer war on the Continent.

Strategically Bold but Devoid of Operational Nerve, Hitler Had Two Personalities

In the military campaign, Hitler was anything but daring. While clamoring for military victories in the campaigns and advances of 1939–1941, he refused to assume risks and slowed German army advances more effectively than the French and Red armies and the British expeditionary forces. Hitler personally stopped the German army short of Dunkirk and, more importantly, halted it again in front of both Moscow (August–September 1941) and Leningrad (September 1941). These aberrant decisions exemplify similar decisions made concurrently and affirm that Adolf Hitler marched to some arcane, extraneous drumbeat in his military operations. He was presented with strong possibilities of victory through bold political decisions for war in Poland, Norway, France, the Balkans, and Soviet Russia, yet the contrast between his bold decision to campaign and the circumscribed military decisions demand explanations. Hitler's fears about attacking France appear identical to those at the beginning of the Russian campaign, under similar circumstances against a major enemy. Just what caused the concern, the inner fear, deduced from the unmistakable pattern of halt, paralysis, and extraneous excursion that characterized the two victorious campaigns?

Adolf Hitler made not only bold political decisions but also the most remarkable tactical military move by any head of state with his personal organization of the glider and shaped-charge attack on the Belgian fortress of Eban Emael.[11] Between the greater Hitler of grand strategic decisions and tactical insights of unsurpassed acumen, a lesser Hitler operated to disrupt the French campaign and lose the Russian campaign—and the war. The greater Hitler apparently knew no strategic fear and would suffer no tactical impasse. The lesser Hitler lacked the psychological makeup to accept risks to effect the grand operational concepts concocted by the army for France and Soviet Russia. An inspired disregard for time and some complex fear of the consequences of daring operational moves let him come close to losing the battle of France and throw away almost certain victory in Russia. We cannot psychoanalyze a missing or deceased Hitler,[12] but the circumstances surrounding his lesser decisions and the pattern comparing France with Soviet Russia may provide adequate descriptions of his fear, if not a psychoanalytical explanation.

Cracking the Code of Explanation, 1935–1945

Hitler at no time seems to have envisioned immediate, decisive military victories in France and Soviet Russia. Manstein's dictum that military victory paves the way to achieving political and economic goals of a war seems to have been lost on Hitler. Yet Hitler was as aware of the importance of military victory as anyone; after all, he made the strategic decision to go to war. In France and in the opening phases of Barbarossa in Russia, he nevertheless made operational military decisions that betrayed a fearful compulsion to avoid decisive military encounters. His compulsive decision on 17 May 1940 to halt Guderian at Marle and Dercy and abort the grand concept of the French campaign (to encircle and annihilate the Allied forces in Belgium) shows an almost inexplicable fright at his own temerity.[13] Unlike his later decision to halt the German forces outside Dunkirk (but on the English Channel), the earlier decision to halt at Marle and Dercy (short of the English Channel) would have allowed the Allied forces to escape by land out of Belgium. Successful withdrawal of these forces into northern France would have presented the Allies with the strong possibility of blocking further German advances and held the German field armies to a stalemate.

Halting Guderian on 17 May, Hitler showed such great fear of further advances that he was willing to throw away an impending military victory. What are the possible explanations for such behavior by the supreme commander? He may have felt that real danger threatened the advancing forces, requiring adjustment and a shift to the defensive—essentially a halt to meet and overcome the perceived threat. He may also have sensed that if the attack continued at the same pace, he would have faced a crisis in the campaign in which certain victory or severe defeat would be realized—a juncture he was unwilling to face. At a higher level of generalization, he must have felt that he had blundered into the attrition-style, conventional war he had hoped to avoid by propaganda undermining the opposition's will to resist and lightning motorized attack against states where propaganda and occupation would not succeed. Hitler faced a nightmarish situation on 3 September 1939—a potentially long war with two major powers—one in which he had been saved from immediate disaster only by the opportunistic brilliance of his liaison with the Soviet government in the summer of 1939. The situation thrust Hitler into the realization that Germany now lay gripped in siege lines manned by the armies and navies of two great powers.

Hitler probably saw that the utility of motorized forces had been expended in the quick unopposed moves into the Rhineland, Austria, Czechoslovakia (1938 and 1939), and in the west Germany would face armies and a warfare style he had seen in the First World War. He might have seen armored forces as useful only in special cases where surprise could be achieved and thereafter be of no particular advantage as Germany's enemies developed similar forces. Hitler expressed similar thoughts in his pronouncement after Operation Mercury (a parachute attack on Crete, May 1941) that parachute forces would no longer be used by Germany because the element of surprise so important to their success had been expended by 1941 and similar victories could no longer be expected.[14] After 1941 the Germans had little opportunity to employ parachute troops. One must suspect, however, that Hitler had decided that parachute troops no longer offered substantial chances of success, and he would not allow their employment in large numbers in future operations. The Germans went on to achieve substantial, even dramatic success with parachute troops, but in an eclectic way, supporting a generalization that Hitler had lost faith in large-scale landings.

Hitler's extraordinary and deeply revealing comment to Heinz Guderian after a demonstration of motorized troops in 1935— "That's what I need; that's what I want to have"[15]—shows him seizing brilliantly on motorized troops to achieve the rapid successes he saw possible through propaganda, psychology, and dramatic moves of motorized forces into one unresisted fait accompli after another. He lost the initiative in continuing the *Blitzaussenpolitik* of 1936–1939 (Rhineland through Poland) when the British and French governments challenged him in a general preventive war over the localized issue of German demands for change in Poland. In what was essentially an abrupt transition from *Blitzaussen-politik* to war against Poland, Britain, and France, he plunged through miscalculation into an entirely different situation from the earlier, fluid, peacetime, political scene. Overnight he was at war with two major European powers, for whom he and the German armed forces had enormous respect from the recent Great War. The propaganda-conditioned moves of the German army, led by modest but psychologically impressive motorized forces in the "flower wars" of the 1930s, were decisively terminated on 3 September 1939.

In the new circumstances, and diametrically opposed to the existing interpretation, in which Hitler is credited with continuing *Blitzaussenpolitik* into blitzkrieg, he perceived Germany under siege and reacted not with a blitz mentality but rather a siege mentality. The revised interpretation accepts and explains Hitler's contradictory, self-defeating decisions of 1939–1941 more naturally and convincingly than the often strained and inadequate current interpretation. That the Germans won quickly and decisively in Poland, Norway, France, the Balkans, and in the opening stages of Barbarossa was a result of the extraordinary battle-winning capabilities of the German army and its leaders' style in translating

Hitler's missions into grand operational concepts leading to great battles of decision in each campaign. Hitler had virtually no share in the military planning of the Polish campaign and less influence on the military maneuvers that resulted in the defeat of the Polish army. Hitler directed the army to attack and finish off Poland as quickly as possible, but it is highly unlikely that he imagined the speed with which the army would accomplish its general mission and just as unlikely that he understood the quick collapse of Poland.

Revising Hitler: the Concept of Siege Führer

Faced suddenly on 3 September 1939 with an unwanted European war, Hitler is seen as lacking confidence in the German motorized forces against major powers. Largely interested in the motorized force for its political effects, Hitler had no real sense of the *military* possibilities of panzer divisions with long-range missions, capable of winning wars quickly. Hitler began to maneuver on 3 September 1939 with a siege mentality, stemming from respect for the toughness and competence of the French and British armies and little comprehension of the possibilities of the relatively small German motorized force. The same conservatively or timidly oriented military outlook explains several hitherto inexplicable decisions of Hitler that seem almost purposely self-defeating in the current interpretation of planned blitz campaigns. Strong evidence supports the view that in preparing and executing the French and Russian campaigns, Hitler made decisions that prove his conscious acceptance that Germany had little chance of winning a quick military victory in Europe. Rather, he was saddled with enduring (after 3 September 1939) a long siege in which securing several fundamental economic targets would bring about eventual German victory and survival.

What decisions did Hitler make that remain largely inexplicable in the existing interpretation of purposeful, optimistic and decisive blitzkrieg on his part? Ordering a halt to the further movement of German panzer forces toward the channel on 17 May 1940, he showed that he was satisfied to accept the defeat of the Allied forces in Belgium, demanding neither their destruction nor the associated immediate conquest of France. With impressive consistency, several days later he halted the German panzer forces on the channel coast outside (southwest) of Dunkirk, showing he was satisfied with an incomplete victory. His reason for the halt—the ground outside of Dunkirk was unsuitable for tank operations—is plausible for a man who ordered an attack by the German army and air force against Belgium with the limited mission of preventing the Allies from seizing it and, incidentally, to conduct the war more effectively by sea and air against Britain.

Hitler saw the Manstein plan not as a decision against France but as a more certain means of taking Belgium. He was more concerned with securing Belgium than smashing the Allied armies in it. With that perspective, he would have been in no particular hurry to destroy the Allied armies there because they were cut off from France, and in a pocket that could be reduced safely with air and artillery bombardment and cautious infantry attack. Hitler can be assumed deeply concerned about a prestige-damaging setback of the panzer force in marginal tank country on lines around strong Allied forces tightly pressed against the Belgian coast. In short, with a siege mentality after the British and French declarations of war, he was primarily concerned with the occupation of Belgium. This would enable Germany to withstand an encirclement, provide as much protection as possible for the Ruhr, and assure supplies of iron ore from Sweden and oil from Romania. To explain adequately the initial *Fall Gelb*, the eventual Manstein plan, the decisions to halt at Marle, Dercy, and Dunkirk, and the planned offensive into the fortified zone in northeastern France, Hitler was concerned not with the blitz conquest of France but with the limited goals of seizing Belgium and the iron ore of Lorraine. Once those goals were assured, he was not averse to a further advance into France.

Hitler's apparent disregard of time, so important in blitzkrieg—the senseless halts at Marle and Dercy, Dunkirk, and later Smolensk—are explained by a mentality compulsively driven by the need to improve Germany's economic position against siege. That he could have had the buffer of Belgium and the iron ore and industry of Alsace and Lorraine by a blitz offensive aimed at destroying the Allied armed forces does not seem to have entered his mind. Similarly, in the Russian campaign, the point that he could have had Leningrad, the Ukraine, and the Crimea more or less automatically with the defeat of the Soviet armed forces does not seem to have been part of his outlook.

In planning for the Russian campaign, Hitler emphasized that the campaign made sense only if the Soviet state could be quickly overthrown in a single campaign. The German army high command planned to destroy the main concentration of Soviet armed forces enroute to the strategic terrain around Moscow. Hitler's words and the OKH's plan support the idea of an intended blitz culminating in the overwhelming defeat of Soviet Russia. Hitler's additional words in planning and his actions in the opening weeks of the campaign, however, run directly counter to any such decisive blitz picture. Hitler operated with a siege mentality, of which his military commanders were unaware while they planned a series of elegant blitz campaigns culminating in Barbarossa. Hitler did not envision the quick overthrow of the Soviet Union by defeating its armed forces and seizing space to bring about their defeat. From the beginning of planning, Hitler repeated the theme that the Russian campaign pivoted around the seizure of Leningrad, and he varied the theme only by adding additional economic targets, including the eastern Ukraine and the Crimea. The latter was an economic target, crucial in Hitler's mind to removing a Soviet air threat to the Romanian oil fields.

Among the most decisive evidence supporting Hitler's siege mentality are the words in the Barbarossa directive of 18 December 1941, which have been cited without challenge by four decades of professional and lay historical scrutiny: "The final objective of the operation is to erect a barrier against Asiatic Russia on the general line Volga-Archangel," essentially "a line from which the Russian air force can no longer attack German territory."[16] Commentators have used these words, penned under the "general intention" in the Barbarossa directive, to support their view that Hitler unrealistically overestimated the possibilities of a blitz in Russia. What the words show is Hitler's astoundingly conservative cast of mind, pivoting around a Germany-under-siege mentality. Assigning a territorial goal for the German armies to prevent an intact Russian air force from attacking German territory does not fit the picture of either a blitz campaign or overthrow of the Soviet government. Although Hitler stated his intention "to crush Soviet Russia in a rapid campaign," his interpretation of those words is clearly limited to the occupation of territory (to the Volga) and acceptance of an intact Soviet air force and, one must assume, intact ground forces. The scene that emerges reflects a Germany with an immensely improved position from which to withstand a seige by British naval power in the Atlantic and Mediterranean, and Soviet ground and air forces along the Volga.

In a high-level conference on 29 November 1941, one hidden from political and military historians of the Second World War because it concerned tank production and antitank defense, (i.e., a limited technical area), Hitler expounded in great generalities on the course of the war. The comments were made when the Germans were close to Moscow and still on the offensive. They reveal an outlook one can characterize as concerned and cautious, representing siege thinking. Hitler, in his messianic style, said:

> The age of tanks may soon be over. For the fulfillment of our tasks, it is important for us to exploit the time in which armored units can still be employed as weapons of attack. If we accomplish our European missions our historical evolution can be successful. Then in the defense of our heritage, we will be able to take advantage of the triumph of defense over the tank to defend ourselves against all attackers.[17]

This statement was made when Moscow seemed about to fall. The Germans had seized the central and eastern Ukraine and largely encircled Leningrad. The statement is evidence that Hitler was prepared momentarily to shift to the defensive on the eastern front and exploit his perceived triumph of antitank weapons over tanks into a successful defense of Germany along siege lines deep into European Russia. In the transcript of the conference, Hitler ordered a shift in production toward antitank weapons and heavier tanks suited for defense. These words to high-level figures in the armed forces, government, and industry, including Brauchitsch, Keitel, Minister Dr. Fritz Todt, and Professor Dr. Ferdinand Porsche, connote a shift to the defensive to protect political and economic gains in the eastern campaign, which were seen as the goals of the attack. The objectives—seizure of several economic targets in western European Russia and the almost incidental advance to Moscow—and a shift to this resolve to "defend ourselves against all attackers" show Adolf Hitler as a siege Führer at the high point of the blitz phase of the Second World War. The role was almost perfectly suited to his deeply etched fanatical will. This interpretation explains the apparent aberrant decisions of 1939–1941 and links them with the stiff, inflexible conduct of the defensive phase of the war from late 1942 onward.

Chapter Fourteen

World War II: Barbarossa, the Hinge of Fate?

Point: "Coupled with the earlier Allied victories at Midway and in North Africa, Stalingrad prompted Churchill to observe: 'the hinge of fate has turned.'"

Forster, *Recent Europe: A Twentieth Century History*

Counterpoint: In 1941, the Germans did not launch an attack against the Soviet Union to lose; they launched the attack to win and to win immediately. The dominant thesis of this work (*Hitler's Panzers East*) is that they had the clear possibility in August 1941 of doing just that.

IN any war in which one side won and the other lost, there had to be a time interval during which the war turned to the disadvantage of the ultimate loser and after which he was locked into defeat. This chapter searches for that interval in the Second World War in Europe and discovers it in the summer of 1941. That brief time can be designated the turning point and is offered as an event demanding reevaluation of the European conflict.

Popular Identification of Turning Points of World War II in Europe

Among the turning points of the Second World War in Europe, the Stalingrad battle is the one that most agree was decisive.[1] Western military commentators and East European and Soviet Communists agree that Stalingrad "was not simply a big victory," but that it marked a turning point in the Second World War.[2] This consensus is not particularly useful because almost every battle of major dimensions pointed analysts toward a following different phase of the war. Few doubt that Stalingrad was a "big victory" and *a* turning point, but the great question is whether the battle was *the* turning point and hence a matter of unique concern in interpreting the war. Soviet historiography would have us believe that Stalingrad "marked a decisive turn of the tide in the whole Second World War."[3] Although most Western historians and commentators consider Alamein (October–November 1942)) and Stalingrad (November 1942) as the turning points in the war, if pressed to choose only one, they would probably select Stalingrad because of its greater dimensions and more direct consequences for Germany.[4]

There are other contenders for the turning point. Both Eastern and Western European writers have made strong cases for the Kursk battle (German Operation Citadel) as decisive in the Russian campaign, and probably also in the war in Europe.[5] Among the East Europeans, Soviet writers stress the importance of Kursk and create the impression that dualism has been forced on Soviet commentators because of the similar, obvious importance of Stalingrad and its reflected extravagant praise. Forced to take propaganda advantage of the victory at Stalingrad, the Soviets have been forced ever since to expand the dimensions of the victory to include the claim of turning point. Inundated by Soviet claims and assailed by the great but exaggerated dimensions of the victory,[6] most historical opinion in the West on the Second World War in Europe considers Stalingrad the turning point in the East. Noting the similar importance of El Alamein, which by chance was fought concurrently, the same Western interpreters have convinced themselves that the two battles were the hinge of fate in the war in Europe. However, Kursk could not easily be ignored as decisive in Europe because of the battle's dimensions.

Kursk as Contender for Turning Point in World War II in Europe

In the early postwar period, noting the Soviet emphasis on Kursk and other knowledgeable evidence on the war in the East, a few Western commentators pointed out that both Stalingrad and Kursk were important battles, and a shift in consensus developed. The shift, never completed, was toward Kursk as the more important of the two.[7] Stalingrad fails as the turning point in the east, however, because the Germans regained the strategic initiative in the aftermath of Generalfeldmarshall Eric von Manstein's post-Stalingrad counteroffensive, retaking Kharkov in March 1943, four months after the Soviet encirclement of Stalingrad. From the Kursk perspective, Stalingrad was a Soviet offensive from which the Germans recovered quickly. Only six weeks after the 6th Army capitulated (2 February 1943), the Germans had regained the initiative in the war in the east. Considering the Stalingrad battle from that perspective, it can hardly be claimed that it "marked a decisive turn of the tide in the whole Second World War."[8] It came months prior to Operation Citadel, a great German strategic offensive near Kursk in July 1943. When the Germans offensive at Kursk roughly handled but did not defeat the defending Soviet forces, the strategic initiative shifted finally to the Soviets. From that time on (July 1943), the Soviets generated uninterrupted offensives to the end of the war, and logic demands, at least if Stalingrad and Kursk are accepted as the crucial battles in the eastern campaign, that Kursk be the turning point.[9] The following points support that view and a reevaluation in favor of Kursk:

1. The centerpiece of the Stalingrad battle—the envelopment and destruction of the German 6th Army—pales in comparison to similar action against Soviet forces in Barbarossa. At Bialystok-Minsk (June 1941), Smolensk (July 1941), Kiev (September 1941), and Vyasma-Bryansk (October 1941), the Germans captured approximately 1,920,000 Russians, compared to 90,000 German prisoners at Stalingrad (November 1942–February 1943). Although extended Stalingrad operations resulted in 240,000 additional casualties in killed and evacuated wounded among the German troops in the pocket, the encirclements in Barbarossa caused similar immense additional casualties in killed and evacuated wounded among the Russians in the pockets and during unsuccessful attempts at breaking out. The Soviet prisoner bag at Stalingrad in 3.5 months is small compared to the brief "coordinated" series of encirclements in Barbarossa in 3.6 months.

2. The Soviets expanded their operations at Stalingrad to include additional offensives designed to collapse the German fronts in the Caucasus (south of Stalingrad) and along the Don River to Voronezh (north of Stalingrad). The great Soviet strategic offensive, however, overextended itself and was collapsed by the Manstein counterstroke of March 1943, which forced the Soviets to assume the defensive in the war in the East.

3. Only after Kursk did the Soviets seize the strategic offensive, and then largely because of German exhaustion resulting from the failure of Operation Citadel, rather than the earlier disaster at Stalingrad.

These arguments suggest then that if the turning point in the Russian campaign were dependent on utility, it would be the Kursk battle. However, the turning point in the war in Europe is uncertain because of the difficulty in measuring the contribution of the eastern front to the entire war. Athenian-style Western allies—especially Britain and, after December 1941, the United States—were conducting massive sea and air operations against the Axis powers in the Atlantic, Mediterranean, and in the skies over Germany. Notwithstanding the penchant of the great naval powers for a strategy of indirect approach, the Western war effort— sea, air, and land—was concentrated in 1941 and 1942 on the land campaign in the Libyan and Egyptian coastal regions. The unanswered question of the turning point of the conflict in Europe and its application to reinterpretation of the war is: What is the relationship between El Alamein (October–November 1942) on the one hand and Stalingrad (November 1942) and Kursk (July 1943) on the other?

Since the El Alamein and Stalingrad battles were virtually concurrent, it is tempting to accept most of the existing interpretation and consider Alamein and Stalingrad as a joint turning point in the war. Despite the convenience of this interpretation in mollifying both Western and Eastern war analysts, Stalingrad does not meet reasonable criteria even as the turning point in the Russian campaign, let alone the entire war. Eliminating Stalingrad from contention, one must relate Alamein to Kursk and then reach a decision on which was the turning point or whether the two must be considered joint turning points.

Sorting Out Alamein, Stalingrad, and Kursk

Just what is the value of pitting El Alamein against Kursk and considering the somewhat academic issue of the turning point of the war in Europe? Almost immediately a competition can be seen to exist between West and East on the issue of whether the Soviet victory at Kursk was more important than the Western triumph at Alamein. A natural competition is brought out by the question, and it is surprising that little argument has taken place over this issue. Soviet historiography has presented the greater importance of Kursk (and Stalingrad), while Western historians assigned equal importance to Alamein, Stalingrad, and Kursk. It is difficult to assign equal importance to battles so different in background and circumstance as Alamein and Kursk. Perhaps it is possible that Alamein was the turning point from the view of the Western Allies in the war against Germany, and Kursk the turning point from the view of the Soviet Union.

Such an interpretation, associated with an era of propaganda, peace, pacifism, and conservation, blurs the picture that might be more usefully painted of the turning point in the war. Most strategies depend on battle—land battle—for their final success. The Western Allies would have preferred to maneuver the Germans into surrender by blockade, aerial bombardment, and accumulating pressures—anything to avoid decisive major ground engagements with them. They were forced, however, to fight great decisive ground engagements by the logic of war pieced together by the great nineteenth-century philosopher of war, Carl von Clausewitz.

If the war in Europe can be viewed as a coherent whole dominated by several concurrent ground campaigns, it is easier to judge the turning point. Considering the Mediterranean and English Channel as western geographical areas of operation, the antitank ditches of the channel and Mediterranean and the south Alpine remoteness of Italy presented special defensive strengths to the Germans. The Germans could collapse with relative impunity in North Africa as they could not in the central Ukraine, a scant 375 miles from the 1941 Russo-German boundary. If the Second World War in Europe were looked at as a coherent whole, the Kursk battle would earn the palm as the turning point in the war, a conclusion within the traditional framework of interpreting the war—as it were, on the basis of the Newtonian historical physics of Alamein, Stalingrad, and Kursk.

Rejecting Alamein, Stalingrad, and Kursk as the Turning Point of the War in Europe

When commentators apply the modest rigor of defining turning point in practical fashion, problems develop with the above picture. They face even greater problems if they research the Russian campaign because it is apparent the Germans had a strong possibility of winning the Russian campaign in the first weeks of the fighting in 1941, when they were strongest. After all, the Germans did not launch an attack against the Soviet Union to lose; they launched the attack to win and win fast. It is my thesis that they were clearly succeeding on 22 June 1941. Looking back, it is difficult to acknowledge the high probability of German victory, largely because it is necessary to march back through a series of German defeats. The events, however, did not take place retrospectively. They began in the summer of 1941 with a German offensive of unprecedented magnitude and a set of psychological and physical interactions between the German and Soviet armed forces in which the Germans dominated.

As Barbarossa unfolded, the war in Europe was ready for the turning point. To define the narrow window in which a war turns finally to the advantage of the eventual winner has a ring of the platonic to it. It suggests, indeed demands, that the war ideally have a single turning point. The concepts of time and physical and psychological circumstance are important in that definition. There is a special time in every war for the attacker to win, after which his failure to do so swings the war into a new phase to his detriment. That is especially true of the blitzkrieg attacker. The Germans combined operational boldness and initiative uneasily with thinness and inefficiency in war production, paucity of productive resources, and subjection to strategic maritime blockade. They could not fight a long war with reasonable prospects of success.

It can be generalized that the Germans entered the Second World War with a significant chance of victory, which increased with the blitz victories in 1939–1941 and the great "offensive-defensive"[10] achievements of Erwin Rommel in North Africa in 1941, and which neared certainty during the opening stages of Barbarossa. The near-certain German victory rests on the contention that continuing the German attack toward Moscow in early August 1941 would have led to its seizure the same month, defeat of the Soviet armies defending it, and control over additional territory, causing the political collapse of the Soviet Union. This revises the present consensus, in which numerous turning points are noted—Dunkirk, the battle of Britain, Moscow (December 1941), Stalingrad, Kursk, and the battle of the Atlantic. The conventional view suggests a war in which the Germans muddled about until a grand coalition eventually collected itself and trounced them. It pictures the Germans as gradually worn down after a series of largely meaningless early victories, only incidental actions prior to an Allied wartime effort preordained to win. The implication of certainty in the Allied victory is based on the attrition style of coalition members and the demonstrable lack of German war production and resources.

The Summer of Barbarossa

Such a view of the Second World War may seem reasonable, having been repeated by so many, so often, from so different ideological directions, from Western democratic to communist authoritarian. Recreating the Second World War, historians dismiss the logic and realism of the period of German victories, treating them as an interesting prelude but one that led nevertheless to German defeat. If, however, Operation Barbarossa were the juncture in the war at which it could be shown that the Germans were clearly capable of winning, then the preceding German victories must have contributed substantially to the possibility of success. The German victories lead toward Barbarossa, and each increased the probability that, in the finely drawn German style in war as operational battles (instead of logistics enterprises), Barbarossa would succeed and bring victory. The German victories in the Second World War have meaning only as they relate to Barbarossa and contributed to the German capability for victory in that operation.

Reinterpreting World War II as suggested by this study, one can diagram historically the early German victories, Barbarossa, and the aftermath (using a bit of mathematics), as in Chart 1. The probabilities of German victory in the war, shown on the time line, are general approximations of realistic historical possibilities (as opposed to technical mathematical probabilities with confidence levels) for both sides in World War II. The diagram indicates that the Germans had a significant possibility of winning a Europe-wide war from the beginning. It also shows that each successful German campaign increased the possibility of German victory up to Operation Barbarossa because the Germans held the initiative and fought battles largely of their own choosing. The diagrammed interpretation is most challenging to the conventional wisdom at the extreme interval of change, where the possibilities of German success veer from almost certain victory (about 31 July 41) to near-certain defeat (about 31 August 41). During this time, Hitler's dilatory orders strayed from the army strategic concept to smash immediately the Soviet armies defending Moscow and move into the Moscow-

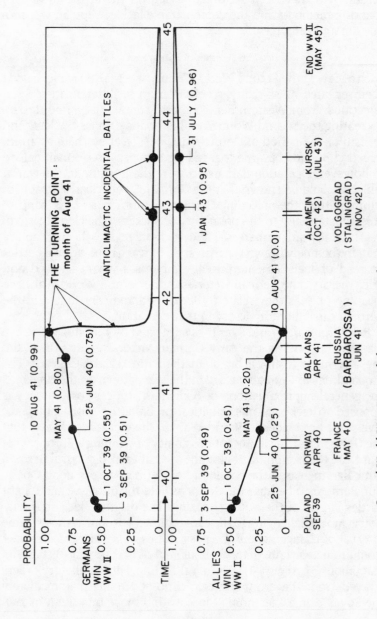

Second World War: Essential characteristics and turning point.

Gorki space. He missed the golden opportunity to defeat the Soviets quickly and shifted the entire war into one of attrition, logistics, and production.

It might be argued that this historical reanalysis concentrates too much on the ground warfare of the great German offensives of 1939–1941 (excepting the amphibious operation in Norway) and does not address air and naval strategy. The argument is important but not germane to the German offensives. With almost complete initiative in the war, the Germans could impose on adversaries their style of warfare—short, decisive ground battles with powerful tank and infantry armies supported by a strong tactical air force. German initiative and success in ground and tactical air operations from 1939 to 1941 negated at least two potential Allied trumps, strategic air operations (and strategy) and naval operations (and strategy). Once the Germans faltered in Barbarossa's ground and tactical air operations, Western strategic air and naval operations and several ground campaigns would become roughly as important as Soviet ground operations in the eventual defeat of Germany.

Ground Versus Naval and Air Strategies for Germany

Without adducing convincing arguments, historians emphasize the lack of German strategic air and naval power, noting opportunities missed by the Germans in the battle of Britain (1940), the Mediterranean area in late 1940 and 1941, and even in the Russian campaign. They aver that a strong German strategic air force and suitable strategy would have given the Germans a better chance of defeating Britain after June 1940. Similarly, they argue that the same hypothetical strategic air force might have been crucial in the defeat of the Soviet Union in 1941. That argument is strained, however, because the tactical air force that the Germans built from 1933 to 1941 could support the German field armies in the battles of 1939–1941, with little strength left for strategic missions and with inappropriate aircraft. Given the limited German economic resources on balance with those of the potential enemy states, the Germans could choose either an effective tactical air force or a strategic air force, not both. The Germans debated the issue in the 1930s and, probably correctly, developed an air force designed for operational support of great offensives launched by ground forces. It is also doubtful, considering the characteristics of conventional strategic air attack as long-range bombardment, that the British would have been seriously hurt by German aircraft that might have been produced had they pursued the strategic air option between 1933 and 1940. It was extremely doubtful against a large, more primitive ground opponent like the Russians.

Historians also note that the Germans failed to develop an effective maritime strategy, claiming they missed opportunities for greater success politically and militarily in the period of 1898–1945. Historians criticize the German governments in 1898–1914 for developing a strong navy rather than seeking Britain as a diplomatic ally, using its navy to defend Germany against the Franco-Russian coalition arising from the military convention of 1894. The same historians note the German lack of awareness of the significance of navies in modern wars and the possibilities of an effective naval strategy. The Germans can indeed be criticized for not pursuing an alliance with the British, but few countries have reacted with more intransigence to the expansion of influence of another state than the British during the same period.[11]

The Germans can be faulted for not pursuing a more effective diplomatic and naval strategy toward the United States in the First World War, appearing inept in their decision to pursue unrestricted submarine warfare in 1917. Still, the same Germans defeated the British tactically in the last major surface navy gun engagement on the final day of May 1916 off Jutland and had come dangerously close to defeating them through submarine warfare by April 1917.

Under revolutionary and postrevolutionary republican governments in the interwar period (1918–1933), the Germans were largely paralyzed by the Treaty of Versailles in developing surface ships and submarines. With Hitler in power in 1933, they began to slowly catch up in naval armaments, although they managed a striking diplomatic victory—signing the Anglo-German Naval Treaty of June 1935. This allowed them to build a surface fleet up to 35 percent of the size (tonnage) of the British and 100 percent of the number of submarines. Between the advent of Hitler and the outbreak of the war, the Germans produced only a modest-sized surface and submarine fleet because of the even greater necessity to produce ground weapons and tactical aircraft in the recovery from the disarmament controls of the Versailles treaty.

Forced to choose between a large navy or a large army, the Germans chose the army—and the continental strategy for its employment. Geographical factors and resource limitations forced the choice, and as long as they held the initiative they could force their ground strategy on opponents and reduce the effects of sea power and strategic air attack. Once German ground offensives had seized the space and resources of the two great land powers of Europe— France and the Soviet Union—they would be in position to reduce the effects of naval blockade and long-range air bombardment to manageable proportions. Possessing the resources of the continent, the Germans could have ignored the British, perhaps using a formula similar to Leon Trotsky's "no war, no peace." Unlike the Bolsheviks, the Germans would be dealing from strength and would have had the initiative to pursue such a policy.

My arguments support a view that the German ground strategy, supplemented by the successful invasion of Denmark and Norway and the alliance with the Italians in the Mediterranean, was sound. The central position of Germany in continental Europe provided the opportunity to take over the resources and space of Europe from the Atlantic Ocean to the area east of Moscow. Possessing this space, with or without Britain, Germany could have negated the maritime blockade associated with naval strategy because it would not depend on overseas imports. It is also hard to resist the conclusion that a viable British strategic air offensive would have been improbable based on the limited space available to them, and it would have been natural for the Germans to adopt such a strategy themselves after smashing the French and Soviet ground forces.

The Germans' Style Made Them Independent of the Usual Attrition Logic

The Germans' fighting style made them independent of the usual attrition logic that numbers and productive capacity predominate in war. Commentators and historians, overwhelmed by the coalition victory in the war, have failed to discern many lessons from military operations that marched to a drumbeat different from that of the Allies. From the beginning of the Polish campaign, historians and commentators of the former Allies have dominated the interpretation of events, largely ignoring Poland based on their contention that German numbers and productive capacity ensured a German victory. In a cautious war and with little regard to time, that attrition logic is faultless. The Germans deemed it necessary, however, to end the war as quickly as possible and use a bold attack to achieve the immediate victory. The superior German economic production and output of war materiel could not be applied to winning the campaign in the little time demanded by the Germans. In Poland, and ultimately also in Norway, France, the Balkans, and the Soviet Union, the opening battle was everything. The Germans were clearly unprepared for the war in 1942–1945, when they were finally defeated, but they won the opening battles in Poland, Norway, France, the Balkans, and the Soviet Union in 1939–1941. They suffered almost negligible losses, measured by the results achieved on the brink of victory in August 1941.

Although these generalizations can be argued further, they suggest a lesson of the Second World War in Europe: Being capable of winning battles may be more important than being prepared for winning wars. It would be ideal, of course, to have both these factors in hand to assure a successful defense policy. In striking disregard of the ideal situation, the Germans produced among their trump weapons only 1,368 armored vehicles and 10,371 military aircraft in all of 1940.[12] This effort is feeble compared with British production alone in 1940, which amounted to 1,232 tanks and 15,049 military aircraft;[13] and German capabilities later, in the defensive stages of an attrition-style defensive war against the Allies, in which German production amounted in 1944 to 19,326 armored vehicles and approximately 40,000 military aircraft.[14] The Germans won the opening battles in Poland, Norway, France, and the Balkans so decisively, however, that what should have been (by Allied logic) lengthier campaigns proved not even to be campaigns. The Germans won the opening battles so decisively that the campaigns never separated from their opening stages. In effect, the Germans won the war from 1939 to 1941 not by winning campaigns but by winning the openings of campaigns; not by producing weapons and ponderous logistical gather-strokes but by winning battles.

The German fighting style in the Second World War can be characterized as battle-winning rather than war-fighting. It evolved from the sensitive multifront strategic calculus, in which Brandenburg, Prussia, and then Germany found themselves for a quarter of a millennium. The ultradecisive, mission-oriented style of the technically skilled German army of 1939–1941 combined with the political leadership of Adolf Hitler to produce astounding results. Hitler contributed much to the synthesis, but his role in the successes of 1939–1941 has not been weighed accurately because of elements of misunderstanding on the European war—the Newtonian historical physics still fastened on the period. This book provides a unified field of explanation in which Hitler intended circumscribed campaigns during 1939–1941 designed to improve the siege position of Germany during a lengthy encirclement. The subtlety that has eluded us in the past is that the army conducted utterly decisive blitz campaigns, while Hitler, with no man comprehending his motives, conducted utterly circumscribed siege operations. Dominated by concern over the flawed resources situation of Germany at war with varying combinations of Britain, France, and the Soviet Union, he pressed the army at a dizzying pace into campaigns mistakenly seen as blitz oriented but designed by Hitler to expand the siege lines around Germany to acceptable proportions. This outlook links the German victories of 1939–1941 with the half-victories and defeats of 1942–1945 and transforms previously inexplicable event and strained interpretation into credible new shapes. Most important for the reality and lesson of World War II, the new outlook shows that German blitz operations in summer 1941 must now be considered to have given Germany an overwhelming probability of victory over the Soviet Union and resultant triumph in the Second World War in Europe.

Notes

Chapter One

1. Even in defeat, the Germans have gained the reputation of superiority in military operations in the First and Second World Wars. See, for example, Hart, *German Generals Talk*, p. 300; Dupuy, *A Genius for War*, p. 257; and Creveld, *Fighting Power*.
2. See, for example, Dornberg, *Munich 1923*, pp. 248–315; Richard Hanser, *Putsch!*, pp. 345–65, for the dangers; and Fest, *Hitler*, pp. 221–37, for the disruption of the party.
3. See the particularly emphatic comments in Helmuth Greiner, Operation Barbarossa (c. 1947), pp. 4,5. U.S. Army, European Command, Historical Division, MS C-065i.
4. See Waite, *Psychopathic God*, p. xi.
5. Observe the operative psychology in Schmidt, *Hitler's Interpreter*, pp. 153, 154, in which the author quotes Hitler: "I needed an alibi . . . with the German people to show them that I had done everything to maintain peace. That explains my generous offer of the Danzig and Corridor questions."
6. Particularly from 1929 to 1939, Göring was probably right when he is quoted in Manvell and Fraenkel, *Goering*, p. 353, as saying, "I want to emphasize in all important political questions I was, of course, included." Once the war began, however, it is accurate to generalize that Göring was eclipsed as an influence over Hitler and that "even to Göring it must have become clear in the war that his influence had diminished to the vanishing point." See in Bweley, *Hermann Göring*, p. 387.
7. Warlimont, *Inside Hitler's Headquarters*, pp. 115–17. See also Manstein, *Lost Victories*, p. 165.
8. See, for example, Fest, *Hitler*, p. 600.
9. See especially Maser, *Hitler*, pp. 210, 212, 213.

Chapter Two

1. *XXXXVII. Panzer Korps, Kriegstagebuch Nr. 2. Anlagen Nr. 1–100, 20.5–27.6. 1941*, 13468/1, Bundesarchiv Militärarchiv, Freiburg, FRG.
2. See the succinct discussion of daring and boldness in Ziemke, *German Northern Theatre*, pp. 109, 110.
3. *The German Campaign in Russia, Planning and Operations (1940–1942)* (Washington, D.C.: U.S. Government Printing Office, 1955), p. 4.
4. Generalmajor Peter von der Groeben, interview Celle-Boye, FRG, 24 January 1980. Commenting retrospectively, Groeben noted, "We did not believe in the success of the war."
5. See in *Der Oberbefehlshaber des Heeres, Gen. St. d. H. Op. Abt. (Ia) . . . H.Qu. O.K.H., den 8.3.1941*, U.S. National Archives, Records German Field Commands, Army Corps, Microcopy T-314, Roll 1389, Frs. 000087–000089, which contains OKH directions for training for the war in the east. The directions list virtually every situation that the Germans met and show an almost uncanny grasp of the challenges of a war in Soviet Russia.

6. See, for example, *Anlage 5c zu OKH Gen. St. d. H. Op. Abt. Nr. 050/41 a. Kdos. (Chefsache), Weisung für den Einsatz der Flakverbande*, U.S. National Archives, Records German Army High Command, Microcopy T-78, Roll 335, Fr. 6291343, in which OKH states, "In contrast to the Polish and Western campaigns . . . heavy air attacks must be expected against troops."

7. Halder, *Diaries*, vol. 6, p. 34. Entry of 24 March 1941.

8. Halder, *Diaries*, vol. 6, p. 9. Entry of 27 February 1941.

9. One must be struck by the realism of Halder in comments such as, "The imposing vastness of the spaces in which our troops are now assembling cannot fail to strike a deep impression . . . all the work of decades that was undertaken to train the division commanders for independent leadership must pay dividends here." See Halder, *Diaries*, vol. 6, p. 147.

10. Guderian, *Achtung Panzer!* p. 148.

11. See *Questions Asked General Guderian and Answers Given by General Guderian* (Steinlager Allendorf, 16 December, 1946), p. 1, U.S. Army, European Command, Historical Division, MS B-271. Guderian notes, "[He] reckoned on 17–20,000. But Hitler and the Supreme Command of the *Wehrmacht* did not believe it."

12. Generalmajor Rudolf Loytved-Hardegq, interview, Nürnberg, FRG, 18 January 1980.

13. *OKW Operations Staff, Section L, War Diary, 9 January 1941*, as cited in Warlimont, *Inside Hitler's Headquarters*, p. 140.

14. See for example, *Combat in the East, Experiences of German Tactical and Logistical Units in Russia* (1952), p. 58, U.S. Army, European Command, Historical Division, MS B-266. The comment is made: "The only possible solution for this catastrophe—and this is the proper term for it—[would have] consisted of having strong details equipped with heavy cross country tractors tow the columns from the mud by working day and night."

15. Halder assigned Generalmajor Erich Marcks the job of putting together the army plan of attack on the Soviet Union and Marcks's plan served as the basis for army thinking from that point forward (5 August 1940). Prior to assigning Marcks the job, Halder had worked out the possibilities for an advance in the east and had passed on those ideas to his planner. Halder also represented complete continuity in the planning for Barbarossa, making it most reasonable to generalize about the army plan as being that of Halder. See also Halder, *Diaries*, vol. 4, pp. 132, 146, entries for 26 July and 1 August 1940, respectively.

16. See, for example, Greiner, *Operation Barbarossa*, pp. 43–51, U.S. Army, European Command, MS 065-i.

17. See Franz Halder, *Decisions Affecting the Campaign in Russia (1941–1942)* (September 1949), p. 1, U.S. Army, European Command, Historical Division, MS C-067a.

Chapter Three

1. As quoted in English in Manstein, *Lost Victories*, p. 97. See also the similar wording in Trevor-Roper, *Blitzkrieg to Defeat*, p. 13, for the OKW directive.

2. The chief of staff of German Army Group A in the west, Generalmajor Erich von Manstein, notes this point with deadly precision and concern, leading to a revised plan for the offensive in the west. See Manstein, *Lost Victories*, p. 99, where he states: "*The 1939 operational plan . . . contained no clear cut intention of fighting the campaign to a victorious conclusion. Its object was quite clearly partial victory* [italics in original]."

3. See Hitler's comments in Halder, *Diaries*, vol. 2, p. 23, entry for 7 October 1939.

4. Hitler had good reason for being concerned about a preemptive allied move into Belgium and Holland. See International Military Tribunal, *Trial of the Major War Criminals*, vol. 41, pp. 126–30, which presents German translations of Allied documents that in turn show Allied planning in April–November 1939 for the potential occupation of Belgium and parts of the Netherlands.

5. See, for example, the comments in Warlimont, *Inside Hitler's Headquarters*, p. 138.

6. See the unelaborated comments in Halder, *Diaries*, vol. 2, p. 43, entry for 3 November 1939.

7. See, for example, the comments in Halder, *Diaries*, vol. 2, p. 18, entry for 29 September 1939: "Techniques of Polish campaign no recipe for the West. No good against a well-knit army."

8. See Jacobsen, *Fall Gelb*, pp. 32, 39ff.

9. Photostat copies of partially burned originals now in archives of the Historical Section of the Belgian army, Hoover Institution Archives, Stanford, California. The photostats show that the Belgians seized enough of the German operations order to have an accurate impression of the attack through Belgium. The Germans, of course, did not know the extent of the intact papers in the hands of the Belgians and could only assume that the plan was known to the Belgians and they had passed on the same information to the Western Allies. Recent historical research indicates that the latter assumption was false.

10. See Manstein, *Lost Victories*, pp. 121, 122, comments about 17–20 February 1940. See also the comments of the army chief of staff earlier in the month of February, which confirm the swing of OKH towards Manstein's ideas in Halder, *Diaries*, vol. 2, pp. 61–63.

11. Hitler still managed to interfere partially, particularly in the details of the surrender of Greece, but not in a way that threatened the swift completion of military operations. See, for example, Warlimont, *Inside Hitler's Headquarters*, pp. 128–31, and Halder, *Diaries*, vol. 6, pp. 36, 53, 64, for details of Hitler's interference.

12. Halder commented laconically that "rapid preparations based on skill and flexibility of general staff allow attack day morning of 6 April 41." See also Halder, *Diaries*, vol. 6, p. 52.

13. Geisler et al., *Unser Kampf auf dem Balkan*, p. 281. The number includes army, *Waffen SS*, and air force.

14. See in, Alfred Philippi and Ferdinand Heim. *Der Feldzug gegen Sowjetrussland*, p. 49, where late spring thaws are noted as delaying the opening of Barbarossa over and above the engagement in the Balkans.

Chapter Four

1. See Greiner, *Operation Barbarossa*, p. 51ff, U.S. Army, European Command, Historical Division, MS C-065i.

2. See, for example, Trevor-Roper, *Blitzkrieg to Defeat*, p. 49. See also Peter de Mendelssohn, *Die Nurnberger Dokumente*, pp. 318–22, for a complete picture of the Hitler directive, from which the above quote can also be extracted. Note finally *Oberkommando des Heeres, Gen. St. d. H. Op. Abt. (I), Nr. 050/41 q. Kdos., H.Qu/OKH, den 22 Januar 1941. Aufmarschanweisung Barbarossa*, U.S. National Archives, Records German Army High Command, Microcopy T-78, Roll 335, Fr. 6291211, in which is found the Army mission: "to overthrow Soviet Russia in a quick campaign."

3. Greiner, *Operation Barbarossa*, p. 52. See also the similar arguments in Warlimont, *Inside Hitler's Headquarters*, p. 138.

4. Trevor-Roper, *Hitler's War Directives*, p. 51.

5. See, for example, the details on the number of streams (forty-one total) to be crossed by Panzer Group 4 en route to the Dvina in *Anlage 11 zu Kdo. d. Pz. Gr. 4, Ia, Nr. 20/41 g. Kdos., Chefsache vom 2.5.1941*, U.S. National Archives, Records German Field Commands, Army Corps, Microcopy T-314, Roll 1389, Fr. 000166.

6. See *Kommando der Panzergruppe 4, Abt. Ia, 249/41 g. Kdos., Chefsache, den 14.6.1941. Befehl für den Einsatz des "Lehr-Regiment Brandenburg z.b.V. 800,"* U.S. National Archives, Records German Field Commands, Army Corps, Microcopy T-314, Roll 1389, Frs. 000131, 000152, in which Brandenburg special forces are attached to Panzer Group 4, 56th Panzer Corps, and specifically to the 8th Panzer Division.

7. Halder, *Diaries*, vol. 6, p. 174.

8. Guderian, *Panzer Leader*, p. 92.

9. Ibid.

10. Manstein, *Lost Victories*, p. 183.

11. See *Panzergruppe 4, Ia, 14.6.1941, Brandenburg*, U.S. National Archives, Records German Field Commands, Army Corps, T-314, Roll 1389, Fr. 000152, and *Der Kommandierende General, Gen. Kdo. LVI. A.K. (mot), Ia 46/47, g. K. . . . 4.6.41*, U.S. Archives, Records German Field Commands, Army Corps, Microcopy T-314, Roll 1389, Fr. 000162. In the latter source Manstein comments on the possible use of underwater battle tanks (prepared for the potential invasion of Britain) in a crossing of the Dvina River.

12. Manstein, *Lost Victories*, pp. 184, 185.

13. The Germans considered that the engagement took place from 24 to 26 June 1941, with the 41st Panzer Corps free to advance from 27 June onward. See in *Oberkommando 6. Pz. D., Ia*, U.S. National Archives, Records German Field Commands, Divisions, Microcopy T-315, Roll 326, Fr. 000049.

14. See, for example, the details in *Small Unit Actions during the German Campaign in Russia* (Washington, D.C.: Government Printing Office, 1953), pp. 76–84.

15. See in *K.T.B. Nr. 3 der 6. Schützen Brigade für die Zeit vom 21.6.41 bis 22.11.41*, U.S. National Archives, Records German Field Commands, Divisions, Microcopy T-315, Roll 322, Fr. 000865, and Chales de Beaulieu, *Der Vorstoss der Panzergruppe 4 auf Leningrad*, pp. 31–34.

16. See *Der Befehlshaber der Panzergruppe 4, Gr. H.Qu. den 1.7.41, an die Herren Kommandierenden Generals der XXXXI. und LVI. A.K.*, U.S. National Archives, Records German Field Commands, Army Corps, Microcopy T-314, Roll 1389, Fr. 000296.

17. Manstein, *Lost Victories*, p. 186.

18. The Rossenie tank battle was tough but brief. The 1st Panzer Division used 100 percent of its initial issue of 5-cm PAK (antitank) ammunition from 22 to 26 June 1941, most of it in that tank battle, but nevertheless "broke through" to Jakobstadt by 28 June 1941. See in *XXXXI. Pz. K. Munitions Bericht, 22.— 26.6.41*, U.S. National Archives, Records German Field Commands, Divisions, Microcopy T-315, Roll 326, Fr. 000193.

19. Gen. J. A. Graf von Kielmansegg, interview, Bad Krozingen, FRG, 19 January 1980.

20. Later, on 14 July 1941, north of Pskov and well on the way to Leningrad, these same forces would still have a reasonable chance for a quick breakthrough to that city.

21. See Chales de Beaulieu, *Der Vorstoss der Panzergruppe 4 auf Leningrad*, p. 30.

Chapter Five

1. See U.S. Army, *German Campaign Russia, 1940–1942*, p. 34, under "Changes in Plans (March–April 1942)."

2. See *Panzergruppe 1, Ic/AO an OKH Fremde Heer Ost, Abendmeldung, 3.7.41*, U.S. National Archives, Records German Field Commands, Panzer Armies, Microcopy T-313, Roll 9, Fr. 7235678, in which interrogation reports note that Soviet commissars since 1939 had been declaring in front of Polish road workers that the USSR would attack Germany when it was sufficiently weak in the west.

3. *Generalkommando XI. A.K., Ic, den 22.9.1941*, U.S. National Archives, Records German Field Commands Panzer Armies, Microcopy T-313, Roll 11, Frame 7237777.

4. Halder, *Diaries*, vol. 6, p. 209, entry for 7 July 1941.

5. Halder, *Diaries*, vol. 7, p. 6, entry for 1 August 1941, shows, for example, the Army Group South estimate of forty-one German infantry divisions versus twenty-nine Soviet rifle divisions.

6. There are notable exceptions to this generalization. See, for example, Luther, "German Armoured Operations," *Army Quarterly and Defence Journal* 108 (4).

7. Halder, *Diaries*, vol. 6, p. 220, entry for 10 July 1941.

Chapter Six

1. See Fedor von Bock, *Tagebuchnotizen Osten I (Oberbefehlshaber d. H. Gru. Mitte. Unterstellt: Pz. Gru. 2, Pz. Gru. 3, 4. Armee, 9. Armee), 22.6.1941 bis 5.1.42, Bundesarchiv, Militärarchiv, Freiburg, FRG, pp. 3, 7, 12.*

2. See Halder, *Diaries*, vol. 6, p. 183, entry for 28 June 1941. Halder notes after a midafternoon telephone conversa-tion with Keitel at OKW that he "again indicates that the Führer is worried . . . about the possibility that Army Group Center might strike too soon beyond the line Minsk-Bobruisk before the pocket is completely liquidated."

3. See Bock, *Tagebuchnotizen Osten I*, pp. 2, 3, entries for 23–25 June 1941, where the diarist comments, "The further forward movement of Panzer Group Hoth raised the burning question whether Hoth . . . should go into the region north of Minsk or immediately in the direction Witebsk-Polozk [i.e., on to Smolensk]."

4. See Halder, *Diaries*, vol. 6, p. 250.

5. See Bock, *Tagebuchnotizen Osten I*, p. 11, the entry for 2 July 1941, where he notes, "I must also say to [Hitler] that the setting out of the Panzer Groups is naturally from a flying start."

6. See, for example, Maser, *Hitler*, p. 210 and as suggested on p. 220.

7. The Germans took huge numbers of prisoners in the last hours of fighting around the pockets, for example: "The pocket west of Minsk is slowly burning out. Since yesterday morning 52,000 Russians have surrendered." Halder, *Diaries*, vol. 6, p. 201, entry for 5 July 1941.

8. See Bock, *Tagebuchnotizen Osten I*, pp. 12, 13.

9. See *Heeresgruppe Mitte*, Ic/A.O., H.Qu., U.S. National Archives, Records German Field Commands, Panzer Armies, Microcopy T-313, Roll 131, Fr. 7379183, in which German intelligence in Army Group Center notes for the benefit of the panzer army and groups under command that the Soviets instituted war commissars on 16 July 1941.

10. Bock, *Tagebuchnotizen Osten I*, p. 13. He notes: "A big day: the panzer groups continue the advance eastward. Guderian gets across the Beresina to Rogachev . . . Hoth on his left flank to the Dvina."

11. See Halder, *Diaries*, vol. 2, p. 23, entry for 7 October 1939. "Führer emphasizes: a) The Belgians will call the French to come to their aid. We must not wait for that. France will do that in the period of the autumn fogs; b) We must forestall this with an operation designed to gain a decision even if we fall short of the original objectives and attain only a line which would afford better protection of the Ruhr."

12. Halder, *Diaries*, vol. 2, p. 25, entry for 10 October 1939, in which Hitler in a memorandum read to OKH states, "Mobilize everything to the last and as quickly as possible" to extend the safety zone of the Ruhr in the west in the event of an enemy movement into Belgium.

13. Halder, *Diaries*, vol. 3, p. 115, entry for 8 March 1940. Halder was thinking in terms of an attack in force across the Meuse only after fourteen days into the campaign. The actual attack took place at a classical blitz pace on the afternoon of the fourth day of the offensive.

14. See Balck, *General der Panzertruppe*, p. 270, the authoritative opinion that Guderian "alone had believed in success," specifically in the capability of the panzer army to force an immediate crossing of the Meuse and defeat the Allied armies on the continent, "and had led a heavy battle against the whole world."

15. See, for example, Warlimont, *Inside Hitler's Headquarters*, p. 58, and, in a slightly different vein, Halder, *Diaries*, vol. 2, p. 43, entry for 3 November 1939. Halder noted that "none of the higher headquarters thinks that the offensive ordered by *OKW* has any prospects of success."

16. See Greiner, *Operation Barbarossa*, p. 59, where Greiner paraphrases Hitler as saying

in December 1941 that the most important task in Barbarossa is "the rapid cutting off of the Baltic area."

17. See Halder, *Diaries*, vol. 6, p. 172, entry for 25 June 1941, and the timidity revealed: "Later in the evening we receive a Führer order ... it betrays concern that we are already operating too deeply into the Soviet Union ... the same old refrain!"

18. See, for example, *Aufmarschweisung "Barbarossa," Heeresgruppe Mitte, den 12.3.1941,* U.S. National Archives, Records German Field Commands, Army Groups, Microcopy T-311, Roll 216, Fr. 000651, in which Bock unequivocally directs his forces into the space around Smolensk to destroy the enemy forces in White Russia "as the basis for the continuation of further operations in an eastward or northeastward direction," i.e., toward Moscow.

19. See Hoth, *Panzer-Operationen*, pp. 26, 27.

20. See the matter of fact and businesslike way in which the Germans began planning in Jacobsen, *Marcks*, p. 92, and Halder, *Diaries*, vol. 4, pp. 132–35, 145, 146, in which the German army develops a simple, decisive plan requiring boldness and dash in the advance but giving considerable chance of success.

21. See, for example, the introduction of *General der Infanterie Rudolph M. Hofmann: German Army War Games*, U.S. Army, European Command, Historical Division, MS P-094.

22. Halder, *Diaries*, vol. 6, p. 161, entry for Sunday, 22 June 1941.

23. See R. H. S. Stolfi et al., *German Disruption of Soviet Command: Control and Communications in Barbarossa, 1941* (Monterey, California: 1983), pp. 72–75, 79, 80.

24. As stated in an interview with Brigadegeneral Rudolf Loytved-Hardegg, Nürnberg, FRG, 18 January 1980.

25. An additional eighteen aircraft were destroyed in various accidents including especially malfunctioning of bomblet munitions upon landing after return from the combat sorties. See Stolfi et al., *German Disruption of Soviet Command*, p. 225, in which thirty-five German aircraft are noted as lost on the first day of the war. The authors estimate that approximately seventeen were lost to enemy action and eighteen to various accidents and misadventures, for example, explosions of fused and activated cluster bomblets.

26. As described in an interview with Generalmajor Peter von der Groeben, Celle-Boye, FRG, 24 January 1980. See also Fedor von Bock, *Tagebuch-Notizen, Band 4, 20.9.40–21.6.41,* p. 19, Hoover Institution Archives, in which Bock notes the game but gives little detail on the results and concerns.

27. See Bock, *Tagebuchnotizen Osten I,* p. 2.

28. Halder, *Diaries*, vol. 6, p. 164.

29. Halder, *Diaries*, vol. 6, p. 166.

30. Interview, Groeben, January 1980.

31. See Bock, *Tagebuch-Notizen,* vol. 4, pp. 18, 19, entry for 30 March 1941.

32. Ibid., p. 14, entry for 18 March 1940. Bock notes that "Hoth looked at the other side of the Dnieper and Duna from the first and considered the possibilities of only incidentally attacking and smashing the enemy standing farther forward [between Bialystok and Minsk]."

33. In the first three months of Barbarossa, approximately one-third of the fuel used by German army units came from supplies captured from the Soviets.

34. Hoover Archives, Bock, *Tagebuch-Notizen,* vol. 5, pp. 15, 18, 19.

35. *Oberkommando der 4. Panzer Armee, Abt. Ic, den 22.7.1941, Feindnachrichtenblatt No. 4,* U.S. National Archives, Records German Field commands, Panzer Armies, Microcopy T-313, Roll 131, Frame 7378916.

36. A Soviet mechanized brigade, also referred to in the literature as a motorized-mechanized brigade and sometimes as a tank brigade, was a powerful tank-heavy unit holding 160 battle tanks, 19 reconnaissance tanks, and 24 armored cars, that is, roughly as much armor as a German panzer division. See *O.K.H., Gen st d H,* U.S. Archives, Records of Headquarters German Army High Command, Microcopy T-78, Roll 335, Fr 6291307.

37. See the telling comments in Shtemenko, *Soviet General Staff*, pp. 378, 379, in which the author quotes Josef Stalin's great toast to the Russian people at the end of the Second World War. The toast reveals monumental anxiety on the part of Stalin over the issue of the loss of Soviet territory in 1941. The anxiety supports a view that he did not feel that his regime could survive the loss of Moscow.

38. German aerial photography of June and July 1941 tends to confirm the obvious. See in Halder, *Diaries*, vol. 6, pp. 251, 252. The entry for 17 July 1941 notes "photographs of Moscow, very extensive industrial installations with vast railways system. Strong AAA defenses . . . no fortifications." And, "With the elimination of Moscow the entire Russian communications network collapses."

39. *Oberkommando der 4. Panzer Armee, Abt. Ic, den 19.7.41*, U.S. National Archives, Records German Field Commands, Panzer Armies, Microcopy T-313, Roll 131, Fr. 7378936.

40. *Oberkommando der 4. Panzer Armee, Abt. Ic, den 22.7.41, Feindnachrichtenblatt Nr. 4*, U.S. National Archives, Records German Field Commands, Panzer Armies, Microcopy T-313, Fr. 7378916.

41. See, for example, *Gen. Kdo. LVII. A.K. (mot.) Ic, Tätigkeitsbericht, v. 22.6.–31.12.41*, 15683/20, Bundesarchiv Militärarchiv, Freiburg, FRG, p. 2, where the report notes: "Russian Oberleutnant says under interrogation . . . that the war comes as a complete surprise. In his unit no live cartridges had yet been handed out."

42. See, for example, *Pz. Gp. 3, K.T.B. Nr. 1, 22.6.41*, U.S. National Archives, Records German Field Commands, Panzer Armies, Microcopy T-313, Roll 225, Fr. 7488960. The 56th Infantry Regiment of the 5th Army Corps "despite battle, difficult terrain, and hot weather, completed a distance of 40km" in the fifteen hours and ten minutes from 0305 to 1815 on 22 June 1941. The corps was under control of Panzer Group 3 (Hoth) on that day northwest of Bialystok.

43. See, for example, *Pz.Gr. 3, Ic, Abendmeldung, 8.7.41.*, U.S. National Archives, Rec ords German Field Commands, Panzer Armies, Microcopy T-313, Roll 9, Fr. 7235690, in which "according to information from III. A K., 150 German soldiers from 25.1.D. (mot.) have been murdered in Russian captivity. Further reports lie in front of us in two other cases."

44. Manstein, *Lost Victories*, p. 180.

45. Ibid., p. 45.

46. See, for example, in Army Group South, *3. A.K., Ic, an Pz.Gr. 1, Ic, 1.7* [1941], 2250, U.S. National Archives, Records German Field Commands, Panzer Armies, Microcopy T-313, Roll 10, Fr. 7236715, in which the report reads, "German prisoners of I.R. 35 mishandled by Russians . . . other prisoners bestially murdered. Investigation to follow."

47. One must be struck by the use of knives in the killings and mutilations. See, for example, *Panzergruppe 1, Abt. Ic/AO, Abendmeldung, den 25.6.41*, U.S. National Archives, Records German Field Commands, Panzer Armies, Microcopy T-313, Roll 9, Fr. 7235663, which comments: "In front of III. A.K. eleven wounded German soldiers who had fallen into Russian hands in a counterattack were murdered by stab wounds in the back."

48. See, for example, *Pz. A.O.K. 2 (Pz. Gr. 2), Abt. Ia, Anl. k, K.T.B. Nr. 1 (l.Band), 1.7.41*. RH 21-2/V. 113, Bundesarchiv Militärarchiv, Freiburg, FRG, in which appears: "1) Enemy situation, . . . b) . . . The Russian . . . believes the principle drummed into him by his commissars that he will be shot if captured. This is the main reason why he will not allow himself to be captured."

49. *I. Bataillon, Schützen—Regiment 64, an III. Pz.K., Abt. Ic, 30.6/41, Subject. Discovery of the Mutilated Personnel*, U.S. National Archives, Records German Field Commands, Panzer Armies, Microcopy T-313, Roll 10, Fr. 7236663.

50. See, for example, *Fernschreiben, III. A.K. Ic, an Panzergruppe 1, Ic. Zwischenmeldung*, U.S. National Archives, Records German Field Commands, Panzer Armies, Microcopy T-313, Roll 10, Fr. 7236392, and *Inf. Regt. Grossdeutschland, Abt. Ic, Regt. Gefechtsstand,*

den 16. VII.41, . . . Meldungen, U.S. National Archives, Records German Field Commands, Panzer Armies, Microcopy T-313, Roll 131, Fr. 7379074.

51. See, for example, *A.O.K. 6, Ic, an Panzergruppe 1, Ic, 8.8.41, 0735, Intelligence Report*, U.S. National Archives, Records German Field Commands, Panzer Armies, Microcopy T-313, Roll 10, Fr. 7236483.

52. As noted, for example, in *III. A.K., Ic, an Panzergruppe 1, 9.7.41, 1430, Intelligence Report*, U.S. National Archives, Records German Field Commands, Panzer Armies, Microcopy T-313, Roll 10, Fr. 7236434.

53. Ibid.

54. See *Pz. A.O.K. 2 (Pz. Gr. 2), Abt. Ia, Anl. k, K.T.B. Nr.-(1. Band), 1.7.41, 24b: Vernehmung Generalmajor Jegorow*, RH 21-2/V.113, Bundesarchiv Militärarchiv, Freiburg, FRG, where the captured Russian general gives "as a reason for the panic and disintegration . . . the sealing off or flanking fires by German artillery and machine guns."

55. Russian troops were forced by their own officers and commissars to stay in the fight. See, for example, *Inf. Regt. Grossdeutschland, Abt.Ic . . . 18.VII.41*, U.S. National Archives, Records German Field Commands, Panzer Armies, Microcopy T-313, Roll 131, Fr. 7379079, in which the report notes, "Russian Infantry Regiment 130 compelled [by force of arms] to fight by one colonel, two majors, three commissars, and 10 other officers . . . according to prisoner statements."

56. See *Der Oberbefehlshaber der Heeresgruppe Mitte, H.Qu., 19.10.1941, Tagesbefehl*, U.S. National Archives, Records German Field Forces, Copy T-312, Roll 145, Fr. 7684400. The document is reproduced as part of the records of the German 4th Army.

57. As described in an interview with *Generalmajor* Eberhard Wagermann, Rheinbach, FRG, 18 January 1980.

58. Ibid.

59. Jurgens, *Meine Schwadron*, p. 28. Herbert Frisch wrote the piece above based on his combat on 20 July 1941 in the Horse Squadron, 26th Reconnaissance Battalion, 26th Infantry Division, 6th Corps, 9th Army, Army Group Center, near the little Russian village of Besenjata.

Chapter Seven

1. See Map 1, which shows the formidable space to be overcome by the Germans in the western campaign.

2. See Halder, *Diaries*, vol. 4, p. 9.

3. This generalization is based on Guderian's panzer corps' being backed in the second wave by the 16th Panzer Corps (Reinhardt) and 14th Motorized Infantry Corps (Wieterscheim), and thus his corps being associated with enough mass and mobility to comprise the *Schwerpunkt* force in the west. Just to the north, around Dinant on the Meuse, General der Panzertruppe Hermann Hoth skillfully led the 15th Panzer Corps in the 4th Army across the Meuse at approximately the same time as Guderian but without the decisive reinforcing mass.

4. See Halder, *Diaries*, vol. 4, p. 18: "Fuehrer Hq. sees it differently . . . [the Fuehrer] rages and screams that we are on the best way to ruin the whole campaign. . . . He won't have any part of continuing the operation in a westward direction."

5. See Halder, *Diaries*, vol. 6, p. 172, where he notes: "Later in the evening we receive a Fuehrer order on the direction of operations of Army Group Center. . . . It betrays concern that we are operating too far in depth. . . . The old refrain . . . "

Chapter Eight

1. The Germans used the colorful term "burning out" for the end of resistance in the *Kesseln*. See, for example, Halder, *Diaries*, vol. 6, p. 201.

2. Bock, *Tagebuchnotizen Osten I*, p. 12, entry for 2 July 1941.

3. See, Bock, *Tagebuchnotizen Osten I*, p. 12, where diarist notes on 2 July 1941, "By my way of thinking we had already waited too long."

4. Bock notes earlier on 8 July 1941 that Guderian had been forced to give up a bridgehead across the Dnieper at Rogachev, "voluntarily or involuntarily is not clear." See Bock, *Tagebuchnotizen Osten I*, p. 19. Note also *Geschichte der 3*, pp. 126–28.

5. See in *Geschichte der 3*, pp. 124, 125, where the division successfully crossed the Dnieper on 4 July 1941 but drew so much Soviet attention that it was never able to break out from this original bridgehead.

6. Bock, *Tagebuchnotizen Osten I*, p. 23, noted on 13 July 1941 that the one place on the eastern front where the Russians had been smashed was opposite Army Group Center and that the way to Moscow was open.

7. Halder, *Diaries*, vol. 6, p. 233.

8. See the estimate of Soviet strength submitted by Army Group Center in Halder, *Diaries*, vol. 6, p. 215, as supplemented for the estimated number of cavalry divisions from *Panzer Gruppe 4, Ic, Feindlage, 20.5.41*, U.S. National Archives, Records German Field Commands, Army Corps, Microcopy T-314, Roll 415, Fr. 8708963, which shows an estimated six Soviet cavalry divisions in White Russia on 20 May 1941.

9. Bock, *Tagebuchnotizen Osten I*, p. 14, notes that by 4 July 1941, "In front of 12th Panzer Division near Minsk 50,000 men had surrendered."

10. See *Heeresgruppe Mitte, Ic/A.O., H.Qu. den 15.7.41, Gefangene und Beute aus der Doppleschlacht von Bialystok und Minsk*, U.S. National Archives, Records German Field Commands, Panzer Armies, Copy T-313, Roll 131, Fr. 7378942.

11. See *General der Gebirgstruppen, a.D., Georg Ritter von Henzl, Corps von Henzel (20 Apr–6 May 45) (27.4.46)*, p. 10. U.S. Army, European Command, Historical Section, MS B-326. The author, recounting his experiences early in the Russian campaign, notes, "Enemy infantry advances primarily under accompanying armored protection, shoots its way in and practically never uses orthodox infantry tactics."

12. See *Generalkommando XII, A.K., Ia, K.Gef. Stand, 2.7.1941, Kampfbericht des XII. A.K. von 27.6.–1.7.41*, U.S. National Archives, Records German Field Commands, Panzer Armies, Microcopy T-313, Roll 82, Fr. 7320919.

13. Ibid.

14. Ibid., Fr. 7320917.

15. See Halder, *Diaries*, vol. 6, p. 206, in which General Ott reports on a visit to Army Group Center: "Russian attack methods: . . . infantry attacking as much as twelve ranks deep without heavy weapons support; the men start hurrahing from far off. Incredibly high Russian losses."

16. As noted in *48. A.K. (mot.), Ic, an Panzergruppe 1, Ic, 4.7.41, Morgenmeldung*, U.S. National Archives, Records German Field Commands, Panzer Armies, Microcopy T-313, Roll 10, Fr. 7236636.

17. See in Halder, *Diaries*, vol. 7, p. 29. The number—200,000—sits awkwardly in the entry for 8 August 1941 and appears to refer to the Uman encirclement operation, which involved predominantly the actions of the German 17th Army and Panzer Group 1 from 20 July to 7 August 1941.

18. The German SS Division Wiking toward the end of the fighting on the Uman *Kessel* reported, "One can generally observe that the enemy runs up thickly massed, breaks up on the German fire, and is thrown back." See *SS Division Wiking Ic, Div. Gef. St., den 8.8.41*, U.S. National Archives, Records German Field Commands, Panzer Armies, Microcopy T-313, Roll 10, Fr. 7236070.

19. See *Pz. Gr. 2, Ia, K.T.B. Nr. 1, 1.7.41, Meldung über den Einsatz der Brigade vom 28.6. bis 30.6.41*, RH 21.2/V. 113, Bundesarchiv Militärarchiv, Freiburg, FRG, p. 2.

20. Ibid.

21. See Stolfi et al., *German Destruction of Soviet Command*, pp. 72–75, 79, 80.

22. See *Pz. A.O.K. 2, Abt. Ia, K.T.B. Nr. 1 (1. Band), 1.7.41, Anlagen k. Feindlage,* RH 21-2/V.113, Bundesarchiv Militärarchiv, Freiburg, FRG.

23. As stated in an interview with Generalmajor Guenter Pape, Düsseldorf-Benrath, FRG, 11 January 1980.

24. See, for example, *Anlagenband E, Teil I, zum Tatigkeitsbericht Nr. 2, Panzer-Gruppe 3, Abt. Ic, begonnen 22.6.41,* U.S. National Archives, Record German Field Commands, Panzer Armies, Microcopy T-313, Roll 223, Fr. 7487604.

25. Pape, interview, Benrath, FRG, January 80.

26. Ibid.

27. For the arrival of the division east of Minsk, see the colorful description in Scheibert, *Gespenster-Division,* p. 53.

28. See *Pz. Gr. 2, Ia, K.T.B. Nr. 1, 1.7.41, Meldung uber den Einsatz der Brigade vom 28.6 bis 30.6.41,* RH 21-2/V.113, Bundesarchiv Militärarchiv, Freiburg, FRG, p. 2, which states: "The [4th Panzer] Brigade had covered from 27–28 June 1941 around 250 km in 24 hours."

29. See *Generalkommando XIV. A.K., Abt. Ic, K.H. Qu., den 5.7.41,* U.S. National Archives, Records German Field Commands, Panzer Armies, Microcopy T-313, Roll 10, Fr. 7236552, in which the German intelligence report states: Out of several documents, the Soviet's state that resistance will be performed to the last man." See also, *Pz. Gr. 2, Abt. Ia, Anl. k, K.T.B. Nr. 1, 1.7.41, 146: Armee Befehl Nr. 4,* RH 21.1/V.113, Bundesarchiv Militärarchiv, Freiburg, FRG, in which the order notes: "1) Enemy situation . . . b) Enemy defends himself in many cases with extreme toughness, sometimes to the last cartridge, even in a hopeless situation."

30. See *Pz. Gr. 1, Ia, Funkspruch Nr. 136 an Heeresgruppe Süd, 22.7.1941, 2315, Tagesmeldung,* U.S. National Archives, Records German Field Commands, Panzer Armies, Microcopy T-313, Roll 5, Fr. 7230203.

31. See *Pz. Gr. 2, Abt. Ia, Anl. k, K.T.B., Nr. 1, 1.7.41, Abschrift Fernsprechbuch,* RH 21-2/V.113, Bundesarchiv Militärarchiv, Freiburg, FRG, p. 4.

32. See *Generalkommando LVII.A.K. (mot.), Ic, Tätigkeitsbericht von 22.6.31.12.41,* 1568/20, Bundesarchiv Militärarchiv, Freiburg, FRG, p. 7.

33. *Pz. Gr. 2, Anl. k, K.T.B., Nr. 1, 11.7.41, Tagesmeldung XXXXVII. Pz.K.,* RH 21-1/V.123, Bundesarchiv Militärarchiv, Freiburg, FRG, p. 48 of file.

34. Prisoners noted in *Generalkommando, LVII.Pz.A.K., Anlage zu Gruppenbefehl Nr. 7, K.T.B., Feindnachrichtenblatt Nr. 8, 28.6.41,* 15683/3, Bundesarchiv Militärarchiv, Freiburg, FRG.

35. As recounted in *Pz. Gr. 2, Anl. k, K.T.B., Nr. 1, 2.7.41, M.G. Bataillon 5 (mot.), Gefechtsbericht des M. G. Btl.5 (mot.) für die Zeit vom 24.6 N 30.6.41,* RH 21-2/V.112, Bundesarchiv Militärarchiv, Freiburg, FRG.

36. Note *Panzer A.O.K. 1, Abt. Ic, Abendmeldung, 8.7.41,* U.S. National Archives, Records German Field Commands, Panzer Armies, Microcopy T-313, Roll 9, Fr. 7235690.

37. As reported in *Pz. A.O.K. 2, Anlagen, K.T.B., 4.7.41, Abschrift Fernsprechbuch,* no. 2 of index, RH 21-2/V.116, Bundesarchiv Militärarchiv, Freiburg, FRG.

38. See Scheibert, *Gespenster-Division,* p. 54.

39. See *Abwehrgruppe beim A.O.K. 4 und bei Panzergruppe 2, Abschrift den 17.7.41,* U.S. National Archives, Records German Field Commands, Panzer Armies, Microcopy T-313, Roll 131, Fr. 7379104.

40. See *Heeresgruppe Mitte, Ia, Nr. 104/41 g. Kdos., Befehl fur die Weiterführung des Operation,* RH 21.1/V.113, Bundesarchiv Militärarchiv, Freiburg, FRG, in which the order states that "the [infantry] armies must exercise all possibilities, including the throwing forward of mobile forces, to free the mobile divisions employed in encircling the Novogrodek pocket."

41. See *18.Pz. Div., Ic, Div. Gef. Stand. den 19.7.41,* U.S. National Archives, Records German Field Commands, Panzer Armies, Microcopy T-313, Roll 131, Fr. 7379099, where the Germans state, based on prisoner interrogation, that "diverse units thrown back and

forth among one another are completely out of touch with the situation" in the fight opposite Panzer Group Guderian near Smolensk on 19 July 1941.

42. See *VIII. A.K., Abt. Ic, Gefangenenvernehmungen vom 23.6.41–24.10.41, Div. Gef. St. den 7.8.41*, Bundesarchiv Militärarchiv, Freiburg, FRG. The report states that "the deserters are White Russians and had the firm intention to desert since being drafted even though the commissars had told them that the Germans skinned their prisoners alive."

43. See General der Infanterie Guenther Blumentritt, *Thoughts of a Former Soldier on Strategy, Politics, and Psychology of the 1939–45 War* (September 1947), p. 35, U.S. Army, European Command, Historical Section, MS B-647.

44. As early as 20 July 1941, Bock was demanding "to thrust farther to the east immediately, until the last reserves of the enemy are smashed." Bock, *Tagebuchnotizen Osten I*, pp. 36–38, where he also notes that the army group would be able to continue east at the beginning of August.

45. Halder, *Diaries*, vol. 7, p. 11, entry for 2 August 1941, comments, "Situation at Yelnya: the troops are laughing at Russian attacks with armor and infantry."

46. The evidence for a voluntary German halt is decisive. Bock, *Tagebuchnotizen Osten I*, p. 40, states that on 22 July 1941, "Brauchitsch called and said the Führer has ordered that the advance of the armor to the east is no longer a question for consideration."

47. Hauptmann Noack, interview, Freiburg, FRG, 21 January 1980. At the beginning of the campaign, Noack was an *Oberleutnant* in the 7th Panzer Division as part of Panzer Group Hoth. Noack recalled a comment made by Hoth on the eve of Barbarossa to the effect: "The next raid will not be a blitzkrieg but a blitz-blitzkrieg."

48. See Bock, *Tagebuchnotizen Osten I*, p. 12, where he rages against halting the panzer groups on 2 July 1941 to ensure holding the Minsk pocket, noting that it would be a "heavy blunder" to allow the Russians to recover from their crushing defeats.

49. *Heeresgruppe Mitte, Aufmarschweisung "Barbarossa,"* U.S. National Archives, Records German Field Commands, Army Groups, Microcopy T-311, Roll 216, Fr. 000649.

Chapter Nine

1. See in Warlimont, *Inside Hitler's Headquarters*, p. 138, the succinct analysis of Hitler's mentality in going for the incidental. With a stroke of the pen, Hitler fundamentally altered the decisive Halder-army plan in December 1941.

2. Authorities as perceptive as J. F. C. Fuller, as well informed but ideologically constrained as Vladimir Sevruk, and others claim that German casualties were so great that the Moscow time table was thrown off. See, for example, Major-General J. F. C. Fuller, *The Second World War, 1939–45: A Strategical and Tactical History* (New York: Duell, Sloan, and Pearce, 1949), p. 123, and Sevruk, *Moscow*, p. 11. Their claims that German casualties and staunch Russian resistance halted Barbarossa at the end of July 1941 are without foundation.

3. See the map in Guderian, *Panzer Leader*, p. 187.

4. Guderian, *Panzer Leader*, p. 188: "advanced on foot with the leading rifle company and thus assured that there were no needless delays."

5. See Geyer, *Das IX*, p. 114.

6. Ibid.

7. See Bock, *Tagebuchnotizen Osten I*, pp. 33, 34, where the field marshal explains that the *Schwerpunkt* of operations for his army group lay around Smolensk and, "for the defense of the flanks only the least necessary strength would be committed." The diary entry is for 18 July 1941.

8. An early nickname associated with Bock, as noted in Turney, *Disaster at Moscow*, p. 72.

9. Panzer Groups 2, 3, and 4 were redesignated panzer armies on 1 October 1941. See, for example, Scheibert, *Gespenster Division*, p. 72.

10. See Plocher, *German Air Force Versus Russia*, pp. 42, 43, which shows immediate German air supremacy followed by operations that concentrated on support of the army rather than continued primary emphasis on air superiority. The author criticizes the Germans for not continuing to emphasize the suppression of the Red Air Force. The Luftwaffe, however, at least concentrated its attacks against the Red Army with results that could have been the final decisive element in the penetration of the German ground armies into the Moscow-Gorki space until August 1941, thus preventing recovery of the Red Air Force by more direct means.

11. See in Stolfi, "Chance in History," pp. 224, 225.

12. See Bock, *Tagebuchnotizen Osten I*, p. 115.

13. See Haupt, *Kiew—die grösste Kesselschacht der Geschichte*. Note the title: *The Greatest Battle of Encirclement in History*.

Chapter Ten

1. See in Halder, *Diaries*, vol. 6, p. 210, the comment by Col. Eberhard Kinzel at the Army General Staff 1100 review of the Russian situation on 8 July 1941.

2. See Halder, *Diaries*, vol. 6, p. 125, the entry for 20 May 1941, in which Generaloberst Friedrich Fromm, chief of army equipment and commander of the replacement army, presents these figures.

3. Average numbers among nine divisions (four panzer, three infantry, and two motorized infantry) assigned to Panzer Group Guderian on 22 June 1941. See in *Pz. A.O.K. 2, H.Qu. den 27 Dezember 1941, Starken Pz. A.O.K. 2*, U.S. National Archives, Records of German Field Commands, Panzer Armies, Microcopy T-313, Roll 103, Fr. 7346281.

4. Average numbers among eight divisions (five panzer and three motorized infantry) assigned to Panzer Group Guderian on 23 August 1941. See *Pz. A.O.K. 2, H.Qu. den 23.8.1941. Starken Panzergruppe*, U.S. National Archives, Records of German Field Commands, Panzer Armies, Copy T-313, Roll 103, Fr. 7346313.

5. Ibid., Fr. 7346281, in which strength figures are given for the same divisions of Panzer Group 2 on 22 June 1941. Comparison shows the Germans operating at 80 percent of their original strength on the later date.

6. Feist and Nowarra, *German Panzers*.

7. Senger und Etterlin, *Kampfpanzer*, pp. 63, 68, 423.

8. See Brereton and Feist, *Russian Tanks*, pp. 12, 20, 32, 33, 48, as supplemented for road ranges by Senger und Etterlin, *Kampfpanzer*, pp. 357, 362, 386, 391.

9. See in *Hoherer Art.—Kdr. 302, Ia Nr. 588/41 geh. Gef. Stand, den 20.10.1941*, U.S. National Archives, Records German Field Commands, Armies, Microcopy T-312, Roll 145, Fr. 7684409, where the report comments that the 10.5cm howitzer required the 10.5cm antitank projectile and the number 6 load of propellant to knock out the T-34 at that time.

10. See the German analysis in *Pz. A.O.K. 4, Ic, . . . 12.7.1941 . . . Abschrift eines Berichten des Pz. Rgts. 25 über den schwersten Sowjet Panzerkampfwagen*, U.S. National Archives, Records German Field Commands, Panzer Armies, Microcopy T-313, Roll 131, Fr. 7378951, which reveals the challenges of fighting the big Soviet tanks (KV-1, 2) in the Baltic.

11. See in *O.K.H. Gen Sta d H, Op. Abt. (I), Nr. 1503/41, g.Kdos. Chef., Panzerlage*, U.S. National Archives, Records Headquarters German Army High Command, Copy T-78, Roll 335, Fr. 6291784. The numbers do not include German tanks manufactured as command vehicles, e.g., Pz.Kw. I, Pz.Kw. III, and TNHS 38 *Panzerbefehlswagen*.

12. See Foss, *Illustrated Encyclopedia*, p. 173, figure for T-26 tanks.

13. See Senger und Etterlin, *Kampfpanzer*, pp. 386, 391. Figures are for T-34 and KV tanks manufactured by 22 June 1941.

14. See Christensen, Steinlager Allendorf, trans., *Questions Asked Guderian and Answers Given by Guderian*, U.S. Army, European Command, Historical Division, MS B-271.

In answer to the question of how many tanks the Germans expected the Russians to have, Guderian notes, "I reckoned on 17–20,000."

15. See *Zusammenstellung*, U.S. National Archives, Records Headquarters German Armed Forces High Command, Microcopy T-77, Roll 15, Fr. 726363, which presents figures of 13,176 "3.7 cm Pak. u. Pak 38 (5 cm)" for "Bestand 1.5.40." See also *Heereswaffenamt, Wa. Stab Ia 3, Ausschnitt Bestand am 1.7.40*, U.S. National Archives, Records Headquarters German Army High Command, Microcopy T-78, Roll 143, Fr. 6973765. The Germans had produced the vast total of 13,029 of the 3.7cm Pak for the antitank defense of the field divisions by 1 July 1940, according to the source.

16. See, for example, *Fernschreiben, 3. A.K., Ic, an Panzergruppe 1, 4.7.41*, U.S. National Archives, Records German Field Commands, Panzer Armies, Microcopy T-313, Roll 10, Fr. 7236603, which states: "Russian tanks: seldom more than battalion strength at one time."

17. See Selz, *Das Grüne Regiment*, pp. 58, 59.

18. German infantry in Army Group South faced similar, huge Soviet tank forces. See, for example, *A.O.K. 17, K.T.B. Nr. 1, 15.5.41–12.12.41*, U.S. National Archives, Records German Field Commands, Armies, Microcopy T-312, Roll 668, Fr. 8301934, in which headquarters, 17th Army, notes: "Around noon [23 June 1941] the 262nd Infantry Division was in danger from about 150 enemy tanks from the area around Kornie."

19. The most powerful antitank gun used by the Germans in Barbarossa, the 5.0cm Pak, was "effective only at ranges under 200 m . . . the [KV heavy] tanks can also be put out of action by chance hits of 5.0 cm Pak at the turret ring." See *Pz. A.O.K. 4, Ic . . . 12.7.1941 . . . Abschrift eines Berichten des Pz. Rgts. 25 über den schwersten Sowjet Panzerkampfwagen*, U.S. National Archives, Records German Field Commands, Panzer Armies, Microcopy T-313, Roll 131, Fr. 7378951.

20. Note the typical Soviet experience in *Oberkommando der 4. Pz. Armee, Ic, Interrogation Report, T-34 Crew Member Georgiewitsch Kowalenko, July 1941*, U.S. National Archives, Records German Field Commands, Panzer Armies, Microcopy T-313, Roll 131, Fr. 7378923, where the Soviet tank man in the Soviet 107th Panzer Division notes heavy fighting around Orsha on 9 July 1941 followed by the attempt of a pack of sixty Soviet tanks "to fight its way eastward through Smolensk" on 17 and 18 July 41 out of the cauldron, 50 to 60 km to the west. Kowalenko notes that only two of the Soviet tanks escaped over the Dnieper toward Smolensk.

21. Note that approximately one month later, under Guderian, the 18th Panzer Division, 47th Panzer Corps would be "standing ready for insertion in further combat at about 60% of its original strength." See *18. Panzer-Division, XXXXVII. Pz. Korps, Meldung vom 15.9.1941 nachdem Stand vom 10.9.1941*, U.S. National Archives, Records German Field Commands, Panzer Armies, Microcopy T-313, Roll 103, Frs. 7347178, 7347180.

22. See in Halder, *Diaries*, vol. 7, p. 17.

23. See *Fernschreiben, 9. Pz. Div. an Pz. Gr. 1*, U.S. National Archives, Records German Field Commands, Panzer Armies, Microcopy T-313, Roll 4, Fr. 7227458, which notes on the day of the start of the campaign that the 9th Panzer Division had "approximately 80 percent of the wheeled motor vehicles of the division ready for insertion in combat."

24. See Author No. 313, *Antitank Defense in the East* (April, 1947), p. 3, U.S. Army, European Command, Historical Division, MS D-253.

Chapter Eleven

1. See Dahms, *Der Zweite Weltkrieg*, p. 54.

2. Creveld, *Supplying War*.

3. For such details note especially Stolfi, "Chance in History," pp. 221, 225, 226.

4. Halder, *Diaries*, vol. 6, p. 104, entry for 7 May 41, based on the report of the chief of army transportation (Gercke).

5. Philippi and Heim, *Feldzug gegen Sowjetrussland*, p. 52.
6. See Halder, *Diaries*, vol. 6, p. 86.
7. Ibid., p. 241.
8. Halder, *Diaries*, vol. 7, pp. 25, 26.
9. Halder, *Diaries*, vol. 6, p. 248, and Halder, *Diaries*, vol. 7, p. 22.
10. See *Kdr. d. Eisb. Pi. i. Bid. Hgr. Nord (Stab Eisb. Pi. Rgt. 3), Bericht, c. 24.8.1941*, U.S. National Archives, German Records, Headquarters, German Army High Command, Microcopy T-78, Roll 117, Fr. 6041126.
11. See Halder, *Diaries*, vol. 6, p. 12.
12. Note Bock, *Tagebuchnotizen Osten I*, p. 4, entry for 25 June 1941, in which he notes, "The railway led already by today . . . up to 80 km east of Brest—a very substantial relief for the overloaded supply routes of Panzer Group Guderian."
13. See OKH, *General der Eisenbahntruppen, Ausschnitte aus der Lagemeldung, Grukodeis. Mitte 1941*, U.S. National Archives, Records Headquarters German Army High Command, Microcopy T-78, Roll 113, Frs. 6035897, 6035898.
14. The additional track would comprise a substantial 15 percent over and above the track constructed among cities. See, for example, the mileages in *Gen. d. Eisb. Tr. Ausschnitte, Stand der Streckenwederherstellung, 1941–1942*, U.S. National Archives, Records, German Army High Command, Microcopy T-78, Roll 117, Fr. 6041049.
15. *Eisenbahntruppen*, U.S. National Archives, German Army High Command, Microcopy, T-78, Roll 113, Fr. 6035898. See also Bock, *Tagebuchnotizen Osten I*, p. 13.
16. See Halder, *Diaries*, vol. 6, p. 241.
17. Note the use of the rail system through Orsha, Vitebsk, and Smolensk in the first half of August 1941 in Generalmajor Windisch, *Personal Diary of the German 9th Army Supply Officer (German Language Copy) (from 1.8.1941–31.1.1942)*(5 February 1954), p. 7, U.S. Army, European Command, Historical Division, MS P-201.
18. See Halder, *Diaries*, vol. 6, p. 248, in which fourteen trains are noted as available for Army Group Center as of 18 July 1941, and Halder, *Diaries*, vol. 7, pp. 25, 26, in which twenty-four trains daily are noted as running to supply the center after 7 August 1941.
19. As early as 12 July 1941, the quartermaster general of the German army noted in a telephone call to the chief of staff that Army Group Center had enough supplies to maintain an armored drive to Moscow. He also notes that the infantry had only enough to get to Smolensk. It follows that as early as 12 July, the Germans were close to having logistics under control for a push almost straight through to Moscow. See Halder, *Diaries*, vol. 6, p. 231.

Chapter Twelve

1. See Halder, *Diaries*, vol. 7, p. 22, where Generalmajor Eduard Wagner, notes train arrivals in Army Group Center totalling twenty-four and twenty-six each on 4 and 5 August 1941, respectively.
2. See *Oberkommando des Heeres, Gen. St. d. H., Op. Abt., Nr. 1401/41 g. Kdos. Chefs. den 28 Juli 1941. Ausfertigungen, Weisung, für die Fortführung der Operationen, Anlage 1, Feindlage*, U.S. National Archives, Records Headquarters German Army High Command, Copy T-78, Roll 335, Fr. 621729.
3. See *Combat in the East, Experiences of German Tactical and Logistical Units in Russia* (1952), p. 58, U.S. Army, European Command, Historical Division, MS B-266.
4. See Halder, *Diaries*, vol. 7, p. 5, entry for 1 August 1941, which shows a ratio of three German to two Soviet divisions in combat in the area of Army Group North.
5. Generalmajor Detlev von Plato, interview, Grabow, FRG, 25 January 1980. Plato was Ib (logistics officer) of 1st Panzer Division attacking in the Baltic. He noted that the division did not encounter a single road with either bituminous or concrete surfacing. The best road was that connecting Ostrow with Pleskau in Latvia, "surfaced" with broken stone—that is,

a gravel road. These statements and similar ones by other Barbarossa veterans have led me to the conclusion that there were virtually no roads in the Soviet Union in 1941 with bituminous or concrete surfacing.

6. See Map 6 and Table 1 for a more complete view.

7. See Cherdantsev et al., *Ekonomicheskaya geografiya USSR*, p. 95, as cited in Lydolph, *Geography of the U.S.S.R.*, p. 332.

8. The city of Batum, near the Turkish border in Gruzinskaya SSR, was larger under special counting of urban settlements close to the city and under control of the city Soviet. Batum was significantly smaller under the ordinary system applied to virtually all the other cities in the USSR.

9. See Munzel, *Panzer-Taktik*, for the general possibilities in such a tactic.

Chapter Thirteen

1. See Keitel, *In the Service of the Reich*, pp. 28, 29, as summarized by the editor, Walter Goerlitz.

2. See U.S. Army, *German Campaign Russia, 1940–1942*, p. 59, in which the monograph notes that "the conflict over the continuation of operations became acute when Hitler overrode all his advisors—except Keitel—and imposed Directive No. 33 . . . upon the Army."

3. Halder, *Diaries*, vol. 3, p. 35. See also p. 30, where Hitler complains that the "enemy reacted in the past drastically and with promptness" to German moves toward the border. He notes that a new system of assembly and probably a whole new plan of attack were required.

4. See Suvorov, "Who Was Planning to Attack Whom?" pp. 50–55.

5. See *Generalkommando XI. A.K. Ic, Qu., den 22.9.1941*, U.S. National Archives, Records German Field Commands, Panzer Armies, Microcopy T-313, Roll 11, Fr. 7237777, in which a Soviet attack against Romania is noted in a prisoner interrogation report as having been planned for autumn 1941.

6. Groeben, interview, Celle-Boye, FRG, Jan 80.

7. The Crimea was not noted for its economic resources. It was a potential air base for Soviet bombers dangerously close to the Romanian oil fields.

8. Hitler, *Mein Kampf*, pp. 264–66.

9. Taylor, *March of Conquest*, p. 158.

10. Manstein, *Lost Victories*, pp. 83–126. In an impressive, detailed analysis, Manstein describes the development of strategy and plan for the war in the west but does not mention Hitler's fundamental personal fear of the Allied seizure of Belgium.

11. See Mrazek *Fall of Eban Emael*, pp. 31–33. The work is an impressive monograph based on primary sources.

12. Langer, *The Mind of Adolf Hitler*.

13. Halder, *Diaries*, vol. 4, p. 15, entry for 17 May 1940.

14. See for example, Edwards, *German Airborne Troops*, p. 96.

15. Guderian, *Panzer Leader*, p. 30.

16. See English translation in Trevor-Roper, *Hitler's War Directives*, p. 49. For the German original see International Military Tribunal, *Trial of the Major War Criminals*, p. 48.

17. See *Beprechung* [sic] *an 29. November 1941, 1200–1400 Uhr, Ort: Reichskanzlei, Teilnehmer: Der Führer . . . Keitel . . . Grund der Besprechung: Panzerwagenverteidigung* [sic] *und Panzerabwehr*. Document collection of the author.

Chapter Fourteen

1. In the more general literature on World War II, the view predominates, implied or expressed, that the tide turned with the German disaster at Stalingrad. See, for example, Langer, *An Encyclopedia of World History*, p. 1143; Falls, *A Hundred Years of War*, pp. 369,

370; and Liddell Hart, *History of the Second World War*, pp. 260–64. In the more specialized literature, see, for example, the ultra-decisive remarks in Alan Clark, *Barbarossa, the Russian-German Conflict, 1941–45* (New York: William Morrow, 1965), p. 248, and Ziemke, *Stalingrad to Berlin*, p. ix, the latter presenting the chapter entitled: "Stalingrad, the Turning Point." Note also E. K. G. Sixsmith, "Stalin's War with Germany," *Journal of the Royal United Services Institute for Defence Studies* 120, no. 3 (1975): 80.

2. From the Soviet interpretation in Deborin, *Second World War*, p. 285.

3. Ibid. See also Ivanov, "Stalingradskaia Bitva," pp. 3–20, in which the statement stands out: "The battle for Stalingrad, the most important battle of World War II, showed the heroism of the Soviet army. The title of the article can be translated as "The Battle for Stalingrad and its International Significance."

4. See Falls, *Second World War*, pp. 137, 138, in which the western author emphasizes the special importance of Stalingrad.

5. See, for example, Kozlov and Olsen, "La Bataille de Kursk," pp. 144–64, in which the thesis is expressed that the Soviet victory at the battle of Kursk in July and August 1943 was the turning point of the Second World War.

6. Deborin, *Second World War*, p. 285, makes the claim that "the Volga battle was the greatest of all the battles on the Soviet-German front." The claim contradicts similar Soviet claims made for Kursk and runs afoul of the German victories at Bialystok, Minsk, Smolensk, Kiev, and Vyasma-Bryansk during Barbarossa, which were of comparable or greater dimensions.

7. See, for example, Frankland and Dowling, *Decisive Battles of the Twentieth Century*, p. 221.

8. Deborin, *Second World War*, p. 285.

9. See in Renato Verna, "Front e Russo 1943," 24 (4): 437–54 and 24 (5): 536–49, in which the author argues in favor of Kursk as the battle that finally tipped the balance between the German and Soviet armed forces in the east.

10. See the interesting terms used several times in Ministerialrat Helmuth Greiner, *Africa, 1941* (February 1946), pp. 1–16, U.S. Army, European Command, Historical Division, MS# C-065f, to describe the way in which the German motorized force would be employed in North Africa in 1941.

11. Even *Punch, or the London Charivari*, 12 July 1905, shows a somewhat unfair attitude on the part of the British and French in its large lithograph entitled, "Not in the Picture," showing the kaiser dressed as a German sailor being excluded from a photograph about to be taken of a British and a French sailor.

12. See *Tank Industry Report*, Exhibit A, facing p. 20, U.S., Strategic Bombing Survey, in which German production totals 1,368 tanks and assault guns and Czech production under German control totals 275 Czech 385 tanks. See *Aircraft Industry Report*, Exhibit 3, U.S. Strategic Bombing Survey, which shows German production of combat aircraft as 7,103 bombers and fighters for 1940 and an additional 3,268 transport, trainer, and "other" aircraft—a total of 10,371 engined military aircraft.

13. See Hancock, *History of the Second World War*, pp. 176, 185, 484.

14. See *Tank Industry Report*, Exhibit A, facing p. 20, U.S., Strategic Bombing Survey, in which German production totals 19,226 armored vehicles, including tanks, tank destroyers, assault guns, and self-propelled guns.

Bibliography

✠

Published Sources

Balck, Hermann. *Ordnung Im Chaos, Erinnerungen 1893–1948.* Osnabrück: Biblio Verlag, 1980.

Brereton, John M., and Uwe Feist. *Russian Tanks, Evolution and Development, 1915–1968.* Fallbrook, California: Aero Publishers, 1970.

Bweley, Charles. *Hermann Göring and the Third Reich: A Biography Based on Family and Official Records.* Toronto: Devin-Adair, 1962.

Chales de Beaulieu, Walter. *Der Vorstoss der Panzergruppe 4 auf Leningrad—1941.* Neckargemünd: Scharnhorst Buchkammeradschaft, 1962.

Cherdontsev, G. N., et al. *Ekonomicheskaya geografiya SSR: obschly obzor.* Moscow: 1958.

Creveld, Martin van. *Fighting Power: German Military Performance, 1914–1945.* Washington, D.C.: Office of Net Assessment, Department of Defense, 1980.

———.*Supplying War. Logistics from Wallenstein to Patton.* New York: Cambridge University Press, 1977.

Dahms, Hellmuth Gunther. *Der Zweite Weltkrieg.* Tübingen: Ranier Wunderlich, 1960.

Deborin, A. *The Second World War: A Political Military Survey.* Ed. I. Zubikov. Moscow: Progress Publisher, c. 1963.

Dornberg, John. *Munich 1923: The Story of Hitler's First Grab for Power.* New York: Harper and Row, 1982.

Dowling, Christopher, and Noble Frankland. *Decisive Battles of the Twentieth Century, Land-Sea-Air.* New York: David McKay, 1976.

Dupuy, T. M. *A Genius for War: The German Army and General Staff, 1807–1945.* London: McDonald and Jane's, 1977.

Edwards, Roger. *German Airborne Troops.* New York: Doubleday, 1974.

Falls, Cyril. *The Second World War: A Short History.* London: Metheun, 1948.

———. *A Hundred Years of War.* New York: Collier, 1962.

Feist, Uwe, and Heinz Novarra. *The German Panzers from Mark I to Mark V "Panther."* Fallbrook, California: Aero Publishers, 1966.

Feist, Uwe, and John M. Brereton. *Russian Tanks, Evolution and Development, 1915–1968.* Fallbrook, California: Aero Publishers, 1970.

Fest, Joachim. *Hitler.* New York: Harcourt Brace Jovanovich, Random House, 1975.

Forster, Kent. *Recent Europe: A Twentieth-Century History.* New York: The Ronald Press Company, 1965.

Foss, Christopher F. *The Illustrated Encyclopedia of the World's Tanks and Fighting Vehicles.* New York: Chartwell, 1977.

Fraenkel, Heinrich, and Roger Manvell. *Goering.* New York: Simon and Schuster, 1962.

Frankland, Noble, and Christopher Dowling. *Decisive Battles of the Twentieth Century, Land-Sea-Air.* New York: David McKay, 1976.

Geisler, Franz, Liebmann, Josef März, Kurt Meyer, Franz Thierfelder. *Unser Kampf auf dem Balkan.* München: F. Bruckmann Verlag, 1942.

Geschichte der 3. Panzer-Division, Berlin-Brandenburg 1935–1945. Berlin: Verlag Günter Richter, 1970.

Geyer, Hermann. *Das IX. Armeekorps im Ostfeldzug 1941.* Neckargemünd, FRG: Kurt Vowinckel, 1969.

Guderian, Heinz. *Achtung Panzer! Die Entwicklung der Panzerwaffe, ihre Kampftaktik und ihre Operationen Möglichkeiten.* Stuttgart: Union Deutsche, 1937.

————. *Panzer Leader.* Trans. Constantine Fitzgibbon. New York: Dutton, 1952.

Halder, Franz. *The Halder Diaries.* 8 vols. Nuremberg: Office of Chief Counsel for War Crimes, U.S. Military Government for Germany, 1946.

Hancock, W. K., ed. *History of the Second World War.* United Kingdom Civil Series. London: His Majesty's Stationery Office, 1952.

Hanser, Richard. *Putsch!* New York: Peter H. Wyden, Pyramid Books, 1971.

Haupt, Werner. *Kiew—die grösste Kesselschlacht der Geschichte.* Dornheim, FRG: Podzun-Pallas Verlag, c. 1975.

Hegge, Per Egil. "Myten om Stalin 'Pusterom.'" *Samtiden* [Norway] 86, no. i (1977): 58–64.

Heim, Ferdinand, and Alfred Philippi. *Der Feldzug gegen Sowjetrussland 1941 bis 1945.* Stuttgart: W. Kohlhammer, 1962.

Hitler, Adolf. *Mein Kampf.* Trans. Ralph Manheim. Boston: Houghton Mifflin, 1943.

Hoth, Hermann. *Panzer-Operationen, Die Panzergruppe 3 und die operative Gedanke der deutsche Führung, Sommer 1941.* Heidelberg: Kurt Vowinckel, 1956.

International Military Tribunal. *Trial of the Major War Criminals. Proceedings.* 24 vols. Nuremberg, 1949.

————. *Trial of the Major War Criminals. Documents and Other Material in Evidence.* 20 vols. Nuremberg, 1949.

Ivanov, S. P. "Stalingradskaia Bitva i ee Mezhdunarodnoe Znachenie." *Novaia i Noveishaia Istoriia* 1 (1973).

Jacobsen, Hans-Adolf. *Fall gelb: der Kampf um den deutschen Operationsplan zur Westoffensive 1940.* Veröffentlichungen des Instituts für Europäische Geschichte Mainz, Band 16. Wiesbaden: Franz Steiner Verlag, 1957.

Jacobsen, Otto. *Erich Marcks: Soldat und Gelehrter.* Göttingen: Musterschmidt, 1971.

Jurgens, Lutz, comp. *Meine Schwadron.* Muster, Westfalen: Aschendorffsche Buchdruckerei, 1970.

Keitel, Wilhelm. *In the Service of the Reich.* Ed. Walter Görlitz. Trans. David Irving. New York: Stein and Day, 1979.

Kozlov, L., and A. Olsen. "La Bataille de Kursk et son influence sur la course de la Seconde Guerre Mondiale." Trans. A. Constantini. *Revue Historique des Armées* (France) 1, no. 2 (1947).

Langer, Walter C. *The Mind of Adolf: The Secret Wartime Report.* New York: Basic Books, 1972.

Langer, William L., ed. *An Encyclopedia of World History.* Boston: Houghton Mifflin, 1972.

Liddell Hart, B. H. *History of the Second World War.* New York: G.P. Putnam, 1971

Luther, Craig. "German Armoured Operations in the Ukraine: The Encirclement Battle of Uman." *Army Quarterly and Defence Journal* (Britain) 108 no. 4 (1978).

Lydolph, Paul E. *Geography of the U.S.S.R.* New York: John Wiley, 1964.

Manstein, Erich von. *Lost Victories.* Trans. and ed. Anthony G. Powell. Chicago: Regnery, 1958.

Manvell, Roger, and Heinrich Fraenkel. *Goering.* New York: Simon and Schuster, 1962.

Maser, Werner. *Hitler: Legend, Myth and Reality.* Trans. Peter and Betty Ross. New York: Harper and Row, 1973.

Mendelssohn, Peter de. *Die Nürnberger Dokumente: Studien zur Deutschen Kriegspolitik 1937–1945.* Hamburg: Kruger, 1947.

Mrazek, James E. *The Fall of Eben Emael, Prelude to Dunkirk.* 1970.

Munzel, Oskar. *Panzer-Taktik: Raids gepanzerter Verbände im Ostfeldzug 1941–42.* Heidelberg: Kurt Vowinckel, 1959.

Philippi, Alfred, and Ferdinand Heim. *Der Feldzug gegen Sowjetrussland 1941 bis 1945.* Stuttgart: W. Kohlhammer, 1962.

Plocher, Hermann. *The German Air Force versus Russia, 1941.* USAF Historical Studies No. 153. New York: Arno, 1955.

Postan, M. M. "British War Production." In Hancock, *History of the Second World War.* United Kingdom Series. London: His Majesty's Stationery Office, 1952.

Scheibert, Horst. *Die Gespenster-Division, Eine Deutsche Panzer-Division (7.) Im Zweiten Weltkrieg.* Dornheim, FRG: Podzun-Pallas, n.d.

Schmidt, Paul. *Hitler's Interpreter.* Ed. R.H.C. Steed. London: Heinemann, 1951.

Selz, Barbara. *Das Grüne Regiment: Der Weg der 256. Infanterie-Division aus der Sicht des Regiments 481.* Freiburg: Verlag Otto Kehrer, 1970.

Senger und Etterlin, F. W. von. *Die Kampfpanzer von 1916–1966.* München: J. F. Lehmanns Verlag, 1971.

Sevruk, Vladimir, comp. *Moscow 1941, 1942 Stalingrad, Recollections, Stories, Reports.* Moscow: Progress, c. 1970.

Shtemenko, S. M. *The Soviet General Staff at War, 1941–1945.* Moscow: Progress, 1970.

Stolfi, R. H. S. "Barbarossa Revisited: A Critical Reappraisal of the Opening Stages of the Russo-German Campaign (June–December 1941)." *Journal of Modern History* 54 (March 1982).

————. "Chance in History: The Russian Winter of 1941–42." *History* (Britain), June 1980.

Stolfi, R. H. S., Lonnie O. Ratley III, and John F. O'Neill, Jr. *German Disruption of Soviet Command: Control and Communications in Barbarossa, 1941.* Naval Postgraduate School Technical Report NPS-56-84-001. Monterey, California: Naval Postgraduate School, 1983.

Suvorov, Victor. "Who Was Planning to Attack Whom in June 1941, Hitler or Stalin?" *Royal United Services Institute* (Britain), June 1985.

Taylor, Telford. *The March of Conquest: The German Victories in Western Europe, 1940.* New York: Simon and Schuster, 1958.

Trevor-Roper, H. R., ed. *Blitzkrieg to Defeat: Hitler's War Directives, 1939–1945.* New York: Holt, Rinehart, and Winston, 1964.

Turney, Alfred W. *Disaster at Moscow: Von Bock's Campaigns, 1941–1941.* Albuquerque: University of New Mexico Press, 1970.

U.S. Department of the Army. *The German Campaign in Russia, Planning and Operations (1940–1942).* Pamphlet No. 20-261a. Washington, D.C.: Government Printing Office, 1955.

————. *Small Unit Actions During the German Campaign in Russia.* Pamphlet No. 20-269. Washington, D.C.: Government Printing Office, 1953.

Verna, Renato. "Fronte Russo 1943, Il Canto del Cigno della 'Panzerwaffe'—la Battaglia di 5–16 Juglio." *Revista militare* 24, nos. 4, 5 (1968).

Waite, Robert G. L. *The Psychopathic God, Adolf Hitler.* New York: Signet, 1978.

Warlimont, Walter. *Inside Hitler's Headquarters, 1939–1945.* Trans. R. H. Barry. New York: Praeger, 1964.

Ziemke, Earl F. *Stalingrad to Berlin: The German Defeat in the East.* Washington, D.C.: U.S. Government Printing Office, 1968.

————. *The German Northern Theater of Operations, 1940–1945.* Department of the Army Pamphlet No. 20–271. Washington, D.C.: U.S. Government Printing Office, 1960.

Archives

FRG. BUNDESARCHIV MILITÄRARCHIV

Generalkommando, LVII. Pz. A.K., Anlage zu Gruppenbefehl Nr. 7, K.T.B., Feindnachrichtenblatt Nr.8, 28.6.41., 15683/3.

General Kommando, LVII. A.K. (mot.), Ic, Tätigkeitsbericht von 22.6.– 31.12.41, 1568/20.

Gen. Kdo. LVII. A.K. (mot.),Ic, Tätigkeitsbericht, v. 22.6.–31.12.41, 15683/20.

Heeresgruppe Mitte, Ia, Nr. 104.41 g. Kdos., Befehl für die Weiterführung des Operation, RH 21.1/113.

Pz. A.O.K. 2, Abt. Ia, K.T.B. Nr. 1 (1.Band), 1.7.41, Anlagen k, Feindlage, RH 21-2/113.

Pz. A.O.K. 2, Anlagen, K.T.B., 4.7.41, Abschrift Fernspruchbuch, no. 2 of index, RH 21-2/v.116.

Pz. A.O.K. 2 (Pz. Gr. 2), Abt. Ia, Anl. k, K.T.B. Nr—(1. Band), 1.7.41, 24b: Vernehmung Generalmajor Jegorow. RH 21.2/v.113.

Pz. A.O.K. 2 (Pz. Gr. 2), Abt. Ia, Anl. k, K.T.B. Nr. 1 (1. Band), 1.7.41. RH 21.2/v.113.

Pz. Gr. 2, Abt. Ia, Anl. k, K.T.B. Nr. 1, 1.7.41, Abschrift Fernspruchbuch. RH 21.2/v.113.

Pz. Gr. 2, Abt. Ia, Anl. k, K.T.B. Nr. 1, 1.7.41, 146: Armee Befehl nr. 4. RH 21.2/113.

Pz. Gr. 2, Anl. k, K.T.B. Nr. 1, 2.7.41, M.G. Bataillon 5 (mot.), Gefechtsbericht des M.G. Btl. 5 (mot.) Für die Zeit vom 24.6–30.6.41, RH 21.2/112.

Pz. Gr. 2, Anl. k, K.T.B. Nr. 1, 11.7.41, Tagesmeldung XXXXVII. Pz. K., RH 21.1/113.

Pz. Gr. 2, Ia, K.T.B. Nr. 1, 1.7.41, Meldung Über den Einsatz der Brigade vom 28.6 bis 30.6.41. RH 21.2/113.

VIII. Abt. Ic. Gefangenenvernehmungen vom 23.6.41–24.10.41, Div. Gef. St. den 7.8.41.

XXXXVII. Panzer Korps, Kriegstagebuch Nr. 2, Anlagen Nr. 1–100, 20.5.– 27.6. 1941. 13468/1.

Generalfeldmarschall Fedor von Bock. Tagebuch Osten I (Oberbefehlshaber d. H.gru. Mitte. Unterstellt: Pz. gru. 2, Pz gru 3, 4. Armee, 9. Armee), 22.6.1941 bis 5.1.42. H 08-22/9.

HOOVER INSTITUTION

Fedor von Bock. Tagebuch-Notizen, May 1939–May 1945. 7 vols. (MS) D743, B665.

Fedor von Bock. Tagebuch-Notizen, May 1939–May 1945. 7 vols. (MS) D743, B665.

U.S. Army, European Command, Historical Division

Manuscript B-266. No author acknowledged. *Combat in the East: Experiences of German Tactical and Logistical Units in Russia.* 1952.

Manuscript B-271. *Questions Asked Guderian and Answers Given by Guderian.* Trans. Christensen, Steinlager Allendorf, 16 December 1946.

Manuscript B-326. *Georg Ritter von Henzl. Corps von Henzl (20 Apr–6 May 45).* 27 April 1946.

Manuscript C-065f. Helmuth Greiner. *Africa, 1941.* February 1946.

Manuscript C-065i. Helmuth Greiner. *Operation Barbarossa.* C. 1947.

Manuscript C-067a. Franz Halder. *Decisions Affecting the Campaign in Russia (1941–1942).* September 1949.

Manuscript D-253. Author No. 313. *Antitank Defense in the East.* April 1947.

Manuscript P-094. Rudolph M. Hofmann. *German Army War Games.* C. 1947.

Manuscript P-201. Generalmajor Windisch. *Personal Diary of the German 9th Army Supply Officer* (German language copy; 1.8.1941–31.1.1942). 5 February 1954.

U.S. NATIONAL ARCHIVES

Records German Armed Forces High Command. T-77, Roll 15, Fr. 726363. *Zusammenstellung.*

Records German Army High Command. T-78, Roll 335, Fr. 6291343. *Anlage 5c zu OKH Gen. St. d. H. Op. Abt. Nr. 050/41 a. Kdos. (Chefsache), Weisung für den Einsatz der Flakverbände.*

Records German Army High Command. T-78, Roll 113, Fr. 6035898. *Eisenbahntruppen.*

Records German Army High Command. T-78, Roll 117, Fr. 6041049. *Gen. de. Eisb. Tr. Ausschnitte, Stand der Streckenwederherstellung, 1941–1942.*

Records German Army High Command. T-78, Roll 143, Fr. 6973765. *Heereswaffenamt, Wa. Stab Ia 3, Ausschnitt Bestand am 1.7.40.*

Records German Army High Command. T-78, Roll 335, Fr. 621729. *Oberkommando des Heeres, Gen. St. d. H., Abt., Nr. 1401/41 g. Kdos. Chefs. dem 28 Juli 1941. Ausfertigungen, Weisung für die Fortführung der Operationen, Anlage 1, Feindlage.*

Records German Army High Command. T-78, Roll 335, Fr. 6291211. *Oberkommando des Heeres, Gen. st. d. H., Op. Abt. (I), Nr. 050/41 g. Kdos., H.Qu/OKH, den 22 Januar 1941.*

Records German Army High Command. T-78, Roll 113, Frs. 6035897, 6035898. *OKH, General der Eisenbahntruppen, Ausschnitte aus der Lagemeldung, Grukodeis. Mitte, 1941.*

Records German Army High Command. T-78, Roll 335, Fr. 6291784.

O.K.H. Gen Sta d H, Op. Abt. (I), Nr. 1503/41 g. Kdos. Chef., Panzerlage.
Records German Field Commands. Army Groups. T-311, Roll 216,
Fr. 000651. *Aufmarschweisung "Barbarossa," Heeresgruppe Mitte, den
12.3.1941.*

Records German Field Commands. Army Groups. T-311, Roll 216,
Fr. 000649. *Heeresgruppe Mitte, Aufmarschweisung, "Barbarossa."*

Records German Field Commands. Armies. T-312, Roll 668, Fr. 8301934.
A.O.K. 17, K.T.B. Nr. 1, 15.5.41–12.12.41..

Records German Field Commands. Armies. T-312, Roll 145, Fr. 7684409.
Hoherer Art.—Kdr. 302, Ia Nr. 588/41 geh. Gef. Stand, den 20.10.1941.

Records German Field Commands. Panzer Armies. T-313, Roll 131,
Fr. 7379104. *Abwehrgruppe beim A.O.K. 4 und bei Panzergruppe Z,
Abschrift den 17.7.41.*

Records German Field Commands. Panzer Armies. T-313, Roll 223,
Fr. 7487604. *Anlagenband E, Teil 1, zum Tätigkeitsbericht Nr. 2,
Panzer-Gruppe 3, Abt. Ic, begonnen 22.6.41.*

Records German Field Commands. Panzer Armies. T-313, Roll 10,
7236483. *A.O.K. 6, Ic, an Panzergruppe 1, Ic, 8.8.41, 0735.*

Records German Field Commands. Panzer Armies. T-313, Roll 145,
Fr. 7684400. *Der Oberbefehlshaber der Heeresgruppe Mitte, H. Qu.,
19.10.1941, Tagesbefehl.*

Records German Field Commands. Panzer Armies. T-313, Roll 10,
Fr. 7236603. *Fernschreiben, 3. A.K., an Panzergruppe 1, 4.7.41.*

Records German Field Commands. Panzer Armies. T-313, Roll 10,
Fr. 7236392. *Fernschreiben, III. A.K. Ic, an Panzergruppe 1, Ic.
Zwischenmeldung.*

Records German Field Commands. Panzer Armies. T-313, Roll 4,
Fr. 7227458. *Fernschreiben, 9. Pz. Div. an Pz. Gr. I.*

Records German Field Commands. Panzer Armies. T-313, Roll 11,
Fr. 7237777. *Generalkommando XI. A.K. Ic, Qu., den 22.9.1941.*

Records German Field Commands. Panzer Armies. T-313, Roll 82,
Fr. 7320919. *Generalkommando XII. A.K., Ia K.Gef. Stand, 2.7.1941,
Kampfbericht des XII. A.K. von 27.6.–1.7.41.*

Records German Field Commands. Panzer Armies. T-13, Roll 10,
Fr. 7236552. *Generalkommando XIV. A.K., Abt. Ic, K.H. Qu., den
5.7.41.*

Records German Field Commands. Panzer Armies. T-313, Roll 131,
Fr. 7379183. *Heeresgruppe Mitte, Ic/A.O., H.Qu.*

Records German Field Commands. Panzer Armies. T-313, Roll 131,
Fr. 7378942. *Heeresgruppe Mitte, Ic/A.O., H.Qu. den 15.7.41, Gefangene und Beute aus der Doppleschlacht von Bialystok und Minsk.*

Records German Field Commands. Panzer Armies. T-313, Roll 131,
Fr. 7379132. *Heeresgruppe Mitte, Ic/A.O., H.Q., den 30.7.1941.*

Records German Field Commands. Panzer Armies. T-313. Roll 131. Fr. 7379074. *Inf. Regt. Grossdeutschland, Abt. Ic, Regt. Gefechtsstand, den 16.VII.41.*

Records German Field Commands. Panzer Armies. T-313. Roll 131. Fr. 7379079. *Inf. Regt. Grossdeutschland, Abt. Ic . . . 18.VII.41.*

Records German Field Commands. Panzer Armies. T-313. Roll 131. Fr. 7378936. *Oberkommando der 4. Panzer Armee, Abt. Ic, den 19.8.41.*

Records German Field Commands. Panzer Armies. T-313. Roll 131. Fr. 7378916. *Oberkommando der 4. Panzer Armee, Ic, den 22.7.41, Feindnachrichtenblatt Nr. 4.*

Records German Field Commands. Panzer Armies. T-313. Roll 131. Fr. 7378923. *Oberkommando der 4. Panzer Armee, Ic, Interrogation Report, T-34 Crew Member Georgiewitch Kowalenko, July 1941.* (Document partly in English).

Records German Field Commands. Panzer Armies. T-313. Roll 9. Fr. 7235690. *Panzer A.O.K. 1, Abt. Ic, Abendmeldung, 8.7.41.*

Records German Field Commands. Panzer Armies. T-313. Roll 9. Fr. 7235663. *Panzergruppe 1, Abt. Ic/AO, Abendmeldung, den 25.6.41.*

Records German Field Commands. Panzer Armies. T-313. Roll 9. Fr. 7235678. *Panzergruppe 1, Ic/AO an OKH Fremde Heer Ost Abendmeldung, 3.7.41.*

Records German Field Commands. Panzer Armies. T-313. Roll 103. Fr. 7346313. *Pz. A.O.K. 2, H.Qu. den 23.8.1941. Starken Panzergruppe.*

Records German Field Commands. Panzer Armies. T-313. Roll 103. Fr. 7346281. *Pz. A.O.K. 2, H.Qu. den 27 Dezember 1941, Starken Pz. A.O.K. 2.*

Records German Field Commands. Panzer Armies. T-313. Roll 131. Fr. 7378951. *Pz. A.O.K. 4, Ic, 12.7.1941 Abschrift eines Berichten des Pz. Rgts. 25 über den schwersten Sowjet Panzerkampfwagen.*

Records German Field Commands. Panzer Armies. T-313. Roll 5. Fr. 7230203. *Pz. Gr. 1, Ia, Funkspruch Nr. 136 an Heeresgruppe Süd, 22.7.1941, 2315, Tagesmeldung.*

Records German Field Commands. Panzer Armies. T-313. Roll 9. Fr. 7235690. *Pz. Gr. 3, Ic, Abendmeldung, 8.7.41.*

Records German Field Commands. Panzer Armies. T-313. Roll 225. Fr. 7488960. *Pz. Gr. 3, K.T.B. Nr. 1, 22.6.41.*

Records German Field Commands. Panzer Armies. T-313. Roll 10. Fr. 7236070. *SS Division Wiking Ic, Div. Gef. St., den 8.8.41.*

Records German Field Commands. Panzer Armies. T-313. Roll 10. Fr. 7236715. *3. A.K., Ic, an Pz. Gr. 1, Ic, 1.7. [1941], 2250.*

Records German Field Commands. Panzer Armies. T-313. Roll 103. Frs. 7347178, 7347180. *18. Panzer-Division, XXXXVI. Pz. Korps, Meldung vom 15.9.1941 nachdem Stand vom 10.9.1941.*

Records German Field Commands. Panzer Armies. T-313, Roll 131, Fr. 7379099. *18. Pz. Div., Ic, Div. Gef. Stand den 19.7.41.*

Records German Field Commands. Panzer Armies. T-313, Roll 10, Fr. 7236636. *48. A.K. (mot.), Ic, an Panzergruppe I, Ic, 4.7.41, Morgenmeldung.*

Records German Field Commands. Panzer Armies. T-313, Roll 10, Fr. 7236663. *I. Bataillon, Schützen-Regiments 64, an III. Pz.K., Abt. Ic 30.6/41, Subject. Discovery of the Mutilated Personnel.* (Document partly in English.)

Records German Field Commands. Panzer Armies. T-313, Roll 10, Fr. 7236434. *III. A.K., Ic, an Panzergruppe I, 9.7.41, 1430, Intelligence Report.* (Document partly in English.)

Records German Field Commands. Army Corps. T-314, Roll 1389, Fr. 000166. *Anlage II zu Kdo. d. Pz. Gr. 4, Ia, Nr. 20/41 g. Kdos., Chefsache vom 2.5.1941.*

Records German Field Commands. Army Corps. T-314, Roll 1389, Fr. 000296. *Der Befehlshaber der Panzergruppe 4, Gr. H.Qu. den 1.7.41, an die Herren Kommandierenden Generals der XXXXI. und LVI. A.K.*

Records German Field Commands. Army Corps. T-314, Roll 1389, Fr. 000162. *Der Kommandierende General, Gen. Kdo. LVI. A.K. (mot), Ia 46/47 g. k. . . . 4.6.41.*

Records German Field Commands. Army Corps. T-314, Roll 1389, Frs. 000087–000089. *Der Oberbefehlshaber des Heeres, Gen. St. d. H. Op. Abt. Ia . . . H.Qu. O.K.H., den 8.3.1941.*

Records German Field Commands. Army Corps. T-314, Roll 1389, Frs. 000131, 000152. *Kommando der Panzergruppe 4, Abt. Ia, 249/41 g. Kdos., Chefsache, den 14.6.1941. Befehl für den Einsatz des "Lehr-Regiment Brandenburg z.b.v. 800."*

Records German Field Commands. Army Corps. T-314, Roll 415, Fr. 8708963. *Panzer Gruppe 4, Ic, Feindlage, 20.5.41.*

Records German Field Commands. Divisions. T-315, Roll 322, Fr. 000865. *K.T.B. Nr. 3 der 6. Schützen Brigade für die Zeit vom 21.6.41 bis 22.11.41.*

Records German Field Commands. Divisions. T-315, Roll 326, Fr. 000049. *Oberkommando 6. Pz. D., Ia.*

Records German Field Commands. Divisions. T-315, Roll 326, Fr. 000193. *XXXXI. Pz. K. Munitions Bericht, 22.–26.6.41.*

Interviews

Groeben, Peter von der. Celle-Boye, FRG, 24 January 1980.

Kielmansegg, Johann A. Graf von. Bad Krozingen, FRG, 19 January 1980.

Loytved-Hardegg, Rudolf. Nürnberg, FRG, 18 January 1980.

Noack, Hauptman. Freiburg im Breisgau, FRG, 21 January 1980.

Pape, Guenter. Düsseldorf-Benrath, FRG. January 1980.

Wagermann, Eberhard. Rheinbach, FRG, 18 January 1980.

Index